A WALK
THROUGH
WALES

BOOKS BY ANTHONY BAILEY

FICTION
Making Progress (1959)
The Mother Tongue (1961)
Major André (1987)

NONFICTION
The Inside Passage (1965)
Through the Great City (1967)
The Thousand Dollar Yacht (1968)
The Light in Holland (1970)
In the Village (1971)
A Concise History of the Low Countries (1972)
Rembrandt's House (1978)
Acts of Union (1980)
Along the Edge of the Forest (1983)
Spring Jaunts (1986)
The Outer Banks (1989)

AUTOBIOGRAPHY
America, Lost & Found (1981)
England, First & Last (1985)

A WALK
THROUGH
WALES

Anthony Bailey

JONATHAN CAPE
LONDON

First published 1992
© Anthony Bailey 1992
Jonathan Cape, 20 Vauxhall Bridge Road, London SW1V 2SA

Anthony Bailey has asserted his right under the Copyright, Designs and
Patents Act 1988 to be identified as the author
of this work

A CIP catalogue record for this book is
available from the British Library

ISBN 0-224-02776-X

Printed in Great Britain by
Mackays of Chatham PLC, Chatham, Kent

to Candida Donadio

CONTENTS

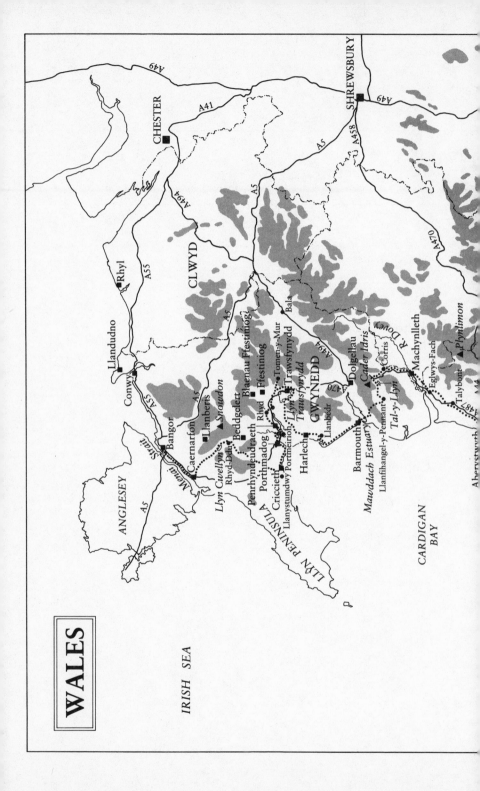

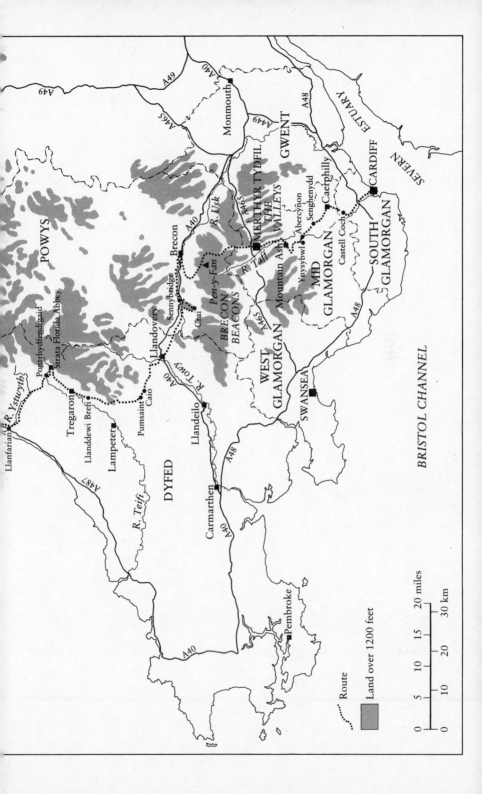

Up into The Valleys

In the spring, the world seemed to be comprehensively thawing. It was going to be the warmest, driest summer in years. And as the glaciers dripped and the seas expanded and people in long-frozen Eastern European states felt the almost unknown thrill of fundamental political change, I felt my annual restlessness. It came with a desire to give it searoom or – more likely – landroom: it is a restlessness which can generally be appeased by a long walk. This time, I told myself, it should be *a really long walk*. I harboured deeply sequestered thoughts of a particular country that I wanted to survey and absorb something of, if only through the soles of my boots. The prickings of race memories, Celtic, British, English, Norman – though less tangible than memories of a dream – perhaps prompted me in the same direction. I took from a cupboard a tubular-framed backpack purchased at a south-east London Greenpeace jumble-sale and crammed it as concisely as I could with clothes for various altitudes and temperatures, with water flask, whisky flask, digestive biscuits, maps, compass, nylon raincoat, knife, laundry-soap powder, notebook, books for reading, language phrasebook, cheque book (no need for a passport), then made a few phone calls to friends of friends who might be helpful, patted the dog, kissed my wife, and with a cheerful 'Who knows? – I may be at least three weeks,' set off. I was departing for the closest-to-hand foreign country: Wales.

The train from Paddington, living up to its 125 mph

billing, whizzed westwards. Slough – Swindon – Severn – a
dark tunnel – Welcome to Wales – *Croeso-i-Cymru* – small
hills – big drops of rain stuttering aft along the windows. I
thought of the shape of the country I was speeding into,
with its two peninsulas stretched unequally west towards
Ireland and dependent on a more-or-less north-south range
of mountains, a strange misshapen animal with small head,
truncated forelegs, and its back for some two hundred
miles pressed against England. I assembled dribs and drabs
of recollection, of thirty- or forty-year-distant Cambrian
forays, of clouds sailing past the windows of a cottage high
on a North Wales mountainside, of an army camp and
confused night-time manoeuvres (rhododendrons lit by
thunderflashes). Interweaved were images of hill-forts and
tumbling streams and an irate farmer with a shotgun and a
shining-eyed girl called Mair. Lloyd George knew my father,
father knew Lloyd George. Taffy was a Welshman, Taffy
was a thief. Welsh Guards, Welsh Fusiliers. Anthracite.
Arthur and Merlin. A grief ago. Ugly chapels. Long names
with too many consonants. Sheep.

A Somali taxidriver proudly pointed out to me a new
mosque abuilding for his community as he drove me from
Cardiff station to the southern end of the nineteenth-century
dockland once called Tiger Bay – the territory presumably
perilous for landlubbers, not the tigers amphibious – and
now reverted to the name of Butetown, after the Bute family
which built the docks and grew rich on them. Here the city
halts beside Cardiff Bay. Here the rivers Taff and Elan,
coming down from the rugged, deeply-rutted coal-bearing
area known as The Valleys, twenty miles or so north of the
city, meet salt water. Here I intended to start my walk.
Here, facing the brown mudflats of the Bay and the grey
prospect of the Bristol Channel beyond, I put my backpack
on a new bench, got out my raincoat, and took note of my
immediate surroundings. The former Pierhead Building still
stood pre-eminent, a Victorian French Gothic concoction

clad in terracotta, with hexagonal chimneys, gargoyles, and a castellated clocktower. Modern regeneration was signalled by newly planted bricks and cobbles, freshly painted black railings at the water's edge, and a bulky man in overalls crouching with a tape measure while a leaner colleague in jacket and tie jotted down figures.

I asked the latter official if there was a specific occasion for the fixing-up.

'One hundred and fiftieth anniversary of the docks,' he said. 'The railway came down here to the pier where the Campbell Line paddle-steamer ferries used to land. Fishing trawlers and Breton onion schooners went through the lock-gates into the West Bute Dock. That closed for ever in 1964. Now a few scrap-iron ships and dredgers use the last remaining docks. You wouldn't suspect it but at the turn of the century this was the busiest coal-exporting port in the world. There were ships out there, queued up halfway down the Bristol Channel, waiting to load Welsh coal.'

'And now?'

'Now we have plans for a barrage across the mouth of the Bay, constant high water within it, marinas, housing developments, thirty thousand new jobs over fifteen years. The legislation is coming before Parliament very soon. We'll get rid of all that mud. Where are you off to?'

I nodded northwards. I said, 'Up into the country,' judging it a bit early to confess to a stranger my ambition, which was to walk through Wales from bottom to top, from Bristol Channel to Menai Strait.

'You're in the right place to start. Bute Street goes up to the city centre. Keep right on for the main road, the A470, which will take you up into The Valleys. Good luck!'

I stood at the railings and took several substantial lungfuls of nutrient low-tide air. I looked at a small collection of ramshackle boats canted over at their moorings. I like mud. I wondered what the permanently raised water-level created by the barrage would do to the foundations and cellars of

Cardiff houses, built on low-lying ground beside the Bay. I wondered how the Bay's waters, fed as they were by two unclean rivers, would be regenerated behind the barrage, walled off from the Channel tides. On the remains of the nearby ferry pier, a pair of railway-type semaphore signals – which had once controlled the berthing of ferry steamers – drooped forlornly. I began to walk: past a new Industrial and Maritime Museum, in whose yard a steam locomotive and a retired lifeboat, the *Sir Watkin Williams-Wynn*, were parked. On the façade of the Pierhead Building the same twin theme was struck in a plaque decorated with both ships and railway engines and in the motto of the railway company – *Wrth ddwr a than*, Through water and fire.

I sauntered slowly around this part of Butetown, past a pub, still thriving, called The Packet, and a shop, with dusty, empty windows, which had last been a Merchant Navy haberdashers. A terrace of spruce-looking sandstone houses with Dutch gables facing out on the Bay had genteel net-curtained windows in which numerous small posters all chorused NO BARRAGE. The Bethel English Baptist Chapel had been re-named the Casablanca Club. The former Cardiff Coal Exchange building – which would have housed the Welsh Assembly if devolution had been approved in the 1970s – had become part of the empire of the barrage-promoting Cardiff Bay Redevelopment Corporation. The Mission for Sick Seamen was now a travel agency offering package tours by air to Tenerife. I paused at the gates to the surviving docks. NO ADMITTANCE EXCEPT ON BUSINESS said a. sign, though within, across derelict land, it was hard to spot what business was going on in the distant warehouses. A battered dark-red pickup truck, containing in the back a lawnmower and digging tools and pulling a very large trailer – almost a mobile home – with huge chrome hubcaps, was turning slowly away from the gates, apparently refused admittance by the security guard. The driver's window was rolled down as the rig stopped alongside me. The man at the

wheel was long-haired, in his thirties, and with a woman
and two small children jammed in beside him. He said,
'Would you be knowing where the travellers' site is?'

'I wouldn't,' I said. 'I'm sorry.'

He had several teeth missing in front and the look of a
man who was used to being sent from pillar to post. I got
out my ordnance map, a twenty-year-old one-inch-to-the-
mile sheet of the Cardiff region, displaying an area of Wales
about twenty-six miles square.

'It's somewhere on the other side of that,' he said, waving
at the gates. 'Tremorfer was where they told us to go.'

After a minute's concentration I found 'Tremorfa' on the
map, apparently an industrial zone on the south-eastern edge
of the city, backed by mudflats. I held out the map and
pointed. I said, 'It looks as if you're going to have to drive
up into the city centre and then back down on the far side of
the docks.' But he barely glanced at the map. A doll in the
costume of a Spanish dancer hung from the driving mirror;
a sprig of dry heather stood in a silvered plastic goblet above
the dashboard. The woman had an arm around one of the
children, whose cheeks were glowing feverishly.

'Back round then,' he said to her.

'Have you been long on the move?' I asked. As someone
who was about to be a nomad, temporarily, I felt sympathy
for as well as curiosity about the travelling family.

'A couple of months now. Burned off we were, from a
site in Dublin. Fled for our lives. Well, we'll be away now.
God bless.'

With a series of clanks and a burst of exhaust smoke the
truck and trailer jolted slowly off. I followed it up Bute
Street and then side-stepped to a skinny park, a filled-in
section of the Glamorganshire Canal, which was dug in the
1790s to link the ironworks of Merthyr Tydfil, twenty-five
miles inland, with the sea at Cardiff. Iron bollards and
mooring rings now set in the footpath provided places where
the pedestrian could pause, without making fast, to ponder

the drab municipal housing which had replaced the canalside
dockland slums. After my encounter with the Irish gypsy
family, I was on the look-out for things Welsh. But as befits
a city which had anti-Chinese race riots early this century
and is one of the few places in the British Isles where baseball
is played regularly, Cardiff continued to present a multi-
coloured, cosmopolitan face. An Indian take-away. Another
mosque. Jamaican greengrocers. A Greek Orthodox church.
A Chinese tattoo parlour. A short, expensively improved
stretch of city-centre roadway named, after Cardiff's twin
city in France, the Boulevard de Nantes.

Yet much of central Cardiff would not be confused with
anything French. Parts have the damn-your-eyes grottiness
of most present-day British cities: some streets thick with
traffic and litter; some so-called shopping precincts thick
with people and litter. And it also has idiosyncratic compen-
sations. The vast rugby stadium, Cardiff Arms Park, is built
beside the river Taff on marsh filled in with slag from the
city's foundries; it is near enough at hand so that Saturday
shoppers in the precincts can hear the crowds cheering,
chanting, and singing. The other great city-centre edifice is a
fully restored Norman castle and Roman fort with eight
acres of grounds. I climbed the White Tower, which was
built of grey stone by the Normans and provided from the
top a grey view of the hills and Valleys where I meant to go.
I, at any rate, felt grateful for the prospect, which King
Henry I denied to his relative Robert, Duke of Normandy,
kept prisoner here for the last twenty-eight years of his life. .
Henry had the Duke's eyes put out 'for greater security'.
Peacocks strutted on the lawns below the tower.

I walked next in Cathays Park, land which the Butes sold
to the city for £159,328 in 1898 and on which numerous
national and civic buildings are disposed in the monumen-
tally bland and formal manner of Washington DC and
Canberra. Portland stone columns and neoclassical façades
bespeak dominion status or federal grandeur – as if to appease

the aspirations of the Heroes of Wales, portrayed in a set of statues within the City Hall. The nearby recent structure housing the Welsh Office – the arm of the British civil service which administers matters Welsh – seems on the other hand to have been influenced by the fortified character of the Castle, perhaps for fear of contemporary riots and insurgence.

Off St Mary's Street I found more congenial architecture. Here are several Victorian and Edwardian arcades, sinuous glass-roofed passages lined with small shops and cafés. I sat in one of the latter with a cup of filter coffee and a slice of treacle tart, my pack doffed, and read the day's *Western Mail*. This paper, published in Cardiff, had the subtitle 'The National Newspaper of Wales', though the specifically Welsh news therein seemed to take up only a few columns, having mostly to do with a child sex-abuse case, a bar-room brawl, and anxiety about how dunlin and redshank would cope without the mudflats if the Bay barrage scheme went ahead. From the real-estate ads I gathered that local property prices remained high. One other ad that took my attention had been placed by BBC Wales for a film about to be made in the Cardiff area. 'Non-Equity Extras' were required, it said, 'to look like Tramps/Down and Outs, with distinctive facial/physical attributes applicable to this life style'. However, 'Locals only need apply.' A pity. In a week or so, I thought, I might look the part.

Restored, I shouldered my pack and marched northwards through Bute Park – more Bute land nicely laid out in 1777 by Capability Brown, the great landscape architect whose first name was in fact Lancelot. The park forms a verdant slice of the city, from the castle to the northern outskirts. I passed through gardens and along paths flanked with herbaceous borders to the river Taff, whose course I followed through bosky areas of the park. (Taff is apparently an Anglicised form of the river's Welsh name, and has nothing to do with the nickname Taffy, which is derived from the

common Welsh Christian name Dafydd.) I crossed the river
by way of a handsome single-pylon suspension footbridge
overhanging a weir. Ducks swam below but there were no
sea trout or elver jumping, as – a sign informed me – they
can be seen doing in season.

A footpath across damp playing fields brought me to
Pontcanna, a sedate residential quarter. There, in Cathedral
Road, spoiled for choice by numerous small hotels, boarding
houses, and bed-and-breakfast establishments, I plumped for
the Ashley Court Hotel. It formed the end of a terrace of
substantial late-Victorian houses. It also displayed on a front
wall a painted sign, THE LAURELS HOTEL, apparently a previous
cognomen, but left there with a carelessness about any
confusion that might arise in the minds of prospective clients.
This seemed – as I walked up the tiled front path – a point of
attraction.

Getting out of bed the next morning, I attempted to restore suppleness to my spinal column by lifting my knees, alternately, to my chin a dozen times. My bed, in a small upstairs front room, had been a bit on the soft side, though Ray Skrines, the ebullient proprietor of the Ashley Court, had said that it was the firmest in the hotel. The Ashley Court, in any event, was full; I had the last available bed. Breakfast provided an opportunity to see assembled the other guests, some of whom had been glimpsed on the stairs or dodging into the shower and toilets: several long-distance truck drivers; an elderly couple on a motoring holiday; a young woman with a serious-looking briefcase; two college students who were apparently long-term residents. Mr Skrines was a Cardiff man by birth, a former steel fitter, whose change of trades seemed to reflect what had happened to his city. 'The industry has mostly gone from here,' he said. 'Now, it's mostly banks, and offices, and government. This is the capital of Wales. We've lots of students, too, and broadcasting people.' He didn't miss working in steel. The Ashley Court, evidently booming, kept him and his wife Doreen busy; today he had to fit and lay new carpet on the upstairs landing.

Mrs Skrines – having asked me whether I'd like 'the full breakfast' – set before me a large plate bearing bacon, eggs, sausage, tomatoes, mushrooms, and fried bread. She was still excited by my walk, which, on arrival, in explanation of my backpack, I had felt the need to allude to. Topping up my

coffee cup, she exclaimed, 'Ray and I were just saying how
we'd like to go on a walk like yours! And go round the
world!' They had driven east to Hereford last Sunday and
walked along the eighth-century border rampart of Offa's
Dyke – 'Just a few miles, mind you. Nothing too strenuous!'

Mrs Skrines made me a neatly packed lunch, to help me
through my exertions when and if breakfast wore off. 'Let us
know how far you get!' she said, seeing me out the front
door. It was nine a.m.; a calm, hazy late-April morning. I
could just see my breath. Adjusting the shoulder straps and
waist strap of my pack for a comfortably tight fit, I set forth
up Cathedral Road, down which some of the last of the
morning rush-hour traffic was moving into the city. Then I
turned into the dewy parkland of Pontcanna Fields, bucolic
and fume-free. I walked north along an avenue of beeches,
birds in the branches loudly twittering. I fell into a quick
stride, almost a light infantry pace, faster (I knew) than I could
manage to maintain for more than an hour or so but just now
matching my spirits. I could feel some of the apprehension
begin to fall away that had so far attended this idea. I was
under way. And as some of the dread faded that had built up
in my mind ('Perhaps I won't get very far. I may have to give
up and creep quietly home'), I was suffused with a wonderful
confidence and expectation. And this was in the first mile, the
first fifteen minutes!

I crossed a busy ring-road – Western Avenue – and followed a footpath along the west branch of the Taff, which
was running white over some shallows – almost a freshet
from rain during the night. Edge-of-city meadows to my left,
damp grass, dandelions, the only other morning walkers
several elderly men accompanied by their dogs.

'*Let us know how far you get!*' I had told the Skrines that
today I was hoping to reach Caerphilly, nine miles or so
walking to the north – an easy beginning. And after that? 'Oh,
I'll follow my nose, see where I get to . . .' There are several
designated routes for long-distance walks on the edges of

Wales: the Pembrokeshire Coast Walk along the Irish Sea cliffs and bays of south-western Wales; and the Offa's Dyke Walk following the border defences set up by the Mercian king in the late 700s to keep the Wealas, 'the foreigners' as the Saxons called them, in their place – the western uplands of Britain. There has also been a route proposed up the middle of Wales, the Cambrian Way, for the most part on high ground, though the precise track has never been agreed or officially adopted, apparently from fears that some mountainous sections might be too arduous or – contrarily – might be so popular they would be eroded by use. I wanted to make my own route, which might coincide now and then with the Cambrian Way but would tend less to day-after-day mountain hiking and would leave me free to take in both highland and lowland, mountain peak and coastal plain, highroad and Roman road, farmtrack, footpath, and field edge, and thereby to encounter not just nature and any other hikers but whatever a haphazard path through Wales might put in my way. At some points I expected to cross the routes of two distinguished earlier travellers – the archdeacon Gerald, who in 1188 made an extensive Welsh journey on horseback in company with Baldwin, the Archbishop of Canterbury, in the course of a trip to gain support and recruits for the Third Crusade; and George Borrow, the determined traveller, linguist, gypsy enthusiast, and Bible proselytiser, who traversed North Wales from east to west and then the whole country from north to south in 1854. 801 years after Gerald, 135 years after George, I thought I would see among other things what similarities and differences were to be found, what and how 'Welshness' presented itself today.

Across the fields the tall tapering spire of Llandaff cathedral thrust up from a tower-top nest of smaller pinnacles. It rose above surrounding trees and the nearby ruins of a bell tower and castle. Llandaff, once a separate village, is now a Cardiff suburb, with a green surrounded by nicely proportioned old houses. A local holy man named Teilo is given credit for founding a church here in the sixth century; he is said to have accompanied Wales's premier saint David on a pilgrimage to Jerusalem and to have spent some years serving the faith in Britanny with another Welsh saint, Samson. (Britons and Bretons were both of Celtic stock. Many Britons are thought to have migrated to Britanny, pushed out by the Saxon settlements.) Llan-daff means the church of the Taff (T and D being interchangeable as first letters of words in Welsh in the same way that – confusingly for those who do not speak the language – C and G, F and B, and F and M sometimes are, when surrounding words or context demand one or the other. Examples are fach/bach, fawr/mawr, and moel/foel.) Gerald was here with Archbishop Baldwin to preach the cross; in their audience, Gerald wrote, 'the English stood on one side and the Welsh on the other'. The travelling party was put up for the night by the local bishop, William, 'who seemed a discreet and honest fellow'. The next morning, before leaving, the Archbishop celebrated Mass at the high altar.

I wandered slowly around the cathedral, struck by how well time pulled together works from different periods. The fine medieval west front is sandwiched between the Jasper Tower, named after Henry VII's uncle, Jasper Tudor, who commissioned it, and the taller south tower and spire, created a hundred years ago by a Welsh architect named John Pritchard. The cathedral was devastated by Cromwell's troops – who committed the usual sins of 'other-side' soldiery, drinking in the nave and using the font as a pig trough – and by Hitler's airforce, whose explosives did great damage in 1941. Within, mild sunlight fell into the tall nave through high, mostly clear glass windows. A Norman Romanesque arch – a slightly flattened semicircle – framed the high altar. In place of a screen dividing nave from choir, as found in most cathedrals, a massive post-war concrete arch spanned the nave, leading one's eye through to the altar, and holding aloft a huge concrete cylinder which seemed almost to touch the massive wooden roof beams. This cylinder formed both a multi-directional case for organ pipes and a support for a piece of sculpture by Jacob Epstein, *Christ in Majesty*, in aluminium. An organist was practising. Short salvoes and long booming runs of sound swelled overhead.

It was quieter in a modern asymmetric side chapel lit by the windows of one slightly curving wall. The chapel was a memorial to men of the Welch Regiment (which amalgamated with the South Wales Borderers Regiment in June 1969 to become the Royal Regiment of Wales and thereby caused the loss of one of the few surviving occasions on which this variant spelling of Welsh was used). On stones set in the walls were inscribed the names of battles and campaigns: Alma, Kimberley, Belle Isle, Detroit, Sebastopol, Mons, Bethune, Loos, the Somme, Macedonia, Jerusalem, Falaise, Benghazi, Crete, Sicily, North-West Europe . . . The slightly nervous style of the incised lettering would have been approved of, I thought, by David Jones, Anglo-Welsh artist, poet, and maker of inscriptions (though Jones had served in yet another Welsh regiment, the Royal Welch Fusiliers, during the First World War). I sat for a moment and said a silent prayer to the Creator, the God of Walkers: a prayer on beginning a walk that begged for divine permission to be able to finish it in a laudable manner.

Upstream along the left bank of the Taff to a busy road bridge at Llandaff Weir, where I crossed to the other bank. I passed through what seemed to be Cardiff's final playing field. The path went under a pair of converging railway embankments. One underpass was flooded but fortunately was also littered with bricks, stones, and pieces of timber which made for haphazard stepping-stones. I passed an old lock cottage for the Glamorganshire Canal – once again filled in – and a restored 1807 water-wheel powered pump which had lifted water from the river into the canal. Ironworks and tinplate works had stood on ground now being developed for housing. Here the path lost its certainty; in fact it soon disappeared altogether among the junior executive residences.

Following one likely street I found myself in a cul-de-sac, with Vauxhall Cavaliers and bottom-of-the-line BMWs in the driveways. A few house-proud housewives were hanging out laundry and shaking doormats. An aged man walking with a small child pointed me toward an exit from the estate, asked me where I was going, and said, 'I'm the babysitter today, otherwise I'd come with you.'

Now I gave up the Taff and took to the canal, roughly a mile of which still existed. The right-hand bank was steeply wooded and I walked along the left bank. The canal was shallow, with big waterlilies carpeting extensive sections; ducks cruised in the clear patches. It was ten-thirty and I was warming up. I was also beginning to hear the whirr of heavy traffic. Built since my map had been produced in 1969, the M4 motorway sliced across South Wales and across my route. The canal ended where a tunnel once carrying it into the hillside had been blocked off, and I took a dog-leg westward, over a stile and along a road which gave access to a striking modern factory, the plant of Amersham International, which makes pharmaceuticals and medical diagnostic equipment, set in brilliant solitude on its Taff-side greenfield site. Following a path to the north, I ducked under the noisy motorway. An abandoned Ford Cortina, windows broken, seats stripped, lay on its hubs, possibly ejected from the rat-race of the M4 up above. Ahead, a mile or so away, what looked like a small enchanted Bavarian castle rose on a wooded hillside above the village of Tongwynlais.

Before it reached the village, my footpath crossed farm- land. I was put to the test by an iron gate, which could be swung open in an elliptical iron enclosure. Apparently intended to keep cattle from getting out, it was by no means easy to enter for bipeds wearing a backpack. Standing on tiptoe, breathing in deeply, I shimmied through. A calf frolicking across the lush pasture caught sight of me and came to a sudden halt, forelegs crossed at the knee, in order to stare.

I didn't pause in Tongwynlais, though several pub doors

were visibly unlocked, even ajar: opening time. It seemed a neat, quiet place, with a proper proportion of houses and small shops as well as the pubs, and a number 26 bus waiting to go into Cardiff. Here was the site of the first charcoal-fired furnace for iron-making in South Wales, built by Sussex ironworkers in the late 1500s. Here was the home of Mrs Mary Ann Wyndham Lewis, widow of a Glamorgan lawyer and industrialist, who in 1839 married Benjamin Disraeli, statesman and novelist, and eventually became Countess of Beaconsfield. I stayed on the rising backroad, which led north-east toward Caerphilly, and turned off after half a mile, up the even more steeply climbing drive to the little castle I had seen – Castell Coch. Lavender-grey stone. Conical turrets. A drawbridge and portcullis. Perhaps a princess in need of rescue. But it was a rather severe girl in a resolutely non-Gothic booth who took my entrance fee – and then changed my first impression by sweetly letting me leave my backpack with her. I stood in the circular central courtyard and looked at open stairs, covered galleries painted a rhubarb-red, lofty tapering chimneys, and the conical towers topped by green-copper vanes. Once again I was made to think, Good for the Butes!

Few dynasties can have had such a successful run of winning commercial gambles and marrying wealthy women. The man who got things going was Lord Bute, the third Earl of that name and George III's least popular Prime Minister, who married Lady Mary Wortley-Montagu and her fortune. His son, the first Marquess of Bute, married two heiresses in succession: first, Charlotte Windsor, who had great estates in these parts; second, Frances Coutts, of the famous banking family. The second Marquess, grandson of the first, also married twice, and well, and went on to expand the Bute fortunes by exploiting the neglected estates in South Wales and by investing in new docks and mines. Port dues, ground rents, and mineral royalties made him one of the wealthiest men in Britain, if not the world. He was a tireless administrator who, despite bad eyesight, wrote at least half a dozen long business letters a day. His son John, the third Marquess, inherited the title at the age of six months and, when he came of age, an income of £300,000 a year. He also inherited thirteen other titles, 117,000 acres of land, and the ruins of Castell Coch. Scholarly, reclusive, a convert to Catholicism at the age of twenty-one, and inclined to frequent fasts, he was passionately interested in the Middle Ages. The celebrations for the end of his minority lasted a week, with balloon ascents, regattas, fêtes, and public dinners, but he was not – despite great generosity to local causes – much attuned to Cardiff and the docks. 'Athens and Assisi', he wrote, 'have spoilt me for anything else.' He intrigued Disraeli, who based on him the hero of his most successful (and utterly soppy) novel *Lothair* – a tremendously rich young nobleman who is convinced 'that life should be entirely religious' but is perplexed 'by the inevitable obstacles which seemed perpetually to oppose themselves to the practice of his opinions'.

The original fortification on this site was a Welsh stronghold belonging to the chieftain of the area, Ifor ap Meurig, Lord of Senghenydd. The Normans built a castle here to guard the gorge through which the Taff approaches Cardiff. It was partly destroyed by fire and fighting in the fifteenth century, and by time and weather thereafter. Bute decided he wanted to rebuild the castle and readily interested William Burges, the architect who was already working for him on the restoration of Cardiff Castle. Burges – nicknamed 'Ugly' to distinguish him from his near namesake J. B. 'Pretty' Burgess, a painter who moved in the same Pre-Raphaelite circles – had found in Bute the perfect patron. The son of one of the partners in the firm which had designed the East Bute Docks in Cardiff, William Burges was as enthralled by the Middle Ages as John Bute; he used vellum-bound notebooks and when at home wore medieval costume – his house was probably the only one in London with a working portcullis. Here the undergrowth was hacked away and the ruins cleared revealing foundations of old red sandstone – hence the name, Castell Coch, the Red Castle. Meanwhile Burges indulged his fantasies of thirteenth-century building, his passion for garde-robes, towers, loopholes, and embrasures. The fact that no Welsh Norman castle had similar conical turrets didn't worry him.

Nor does it matter now. The limestone used for the rebuilding merges neatly with the sandstone foundations. The base of the curtain wall slopes steeply down and outwards, and the bases of two towers are 'spurred' and supported with massive sloping buttresses. At the single gate, so-called 'murder holes' set in the wall overhead allow for stones, boiling water, and heated tar to be poured on to the heads of unwelcome visitors. Slightly higher on the wall above the gate an Italian statue of the Virgin and Child, painted purple, white, and gold, manifests a gentler approach to things.

I climbed to the gallery and wandered around the rooms which are separated by eccentric passages and tortuous little flights of stairs. The Banqueting Hall had unappetising murals that showed the gruesome culminations of the lives of various obscure Christian martyrs. The octagonal Drawing Room was decorated on the restless theme of Life and Death in Nature, with scenes from Aesop's Fables, and with a vaulted ceiling whose gold ribs divided panels showing sky, stars, birds, and butterflies. The fireplace tiles bore the signs of the Zodiac. Above the mantel stood statues of the Three Fates. Everywhere, too much, too much! The nearby Windlass Room came as a relief, being scarcely decorated, given over to machinery for raising and lowering the portcullis and to a fireplace for heating water and other substances that could be poured on the enemies Billy Burges imagined at the gate. On Lord Bute's bedroom walls was a maze of stencilled geometric patterns of a sort that resembled those in a frieze I remem-bered as having figured, in a childhood bedroom, in awful nightmares. The furniture looked immensely uncomfortable. Lady Bute's circular bedroom, on the floor above, was apparently designed for the Sleeping Beauty, with narrow windows and a domed ceiling done with mirrors entwined by carved thorns and brambles. The castellated washstand had end towers containing hot and cold water tanks. Her ladyship's ornate red and gold bed was a double, but Lord Bute is said to have found the paintings of monkeys on the walls 'too lascivious', and I wondered if he ever joined her there. In fact, though the craftsmanship that went into the rendering of Burges's fantasy was intense, almost dementedly so, I was not surprised to read that Lord and Lady Bute seldom visited the place – though their children were occasionally sent to stay when suffering from infectious diseases. Burges himself died suddenly in 1881, and completion of the project was undertaken by his colleagues. Bute became interested in other things: Scottish history; the occult; travelling in Palestine; learning Welsh; sailing; and establishing a vineyard here at Castell Coch. The produce of some years was turned into communion wine, but the vintage of 1893 – which brought forth forty hogsheads – was found 'superb' by some of those who tasted it.

At the entrance booth, where I stopped to collect my backpack, I asked the young castellaine what it was like to work here.

'It's cheerful much of the year,' she said, 'especially when school parties come. The children love it. They run around, pretending they're back in olden times. But I don't like it during the winter, on the days when it's dark and dank and few visitors turn up. Then it's very eery.'

When I set off again, it was with my sweater removed and stowed in the top of my pack. I took a gravelled path through the woods, where bluebells, herb robert, aconite, and wild garlic were growing. I came to the narrow Caerphilly road again but quickly got bored with trudging uphill along it. So I crossed the road into woods beyond and climbed alongside a stream which descended the steep hillside. Perhaps the downward flow of water increased my sense of walking up a down escalator; perhaps I wasn't yet in tiptop condition for Welsh gradients. I arrived at the summit, at another minor road, puffing and sweating. A nearby stile provided a handy seat for rest and map-reading. The map showed the encouraging letters PH less than a mile in the Caerphilly direction and – I was now roughly 675 feet above sea level – a merciful lack of contour lines between me and the public house. Walking on, I recalled that my map was old; a dreadful disappearance might have occurred. But the Black Cock Inn still stood at a fork in the road. I purchased a pint of draught Bass – brewed in Burton-on-Trent, England, and served in a French glass. But it was the only beer being dispensed, non-pressurised, from a proper pump, and I took it gratefully to a trestle table in the garden and ate Mrs Skrine's excellent ham sandwiches. Across the way was a golf course and in the north-west distance something new: a desolate bare-topped hill.

I took the right hand fork. I passed a driveway with a sign advertising a boarding hotel for cats – guarded, however, by two black-and-white dogs. They rushed down the drive, woofing, heading for my ankles, and saw me off. A woman riding past on a chestnut mare gave me a friendlier greeting, a cheerful 'Good day'. The road ran around a hill, part of Caerphilly Common, to whose heathy summit I climbed. At the top, no trees, only grass and ferns and a stone cairn with a plaque inscribed in both Welsh and English with Psalm 104, verse 21:

> O Lord, how manifold are thy works!
> In wisdom hast though made them all.
> The earth is full of thy riches.

The distant view was now of an expanse of blue-grey hills to the north – the hills from whose valleys Welsh coal had come. Below, in the immediate foreground, lay the town of Caerphilly, a large chunk of which seemed to be stone fortifications – another castle. Although this would be my

second castle in a day, my third in two days, I looked forward
to seeing it. For some years as a child I lived in the Hampshire
village of Portchester, in a house in Castle Street. At the far
end, by the muddy harbour, stood one of the finest Roman
and Norman castles in England, where I scrambled on the
walls and watched my father play for the local cricket team on
the grounds below the great Keep. Moreover, at the age of
seven my most prized toy was a bright green clockwork
engine, a Hornby model locomotive of the Great Western
Railway's Castle class. It was called 'Caerphilly Castle' – the
name on an arched plate fastened over the driving wheels on
each side. At the age of eleven, when I returned from four
wartime years in the USA, it was one of the recovered
possessions that made me realise that, Yes, I am really home
again.

   The afternoon was hazing up and the wind on the summit
was cool. I set off downhill. I had to steer around another golf
course, fenced off from the Common, that interposed itself
between me and the town. I found myself on boggy ground
approaching a bridgeless brook. Fortunately there was help
from some mole hills and tussocks, and I crossed the wetness
with only a bit of mud and water on my boots. (Keeping dry
even supposedly waterproof boots is a challenge I try to meet
when walking.) Caerphilly itself, with one main commercial
street, seemed to lack the big-city prosperity of Cardiff; it lost
a good deal of employment in 1964, when its railway workshops were closed. I was forced with my backpack to step off
the narrow footway into the street to let old people with sticks
and young mothers with baby-strollers get past. One hip-
pyish girl said to her punk male companion, as they came out
of a chip shop, 'Oooh, there's a hiker!' I was hailed by the
driver of a delivery van, wanting to know the way to a certain
warehouse. It seems to be my fate, my nature, to attract such
questioning – coming out of the station on my first visit to
Bologna, a car of French tourists stopped and asked me the
way. Wasn't it clear to this van driver, to the Irish gypsy by

the Cardiff dockgates, that I was a traveller, too? Or did they set against that the impression that I seemed approachable, open to questioning?

More crucial to me than Caerphilly's scruffiness was the fact that it lacked obvious accommodation for wayfarers. One inn I passed had a shakily hand-lettered sign offering rooms and meals but failed to convey any substantial promise of cleanliness or comfort. One 'hotel' I looked in was a dark and gloomy pub populated by fruit machines. The town tourist office was not in the street in which a sign claimed it was. But I found it eventually on the edge of the greensward and lake beside the castle – the huge castle. Castell Coch had been a toy; this was the real thing.

I felt I should ensure a night's repose by visiting the tourist office first. The lady within was in her mid-forties, blonde, and loquaciously friendly. Her name was Rita. She described several places that did bed-and-breakfast and telephoned the one I fancied to make sure a bed was available. I paid a ten per cent fee which would be deducted from my bill. As Rita did the necessary paperwork, she allowed that she was just a bit bored with Caerphilly. She liked the progress they were making in Cardiff – the barrage scheme, maybe an opera house like Sydney's. Her favourite TV programme was *The Antique Road Show*, but they'd never filmed it in Caerphilly, which was a shame, didn't I think? Even the tourist office was in a bit of a backwater now. They'd moved it from up the street to here by way of a caravan in the town car park where funnily lots of visitors found them even though a few cars backed into it now and then.

'You have a fine view of the castle, though,' I said, wondering if the sight of my backpack brought out the restlessness in people.

Rita agreed about the view. In the castle, she told me, a hall was being fixed up to accommodate conferences – and compete (it seemed) with Cardiff's enterprise.

Apart from me, the tourist office's only client was a small

boy. He shyly approached the counter and asked if he could have a brochure about the Rhymney Valley, nearest to Caerphilly of the half-dozen valleys that furrow the hills north of here. When he left, smiling and clutching the brochure, Rita said, 'He and his friend take turns coming in here, nearly every day. One brochure after another. They say they're doing a geography project. At least they're not cheeky, like some.'

In South Wales clearly one can't avoid castles and the ruins of castles; but that at Caerphilly is the biggest and best. The site covers thirty acres, not only of land and masonry but of water arranged for defensive purposes in the shape of an outer moat, two artificial lakes, and an inner moat. A huge 'barrage-wall' forms an almost separate, introductory castle, covering the approach to the main structure. The latter is on an island, a concentric brown-grey wedding cake of rough stone towers and an inner wall rising behind and above a lower wall with flanking bastions. The poet Tennyson ('The splendour falls on castle walls . . .') was here in 1856 and exclaimed 'It isn't a castle – it's a whole ruined town!' But in fact the whole thing had a military purpose – with which it still impresses. Gilbert de Clare, Earl of Gloucester and Hereford, spearheaded the Norman advance into these parts, and despite attacks by the natives commenced building his headquarters here. It was high-tech for its day, influenced by the fortifications of Kenilworth, Dover, and Aigues-Mortes – the Provence port of embarkation for many Anglo-Norman knights going crusading. It showed how great an investment the intruders were prepared to make in order to live secure from Welsh assault. Owain Glyndŵr, the Welsh insurgent, captured the castle in the early fifteenth century but his tenure was brief. During the Civil War of the seventeenth century the castle was 'slighted', that is wrecked to make it useless, the power of gunpowder being forcefully demonstrated: a tower at the south-east corner was cleft and blown to a Pisa-like angle, though like a tottering veteran it still just stands.

What's to be seen now is once again thanks to the Butes – this time the fourth Marquess, who rescued the castle from complete dilapidation after 1900 and in ensuing years bought up and demolished all the roundabout houses which stood in the way of the spectacular sight. (Some such houses are visible in a drawing of the castle done in the late 1600s by the Dutch artist Hendrik Danckerts, at which time shrubbery was already growing on the battlements; the castle has long been on the itineraries of artists making tours of Wales.)

I walked in and out, up and down. Weathered wood planking of the bridge across the moat. Cropped turf growing almost up to the stonework, though a little ditch next to the stones kept the blades of the mowers at a safe distance. Cool breeze in the gateways, cold shade in the shadows of walls and towers. Despite a wind-blown collection of plastic lemonade bottles in one corner of the moat, an impression that CADW, the Welsh body which protects ancient monuments, was doing its best to care for the great pile. I took the comfort I usually take in Norman castles from finding my name, Bailey, attached to the inner walled area that was used to house the castle garrison and is overlooked by the mounded motte and tower.

Shafts of sunlight thrust at a low angle against the castle walls; the afternoon was getting on. I walked north up Pontygwindy Road which was lined with gritty little houses, struggling shops, used car lots, and a huge new supermarket which would no doubt finish off many of the small shops. To one side lay a so-called industrial estate, with many ware-houses. On the north edge of town I arrived at a roundabout where five roads came together. End-of-the-working-day traffic rushed around clockwise and I took a moment to spot on the farside, at eleven o'clock, my destination for the night: 'The Cottage'. I had to pick the gaps in the traffic to get there unscathed.

My first inclination was to blame Rita: had I come walking in Wales to spend the night next to a noisy roundabout? But second thoughts soon prevailed. The Cottage was a rambling former farmhouse, several centuries old. It was low-ceilinged and double-glazed. From the window of my bedroom I could see the traffic but hardly hear it. I was handily placed for dinner at a large roadhouse on the east side of the junction; eating there, I had the impression I was the only customer who had not arrived by car. My hosts at The Cottage, the Owenses, were both musicians. Mrs Owens sang in a local choir. Her husband, Barrie, was a pianist and organist who also worked as a guide for parties of foreign musical groups. 'I take them anywhere in Britain – England and Scotland, but I make sure they see Wales, too. I'm not a Welsh nationalist – just a patriot.' He also supported those in Caerphilly who felt that its past should be maximised and marketed, for instance by holding recitals and fêtes in the castle, even if this required some initial investment. 'Some people round here say why spend money on making a conference suite in the castle entrance tower when there's a shortage of council houses in town. I say 120,000 visitors come to the castle every year and come to Caerphilly for that reason – and we should build on that. Mining was our mainstay here for a long time, but, like it or not, it has just about gone. Tourism, and therefore the past, is a vital industry. I think we have to go out and seize it with both hands.'

I said, 'Haven't I read that a lot of non-Welsh-speaking people in these parts are being patriotic by sending their children to Welsh-speaking schools?'

'I think it's a fashion,' Barrie Owens said. 'It could also be a dead-end. What are those children going to do with their lives? They can't all work for the BBC in Wales or for local authorities which want their officials to be not just English-speaking but Welsh-speaking, too.'

When I set out next morning after breakfast it was a dulcet day. I was hoping to reach before evening some friends of my sister's who had a small farm about nine miles away to the north-east as the crow flies but probably at least fifteen as I would walk it. A light headwind was blowing and the sun was warm as I cut through a council housing estate – by no means all local funds went to the castle – at Penyrheol. Women, having seen their children to school, were standing chatting at street corners. I came out of the estate on to a road which ran beside a stream, Nant-yr-Aber, the Brook of the Confluence. This was the southern edge of the South Wales coalfield, and the road went up a valley which introduced me to features to be found in most of the larger, better-known Valleys not far to the north: the sound of running water close at hand; the smell of coal smoke; the sight of small farms on the slopes of hills whose summits were thinly grassed and bare of trees; and the presence of long villages or towns which snaked along the one road down the valley.

Here I encountered two such villages, more or less continuous, the first being Abertridwr, the second Senghenydd. Coal had caused both to expand from small farming hamlets. Now, though their mines had closed, the smell of coal, not just as coal smoke, was in the air. Coal was underfoot. The topsoil of the nearby ground was mostly coal, slag, soot, and grit. (A few nights after this I watched on the television news police digging up a South Wales backgarden for the bodies of a missing woman and child. It looked as if they were digging in pure coal dust.) Nuclear power is not the only source of energy to have disposal problems. The mining of coal left much residue on the surface, and bulldozers were to be seen at the top end of Abertridwr re-arranging mountainous old heaps of shale and spoil, of the kind that cast a fearsome shadow over many Valley communities. The reclamation scheme was also similar to that being carried out in many of the Valleys, with the intention of re-greening them. Near one former Abertridwr mine, a football pitch had been created on recently levelled ground. At the edge of the road daffodils were blaring an announcement of Improvement from the sooty soil.

Both Ray Skrines and Barrie Owens had suggested that although the Valleys had generally lost the industry which had populated them, with the Rhondda Valley for instance at that point reduced to just one working pit, the Valley communities hadn't become ghost towns. Many of the residents commuted to work elsewhere by bus, train, and car. As house-prices rose in Cardiff, a Valley house was all that many young couples could afford. Unsurprisingly there were a number of FOR SALE signs on the terraced houses I walked past; remarkably, there were a number of SOLD signs, too. Video rental outlets and medical practices with plaques bearing the names of Asian doctors were to be seen among greengrocers and pet-food shops. In Abertridwr the largest business appeared to be the Cyril Evans bus company, with its fleet of red and yellow coaches. In Senghenydd, Commercial Street had a few shops and a post office near the stone clock tower which is the war memorial.

'This street used to be all shops, eighty years ago,' said a plump, pretty woman behind the counter in Cavanna's, the general store I went into. 'Most of the life went out of Senghenydd in the mine disaster of 1913. But our heart has kept beating, nevertheless.'

Cavanna's seemed to sell a bit of everything. My eye was taken by a row of tall glass jars holding sweets – Liquorice Allsorts, Chocolate Toffees, Bullseyes, Glacier Mints, and

Humbugs – of the sort that took my fancy and my pocket money when I was six or seven, coming home from school. I asked the woman if Senghenydd still had a school.

'Oh, we've got two, two primary schools,' she said. 'There's the ordinary one along the street and then the Welsh one, Ysgol Ifor Bach, not far up the hill behind the clock tower.'

I bought a quarter of a pound of Humbugs. I only wanted one, to retrieve the taste of childhood, but felt a quarter was the least I could buy. Sucking the sweet, I turned up the hill along a street of small houses built for miners and their families in the late nineteenth century. High-quality steam coal was the lure here, found in relatively thick seams, averaging six feet; it was particularly good for smelting iron and firing the boilers of ships. (The smoke which rose from the funnels of cargo steamers over the oceans of the world was generally Welsh smoke.) With the exploitation of the coalfield, instant towns appeared where farms had been. Villages of one hundred people suddenly held three thousand. Men came to work in the mines from all over Wales and from other parts of Britain – quarrymen, canal boatmen, farm workers, mill hands. There was a sudden need for houses, chapels, pubs, shops, and schools. In this area, several mines were sunk: the Windsor at Abertridwr, which remained open until the late 1970s; the Universal at Senghenydd, which closed during the 1920s General Strike and never re-opened, though its workings went on being used for ventilation by the Windsor colliery; and the Albion, two miles away at the village of Cilfynydd in Taff Vale. It is an area of a few square miles which in ten years had three great disasters. In 1894, an underground explosion at the Albion killed 290 men and boys. In 1901, 81 miners were killed at Senghenydd. And in 1913, the worst mining calamity ever to occur in Britain took place here, when 440 died.

Walking up the street toward the Welsh school, there was nothing in the air or on the ground to prompt the feeling that massive tragedy had happened here. The surface machinery of winding gear and aerial dumping baskets has been removed; yet underground at a depth of up to 1700 feet the levels and roadways and working faces still form miles of empty veins, out of which rock, coal, and human blood have been drained. Only in the graveyards at Eglwysilan and Penyrheol are the memorials visible with the telling dates and such inscriptions as '*Bu farw yn Nancha Senghenydd*' – 'Died in the Senghenydd Explosion.' As I climbed the hill, I felt relieved no working mine remained – for I might have felt duty-bound to make a descent. I know what a coal mine – a modern one, at least – is like, having visited one in Yorkshire ten years ago. On that occasion, I went down in a cage, travelled by tram along a level tunnel, then crawled in expert company half a mile to a coal face. I had been given overalls and pads to strap to my knees, but I lacked the experience of making them fast, and during the interminable rapid crawl under back-scraping rock sharp lumps of coal and stone dug into my knees and elbows. I remember the dark, the dust, and the sound of rock creaking and of beams and props groaning. This was an up-to-date mine, with coal-cutting machines, electric light, powerful ventilation, and much safety equipment, but the work was still immensely difficult and dangerous, and involved physical hardship and courage. What it must have been like in the South Wales pits at the turn of the century is hard to imagine.

At Cilfynydd in 1894 and Senghenydd in 1901 the cause of the disasters was thought to have been the firing of explosive charges which had not been properly tamped or packed in with clay. Explosives were used to increase the height of roadways, as roofs settled, by blasting out the rocks of roofs or the floors, and were meant to be used between mining shifts and only after the surrounding underground area had been dampened with water. For the father and son teams who worked at the seams, the mines of this locality were favourable because of their dryness: little water seeped into the working places. But because of this, danger was increased. Mines are usually warm – at the Universal colliery, it was often 25 Fahrenheit degrees more at the work faces than on the surface; the effect being further to dry out the workings. Moreover, in time much coal dust accumulated. The tramway wagons were overfilled, coal fell out and was crushed along the tracks, making long trails of combustible material. After the first two calamities, recommendations were made about watering the surroundings before blasting and not overloading the wagons. It was evident that the 1901 explosion had been set off by a blasting charge which had blown outwards – had not done its job of breaking rock but, improperly tamped, burst forth as from the barrel of a gun, firing the nearby dust and setting off an explosive flame which expanded through the workings of the pit. Some of the dead were so mutilated, their bodies were unrecognisable fragments; weights were added to coffins to make them feel as if they contained a normal corpse.

If the recommendations of the inquiries after the first two disasters had been heeded, there would not have been one in 1913 at Senghenydd. The cause – the spark – was believed to be different: this time it was officially ascribed to gas being ignited when a miner's lamp was re-lit and the consequent explosion being fed by coal dust. But once again the rules about watering and overloading had been breached. The fire spread through the pit, killing half of those below ground at the time and burning for six days. The town was devastated. In each of three separate homes a father and two sons died. One woman lost her husband, two sons, a brother, and a lodger. One woman who had lost two sons at Cilfynydd and a son and son-in-law in the 1901 Senghenydd disaster now had to bear the death of another son and grandson. A Senghenydd miner who came out alive, William Hyatt, never went back underground. He said, 'My father always said there was more fuss if a horse was killed underground than if a man was killed. Men came cheap – they had to buy

horses.' Fines that the managements had to pay for contra-
vening regulations were ludicrously small – £10 per offence
in 1916. Although at least half the homes in the community
had lost their breadwinners, compensation paid by the
owners was niggardly. A fund to assist the survivors was
more helpful: £1200 was raised by an exhibition in London
of the wedding presents of Prince Arthur of Connaught and
the Duchess of Fife (entrance fee one shilling). The King,
George V, donated £500. A twenty-eight-year-old teacher at
Senghenydd school, Mary Jane Lewis, had been about to
marry a miner, David Davies, who was killed in the 1913
disaster. She died in 1977, at the age of ninety-three. She had
never married.

A year after 1913, the Great War began. 'After the first
death there is no other,' a Welsh poet wrote during the
Second World War, but it did not apply in Senghenydd. The
names on the clock tower memorial recall what from the
village's point of view was a second, longer-drawn-out, and
only slightly less well-stocked tragedy. It was amazing the
place was still there in 1919. In the last week before the
Senghenydd colliery closed for ever in 1926, the miners
broke the pit's previous production record.

As with the M4 motorway, I could hear the school before I
saw it. The sound of children cascaded down the steep little
street from several buildings near the top edge of the village.
In the headmaster's office, waiting for him to finish taking a
class for a teacher who was ill and away, I looked at an old
dark-framed photograph of Caerphilly Castle, taken before
the castle's lakes and moats were reflooded; a shabby, sepia
Camelot. The office was small, crammed with desk, filing
cabinet, photocopier, and a crate of lemonade bottles. On
the filing cabinet sat an open plastic box full of change: the
day's dinner-money offerings. When Gwyn Jones, the headmaster, turned up, apparently glad to see an adult – even if
alien – visitor, he told me that Ifor Bach (meaning Little

Ivor), the school's name, was the nickname of Ifor ap Meurig, Lord of Senghenydd roughly 800 years ago. He had not only held the fort where Castell Coch was built but had, as the high point of his anti-Norman career, attacked Cardiff Castle and taken as hostages the Duke and Duchess of Gloucester. 'Our school song is about the incident,' said Jones, who was in his mid-forties, with a debonair moustache, a light grey suit, and a warm, confident manner. 'What lies behind this school is an attempt to rekindle Welshness in these parts. Many of us feel that at the heart of Welshness is the Welsh language. Here in the Valleys, thirty years ago, we were very close to losing the language for ever.'

At this point Welsh-speakers make up only a fifth of the population of Wales, and are concentrated in the west and north. The language has been on the defensive since at least 1536, when the Act of Union with England decreed that English alone could be used in the administration of law and no one could hold an official post in Wales unless he spoke English. Welsh went through a long period of declining allegiance in the nineteenth century. The writer and artist David Jones noted that, in the 1870s, 'My own father was most definitely discouraged from using that language in his own home by his Welsh-speaking parents; in the day-school the prohibition of Welsh was absolute.' In many schools the prohibition was enforced by an implement which became known as the 'Welsh Not', a piece of wood which was hung around the neck of a child heard speaking Welsh in school. The child wearing it was meant to listen for any other who broke into Welsh and to whom the Not was passed on. At the end of the day, the pupil who had the Not was caned. In the columns of *The Times* a writer declared – as if it was accepted opinion – that the Welsh language was an obstacle to civilisation.

In Caerphilly, in the late 1950s, a few people decided that it was now-or-never time for Welsh in their part of the

country, the county of Glamorgan. Gwyn Jones told me that
in 1959 nine children began to attend a Welsh-language class
in a local chapel. Two years later, a single classroom of an
ordinary state-run English-language school was given over
to instruction in Welsh – eleven children attended. Slowly
interest and numbers increased. A Welsh school was founded
in Senghenydd in 1963 with forty-nine children. Jones joined
the staff in 1965 and became head sixteen years later. His
school took over the buildings of the Senghenydd Primary
School, which moved to new ground, where it now has
about 210 pupils. The Ysgol Ifor Bach has 331.

'Our children range from four to eleven and almost all of
them come from homes in which English is the only
language spoken,' said Jones. 'It may be that their grand-
parents had "Welshness" and their parents do not. But
obviously more and more of those parents want it for their
children.'

Jones's English was more than fluent. When he answered
the phone, however, it was clear that almost all the machinery of education in which he was involved worked in Welsh.
Occasionally he paused to seek the exact English for a term
he had in mind – 'Ah yes, "supply teacher".' His school is
now one of a quarter of mid-Glamorgan primary schools
which have Welsh as their chief medium of instruction.
(Welsh is studied as a separate subject in the other schools.)
At Ysgol Ifor Bach the core curriculum of Science, Maths,
and Music is taught in Welsh. English is taught in English.
Jones admitted, 'You still have to have English to get ahead.'
He also recognised that at the end of the school day most
children went home and heard only English; therefore he
encouraged parents to let their children watch Welsh television programmes. He tried to ensure that most of his
pupils went on to Welsh-language secondary schools – as,
last year, forty-one out of forty-five eleven-year-olds did.
He was aware that some parents chose his school for
convenience, because – unlike the English-language schools

– it bused its pupils to and fro. But he believed most were picking it because of a concern for their Welsh heritage and from a hope that a bilingual education would be best for their children.

'And perhaps because of the standard of teaching?' I suggested.

'The school speaks for itself. Some of our present parents were among our first pupils. So was one of our teachers. I think our commitment to the Welsh language has a powerful effect. We don't want the language to die – and that concern and enthusiasm rubs off, and enlivens our teaching.'

Jones looked at his watch. 'Have you got a sandwich in that backpack of yours?' he asked.

I shook my head.

'Then how about an Ifor Bach school dinner? I should warn you, it's the first sitting – with the infant classes.'

We went by way of a junior classroom, so that I could see a collage mural the children had recently done of Ifor Bach capturing the Duke and Duchess of Gloucester – bright coloured paper the medium; the Bayeux Tapestry a distant, maybe unknown ancestor. One small boy, seeing my backpack which I was lugging by hand, asked me, 'Are you camping?' In the school dining-room I found myself among a hundred small children, four and five year olds, all in bright green sweaters, all apparently talking, all talking Welsh. The noise was terrific. Jones and I perched on child-sized chairs at a corner table, and the smiling ladies who ran the kitchen brought us food in adult portions.

'You picked a good day to be here,' Jones shouted or perhaps simply mouthed – I couldn't really hear him – as he pointed to the roast chicken, mashed potatoes, carrots, and creamy gravy.

I said, equally loudly, 'If the infants make this much noise, what about the juniors?'

Jones grinned and stood up. He said something in Welsh, firm and commanding. There was absolute silence. He said

something else, words in which I recognised my name.
Every eye in the room turned on me – a hundred pairs of
eyes, small, round, and wondering. Jones sat down and the
hub-bub continued at a slightly moderated level.

'What did you say to them?' I asked.

'I said, "Our visitor, Mr Bailey, thinks you're very very
noisy." It had an effect, didn't it?'

Dessert was pink jelly and custard. Jones then helped me
don my backpack. The Ifor Bach infants didn't seem to hold
anything against me for they waved and smiled as Jones
shook hands, seeing me off.

I went down a lane to the top end of Senghenydd, walked past the sawmill which seemed now to be the main industry in the place, and followed a narrow road uphill again, the way north. I passed old coal workings and slag heaps, thinly grassed, which looked like the ramparts of ancient forts. In time nature recovered everything, it seems, even coal dust. Under this hill, Mynydd Eglwysilan, men had worked in deep levels and on cramped coal faces – had even died there; were also dust. It took an effort to switch one's mind from the bright air up here to the dark confines below. At the top of the hill, by a cattle grid which spanned the road, I looked back down the Aber Valley to Senghenydd and Abertridwr. Then I walked on, bypassing the cattle grid through a wide gate marked FOR HORSEDRAWN VEHICLES AND ANIMALS. The track ahead was surfaced with loose gravel embedded in the turf, a sort of droveway. On either side sheep grazed over open land. At one place water welled from damp ground and became a stream. I consulted in turn my map, a small hiking compass, and distant hills to the north: north was where map and compass agreed it should be. For a while I walked not on the track but on the buoyant turf alongside it. I admired a sinuous dry-stone wall; smaller stones now formed the bed of track; dry brown bracken edged the way. Taking a deep breath, I was suddenly aware that a sinusy, city-dweller's condition which had been bothering me for a month had gone.

The track down the north slope of Mynydd Eglwysilan brought me to another gate. I reached it at the same time as a horse, coming the other way, and I opened the gate before the rider, a woman, dismounted to do so. She thanked me and asked where I was walking to.

'Northwards,' I said, looking up at her. 'I started in Cardiff, yesterday. Today to Ynysybwl.' I attempted to pronounce it properly, with the 'y's like 'u's.

She said she lived in Senghenydd and rode daily. Under her black riding hat her face was thin but attractive; her eyes gleamed. For a moment I had a feeling, which I sensed she shared, that we might go on talking, asking questions of each other – strangers at a hillside gate. But the horse moved its head nervously; she gave the reins a slight lift and it moved through the gate, which I closed behind them. 'I wish you well on your walk,' she said. 'You'll reach the pub at Llanfabon before afternoon closing.'

So I did – it wasn't far along a minor road: the inn with three or four houses and a farm nearby. Although clearly dependent on passing trade, the inn seemed to resist entry. The first door I tried was locked and I asked a man who was getting into a car what was the way in. 'Round the side,' he said, 'but it won't do you any good – I've just drunk the last of the beer.' He appended a laugh, in case I was taking him seriously. (I was.) I bought a half of bitter and brought it outside so that I could drink it while looking back at the hill I had just walked over. In a hedgerow along the road birds were sounding off. From somewhere to the west came the noise of rapid gunfire, presumably from an army range, somewhat shattering my rural idyll of hill, birds, and beer.

In the next few miles I met two dogs: a shaggy, evil-looking German Shepherd which sloped out of a farm driveway and sniffed my trousers interrogatively, as if deciding whether to hand me over to the Gestapo, and a black mongrel, walking alone but clearly on an important errand, which overtook me – though I was by no means dawdling. This was near a fine country house, Llechwan Hall according to the map, which had a long roadside stretch of the highest dry-stone wall I'd ever seen. I stood against it and raised my arm but didn't quite touch the top; it was over nine feet tall. Then I was abruptly out of the country and faced with the A470, four lanes of traffic heading to and coming from Cardiff, and beyond it the Taff, near its foaming junction with the Cynon river at the town of Abercynon.

The Cynon valley provided a longer and larger version of Abertridwr and Senghenydd. Interminable rows of grey little houses, grey little shops, knobbly stone chapels, worn-out mines, black slagheaps and – hard to distinguish from the heaps – battered hills. One town stretched into the next like a black mourning ribbon. This is, in European Community terms, an 'Area of Social Deprivation'. I had read that half the households in the Cynon valley live on less than £4000 a year. Here, as in neighbouring valleys, the last mines are closing, putting hundreds of men out of work. Despite various initiatives from Westminster and Brussels, new industry seems to want to be on the coast, near to Cardiff and Swansea. It is tough on those who own their own houses here, as most residents do, and have enjoyed work nearby to which they could walk. In Abercynon I paused in front of a small provisions shop. Inside the bay window were laid out a sparse sampling of goods: a bar of soap; a plastic bottle of washing-up liquid; a single roll of toilet paper. It might have been an illustration for a chapter of social history – How We Shopped Before the Supermarket Age – but a small sign hung in the door said OPEN. A grimy bookmakers in the adjacent premises seemed to be doing better business.

In many large British cities late-Victorian houses like those in the Valleys have been pulled down as slums. Most are built in terraces which run parallel to their valley. But some are in rows which perversely run at right-angles to the valley, up the slopes; and for these the builders had to choose

between two distinctive roof-lines, covering the houses with
roofs that seemed to share a continuous steeply sloping roof-
beam or giving each house a roof with its own slope down
into the valley, with a step down at each party-wall gable.
All the roofs are made with shiny dark slates. But seen at
close hand the houses are not slum-like. Most are well cared-
for. They were generally put up by the colliery owners to
Victorian by-laws that called for separate toilets, private
yards, and streets wide enough for light and air. Post-
Second-World-War subsidised housing, built by district
councils in so-called estates, is often on higher ground and
set on roads that the planners have, for variety, laid out with
bends and curves, but does not seem much of an improvement in terms of the quality of construction or the virtues of
neighbourhood, though the occupants no doubt appreciate
the larger gardens and more extensive views.

I turned up a road which diagonally climbed the hillside
through such an estate. My map told me that this was called
Perthcelyn, though there was no street-name sign or indication of where the road went. (This lack was not exceptional.
One person I asked explained, 'Everyone round here knows
where they are.') In one garden, a man in shirtsleeves was
calling in his homing pigeons with sounds which were half
words, half cries: 'Coom on th'n! Coom on th'n!' Two men
were working on some cars in a shed which seemed to have
been turned into a garage repair-shop, also nameless and
possibly permissionless. A mobile grocery in the shape of a
beat-up van rattled slowly up the hill, screeched to a stop,
and let off a blast of its horn to alert the housewives who
were stranded at this lofty distance from the valley mer-
chants. It was certainly a long haul to the top. I halted by a
playground and leaned against a railing to catch my breath. I
took in a panorama of the Cynon valley: the town of
Mountain Ash to my left; opposite, the long hill called
Aberdare Mountain and Merthyr Mountain, behind which
was the former pit village of Aberfan, where in 1966 a mine

waste tip became unstable and slid down on the school, killing 114 children; and below, in the valley bottom, the Cynon river, a railway, and the continuous gritty settlement.

At the hilltop, the road curled back in a south-westerly direction, past a small sub-post-office-cum-shop and under electric transmission cables hung from tall pylons, and was suddenly in country again: gently-folded pastureland; sheep and lambs. I realised that in the Valleys one needed to balance against 'social deprivation' the fact that the hills are never very far away. In fact, as I sat on a grassy bank beneath a hedge with my pack off, taking a drink from my water bottle and munching a chocolate bar, a boy came past with a dog, presumably from the council estate below, heading for the open spaces.

At this point I consulted not only my ordnance map but a hand-drawn one, which showed the way to a farmhouse called Gelli-Wrgan, a mile or so from here. The latter map had been drawn by Barbara, an old friend of my sister's, who had recently with her partner Mike and their two small boys moved from Pontcanna, Cardiff, to this place in the country, not far from the former mining village of Ynys-ybwl. I turned off along a lane, past a pond where a heron flew away at my approach, and through several gates. Then from a dip beyond came a welcome sight of smoke curling from a chimney. No other house was in view, only a backdrop of drab green firs in a Forestry Commission plantation on the hill behind.

In the front yard as I walked in a birthday party was going on: half-a-dozen children; half-a-dozen adults; candles on cup-cakes; sausages on chunks of brown granary bread; several dogs doing well on items dropped on the grass. I took off my pack and helped sing Happy Birthday and ate several sausages and a cup-cake. In the course of the long evening – light till eight-thirty – other adults, children, and animals came and went. There were introductions of a not very formal kind. Supper was put on the kitchen table. I wondered if this well-worn old farmhouse, part of it built in 1616, had seen such various life until recently, when Mike and Barbara moved in. The small acreage that came with it was no longer enough to support a family wanting to live off the land. Any farming here now had to be part-time, amateur even, while other work paid the bills. Although, having walked here, I felt as if I was in a sort of outback, and one or two of the locals present clearly had no sense of the area as other than their own personal, rural locality, Gelli-Wrgan was also situated in ex-urban Cardiff and, distantly but not remotely, ex-urban London. Among those present were:

Mike Fleetwood, Cardiff art college lecturer, ex-architect.
Barbara Castle, a planner by training, now a public housing consultant in Bristol.
Ben and Jake, respectively five and three, their sons.
Peg, Mike's mother.
Tom, Cardiff lecturer and an automated technology specialist.
Tom's two children.
George Morgan, over eighty, known as 'Mog,' shepherd and farm labourer.

Peg was staying for a month, while she got over an illness. Tom and children had just come for the party. Mog had checked in, as he apparently did on most days, to the place where he had frequently worked over the years when it was a full-time farm. And in the course of the evening among others who dropped by were Allen and Pat and their children. Allen ran the Perthcelyn sub-post office and shop and said to me, 'We saw you going by. I told Pat, "That bloke's walked a fair distance."' Until a year and a half before this they had lived in Plumstead, in the furthest reaches of south-east London. Allen had been a bus driver for London Transport – 'The 99 to Abbeywood,' he said. 'But I couldn't stand the traffic, the stress.' They had seen an advertisement for the Perthcelyn P.O. in a weekly listing such properties and though they had never been to this part of the world before and had no connections here, had bought it.

Allen had come by hoping to get rid of some goats, part of a flock he had bought and surplus to his requirements. Mike and Barbara, it seemed, had been talking of getting some sheep, but either they weren't keen on goats or Allen got the impression this wasn't the time to attempt a deal: the subject of goats was dropped. Pat, wanting to hear about Greenwich, gave the impression of being homesick for Plumstead. Allen talked about driving a number 99 double-decker – 'It's the car-drivers cutting you up all the time that's the worst of it.' Mog told me about his work, shepherding, building dry-stone walls, and 'bodging around' at miscel laneous farm labours. The forested hill to the west fell into deep shadow as the sun sank behind it. Mog said, with a gesture in that direction, 'I remember when that tump there, now the Forestry Commission's, had no trees on it at all. And over that other way, where you see the slag tips on the hill behind Abercynon, well, all that slag and spoil was hauled up over the hill by a sort of cable railway. There used to be a farm under where that tip is now.'

Tom and his children left, followed by Allen, Pat, and their children. Mog drifted away. Tim Wilson arrived. Tim, who was sandy-haired and in his mid-thirties, lived on a small holding near Ynysybwl and had helped Mike and Barbara find Gelli-Wrgan. A Yorkshireman by birth, he was a Gypsy Liaison Officer in Cardiff, where he worked on two levels – trying to get the council to provide services for travelling families, and encouraging self-help among the travellers. One of the dogs present – a brown-and-white terrier named Joe – had belonged to a travelling family which had moved on without it, and had been a present from Tim to Mike and Barbara. I told Tim about the family with the pickup truck and caravan I'd encountered two days before in Butetown.

'They were probably looking for the site in Roverway, Tremorfa,' he said. 'Cardiff has two sites, with pitches or places for about sixty travelling families. The families can be large, sometimes with ten or twelve children, some of whom have children of their own. The demand for pitches is overwhelming. There are always new families turning up, like your Irish travellers, hoping there'll be room for them. Parliament put through legislation in 1968 which was meant to bring about a countrywide network of sites. But many local authorities didn't do anything about it because of public opposition – you can guess the sort of thing, "Gypsies in the neighbourhood bring down property values." This means that the pressure is all the greater on those councils which have built sites, as Cardiff has done.'

Tim told me there were no accurate figures on the number of travellers in Wales; the number for Britain as a whole was believed to be 100,000, about half of whom were still nomadic to some extent. Although there are 'Welsh', 'English', or 'Irish' families, those that still travel regard all of Britain as their borderless domain. Within each national category, some are poor, some wealthy. Some receive social security and housing benefits. Some have successful antique businesses. Many still have the traditional accoutrements of chickens and horses, for which they rent fields if necessary. Some tell fortunes, weave baskets, lay tarmac, or sell carpets door-to-door. Some put their names down on waiting lists for council houses, believing – often rightly – that such a house will be easier to get than a pitch for their trailer or caravan. In Cardiff, several are well-known musicians – the members of the Fury family, for instance.

I asked Tim where those travellers who still moved around tended to go.

'They have circuits that take them about three months and seem to be in the blood,' he said. 'Hop-picking in Kent, onion-tying near Evesham, buying and selling manure in Hampshire, collecting scrap in Salisbury – then perhaps back to Cardiff. I think those hanging on to that way of life may be doing the right thing. The children of those travellers who no longer travel sometimes have identity problems. They're treated as travellers but they have no personal history of travelling. In any case, people are wary of them. They say, "They're not real gypsies anymore." They don't realise that gypsies have changed like the rest of us. We had horses or bikes and now have cars, and so do gypsies. Of course, people also believe that all gypsies and travellers steal, kidnap children, and put curses on you. In fact, they are useful scapegoats, often accused of thefts that others have done. Most travellers I've met are just as suspicious of people who live so-called normal lives. They think those who dwell in ordinary houses are generally immoral, promiscuous, or use drugs. They prefer to keep their children at home once they are of secondary-school age so their children aren't introduced to evil ways. They tend to marry young, within the travelling community.'

I asked what the Irish travelling family might expect to find at Roverway.

'Probably no room,' he said, hand-rolling a cigarette. 'The site is full, despite the fact that it backs on to a sewage works and an electricity transformer station. We need a transit site for families passing through, genuinely travelling or attending weddings and funerals. Recently we had a hundred travelling families turn up for a funeral with their vehicles and trailers and expect to stay for two weeks. The police find themselves having to move the travellers on, when they catch them camped on the roadsides.'

I slept on a couch in a downstairs room and Joe, the travellers' terrier, slept at my feet – whether to be in proximity to a man who was actually travelling or because it was his usual spot, I didn't discover.

Morning: grey, damp, mild. Mike drove off in one car to Cardiff. Barbara in another car took the boys to school and a playgroup in Ynysybwl before going on to Bristol, forty miles away, where she was trying to involve the residents of a run-down council estate in the decision of whether the estate should be demolished or renovated. I let Joe out and the cat in and then sat in the kitchen, by the warm coal stove, with coffee and toast, looking at my map and planning my day's march. No rush. It was hard to leave a warm kitchen on a damp morning. The place felt like home, even if somebody else's. I had a moment or two of vicarious possession of Gelli-Wrgan, as if it were I who would be waiting for the postman on his morning round or having to make decisions about how many sheep to get and how to improve the erratic water supply – rural decisions governed in part by modern livelihoods earned in cities. Then Peg appeared and made me a sandwich for lunch. I asked her to hand on my thanks to Mike and Barbara, barely greeted in the morning rush to school and work. I set off up the lane, careful to close the gates behind me.

At the pond where I'd seen the heron I turned off along a track which Barbara the night before had suggested I take through the neighbouring farm at Penrhiw Cradoc. Brown Highland cattle, docile despite their long horns, grazed on boggy-looking ground. The track actually entered the farm-yard, and I paused at the gate while several dogs barked and a Highland bull gazed at me with large, remarkably interested, liquid brown eyes. I was glad to see a young man, pitchforking fodder, to whom I explained my desire to follow a path towards Mountain Ash. He let me into the yard, hospitably kept between me and the bull, and led me around the farmhouse and barn, through an extremely muddy yard. He pointed across a field to a place where the path disappeared over a wooded escarpment. 'Steep it is, too,' he said, with a smile in which I suspected there might be a trace of Welsh *schadenfreude*. 'Good morning.'

Steep it was. You are aware of your backpack on occasions like this, when gravity – though of no great G-force – takes hold; when your centre of balance seems too high; and when the grip of your boots on loose shale feels insufficient. I held on to thin branches and even to tufts of long grass to control my 500-foot descent. At least it didn't become headlong. The unkempt hillside overhung part of the extended valley settlement called Penrhiwceiber, which used to have three coal pits. Now there were allotments where a colliery yard had been – little patches of vegetables, sheds made of tarpaper and cracked weather-boarding, scruffy but always heart-warming manifestations of man's attachment to the soil, no matter how grimy. But I wondered about the longevity of the allotment holders, ex-miners from the dusty pits – did they have the breath for digging their plots? No one was at work this morning among the spring cabbages.

Mountain Ash at first glance had little to recommend it. Some terraced streets looked as if they had been bombed. The repair of houses had begun and then – lack of cash or failure of morale? – stopped. The town had clearly once been God-fearing: all manner of churches and chapels had vied for the souls and voices of the populace – St John the Baptist vs. St Winifred; St Dyfrig vs. Our Lady of Lourdes. There were English Baptists, Welsh Baptists, English Wesleyans, Welsh Wesleyans, Congregationalists, Calvinistic Methodists, and Primitive Methodists (the latter had four local chapels). Few

of these congregations appeared to be thriving, but there was
no hint of un-Christian behaviour in Mountain Ash. In the
busy street which formed the town centre people were
standing outside shops on the narrow pavements chatting
cheerfully. I edged into a crowded baker's to buy a Chelsea
bun, which I ate as I walked on. The delight of a Chelsea
bun is not just the band of soft bread powdered with sugar
and packed tightly in a square but the way you can slowly
unwind it, breaking off pieces to munch until you finally
reach the sweetest part in the centre.

A bridge took me across the Cynon. Past the town hall
and hospital I came to a little park with a war memorial,
erected by the local workingmen's institute. TO THE GLORIOUS
DEAD. THEIR NAME LIVETH FOR EVERMORE. Also among the
park trees was a small circle of standing stones, a purportedly
megalithic memorial that looked too neatly arranged to be
ancient. I learned later that the stones had been set up for the
Gorsedd ceremonies of the 1905 National Eisteddfod. The
musical and poetry competitions of the Eisteddfod have a
long lineage, going back to occasions like that held by the
Welsh lord Rhys ap Gryffydd at his court in Cardigan Castle
at Christmastide 1176. He had contests for bards and poets,
harpers and pipers, with prizes for the winners and largesse
for all. But the Gorsedd – which means throne – was a ritual
concocted in the late eighteenth century by one Edward
Williams, a Welsh stonemason living in London. Williams
was also a poet, antiquarian, laudanum addict, and long-
distance walker, who hoped to abolish Christianity and set
up a utopian community in the New World (where, he
believed, some of the Indian tribes were of Welsh descent).
Under his bardic name of Iolo Morgannwg, he talked
Eisteddfod organisers into accepting various documents he
had written as evidence of the priestly ceremonial and regalia
of Celtic druids (who, in fact, in their sacred groves had
occasionally gone in for human sacrifice, whether of pris-
oners, poets, or superannuated kings). Many who attend the

annual Eisteddfods say that the Gorsedd adds a colourful and of course unbloodthirsty pageantry, which evokes a distant past despite having been first put on by Edward Williams on Primrose Hill in 1792.

I climbed the hill on the north-east side of the Cynon valley by way of a road which gradually narrowed. One of the last buildings on it was a shop and post office whose window displayed a poster for a public meeting, in a few days' time, on the problem – new to me – of Phurnacite pollution. I bought from the motherly postmistress a bar of chocolate to bolster my Gelli-Wrgan bread and cheese, confirmed my hope that this road would lead to a path over the mountain to Merthyr Tydfil, and got a brief run-down on the Phurnacite question. She said that when the wind was in the west, this side of the valley was wreathed in black smog from the tall stacks of the Phurnacite plant at Abercwmboi, just above Mountain Ash. The plant con-verted coal into smokeless fuel; in creating a product which made for cleaner air in British cities, it had become one of the worst sources of air pollution in Britain. The company claimed they had a new production method which was going to make things better. Local opinion was split: some people wanted to give the company's new method a chance and save the 400 jobs at the plant; others wanted to get rid of the plant altogether and attempt to bring in new, clean, so-called sunrise industries, like the Hitachi electronics factory already established further up the valley at Hirwaun. She said, 'It's all right today, with the wind in the north, but you just come here when it's blowing from across that way!' It was going to be a lively meeting.

For me, climbing, the air in any event grew cleaner. Underfoot, the tarmac of the lane gave way to loose shale. I rested on a stile before setting off on a path up and over the top of Mynydd Merthyr. On the wire of a fence, sheep's wool hung in bunches where it had snagged. Near the top, 1300 feet high, I cut through the edge of a plantation of

young firs. A mist was condensing as thin rain, but despite
this there was a long view north to the Brecon Beacons – the
highest mountains in South Wales – and to loose cloud
scurrying above them. I climbed over a thick green pipe
which snaked over the ridge, unlabelled though carrying, I
assumed, North Sea gas: the still plentiful submarine fossil
fuel being brought to the Valleys where exploitation of
another fossil fuel had left so many relics. At noon I was at
the broad summit, with not a soul in sight. A faint print of a
horseshoe on the track; a lark, heard but unseen, overhead.
A hundred years ago men who lived in Mountain Ash and
laboured in the foundries of Merthyr walked this way to and
from their work. Across the Taff valley, south of Merthyr
town, an artificial ski slope made a long white slash down
the far hillside. Mike Fleetwood had mentioned it – an
artifact of the leisure age that apparently wasn't paying its
way. At this distance, it made me think of the huge figures –
of man and horse – carved in the chalk of the Wiltshire
downs, possibly propitiatory of other gods.

I descended past a small, disused stone quarry and an even
more conspicuously abandoned orchard, with gnarled old
apple trees, some dead, some sprouting high. Here, between
the ruins of a farmhouse and a stream which had just come
to loud maturity, I spread my nylon raincoat on the ground
and ate Peg's bread and cheese. Birds catching their lunch on
the wing fluttered busily in and out of the apple branches.
Then, warmed and cheered by the post-meridional arrival of
the sun, I continued downhill and along a disused railway
track through former mine workings into Merthyr.

Merthyr Tydfil, to give it its full name, is the town of the
martyr Tydfil, the Christian daughter of a local chieftain
who was murdered by Saxon marauders *c*.AD 480. It was
the largest town in Wales in the mid-nineteenth century,
renowned for its iron works. George Borrow, striding in, was
affronted by the 'enormous furnaces . . . streams of molten
metal and millions of sparks flying about . . . dreadful

sounds.' Now the town seemed to be gamely hanging on
to a life for which past inhabitants were given most of the
credit. Monuments have been erected to such worthies as
Lord Buckland of Bwich (outside the Central Library), Lord
Merthyr (outside the hospital), and Richard Trevithick (near
the Theatre Royal). What the two Lords did to be so
commemorated I remained ignorant of, but Trevithick, who
wasn't ennobled, I knew to be the genial Cornish steam
locomotive pioneer. It was in Merthyr, in 1804, twenty years
before Stephenson and his *Rocket* got so much attention, that
Trevithick's 'high pressure tram engine' had its moment of
glory. A thousand pounds had been wagered between two
of the town's iron-masters: Samuel Homfray betting that
Trevithick's machine would allow him to convey a ten-ton
load of iron from his works at Penydarren, just north of
Merthyr, to the Glamorganshire canal nine miles away at
Abercynon; Richard Crawshay, a rival industrialist, betting
it wouldn't. The iron rails rested on stone sleepers. A third,
middle rail was notched to take a cogged driving wheel,
since Trevithick didn't count on the friction with the rails
being sufficient to drive the locomotive forward. A party of
courageous passengers rode along with the iron cargo.
Among the excitements of this novel journey was one
frightening moment when the engine's smoke-stack – made
of bricks – hit an overhanging bridge and collapsed. But
Trevithick had the stack set up again and the train steamed
on at five miles an hour to the canal. Mr Crawshay lost his
thousand pounds. He should have made a wager on the
return trip which – although now unburdened of its freight
– Trevithick's engine failed to complete because the journey
was uphill. Despite this setback, the *Cambrian* newspaper
next day smartly opined: 'It is not to be doubted but that the
number of horses in the kingdom will be very considerably
reduced, and the machine, in the hands of the present
proprietors, will be made use of in a hundred instances never
yet thought of.'

Merthyr's iron went into cannons for British armies in the Napoleonic Wars and then into rails for the railways being built all over the world. In 1831, a three-day rising by discontented workers was put down by military force; for several years following, soldiers were billeted at the Dowlais ironworks. The good image of the town was defended by William Crawshay. He told his dinner guests on one occasion that Merthyr was so salubrious a place that residents never died of natural causes and, to be got rid of, had to be blown up. At that moment, as he may have anticipated, a blast came from a nearby quarry. 'There, you hear them now,' said Mr C., who must have had an imperial sense of humour. Despite this assertion of good health, a cholera epidemic hit the town in 1849, killing 1400 – three-quarters being children under five. A resident who truly devoted herself to the place was Lady Charlotte Guest, wife of the ironmaster John Guest. Not only did she bear ten children in thirteen years, but she translated *The Mabinogion*, a collection of early Celtic tales that had been passed on by word of mouth for centuries until finally written down about the time of the Norman Conquest. She also successfully managed the ironworks after her husband's death, and founded schools for the workers and their children. (Her own first two sons were named Ivor and Merthyr and were taught Welsh.)

Current schemes in the Valleys to generate employment and clean up dereliction didn't seem to be having a joyful impact in Merthyr. I walked along a down-at-heel shopping street, where a number of youths were hanging about as if waiting for someone to suggest to them something to do. I passed the Victorian red-brick Town Hall, which George Bernard Shaw once called a monstrosity. He had been on his way to speak at an election meeting in town in support of the socialist Keir Hardie, who proceeded to represent Merthyr in parliament for the next fifteen years – the first Labour MP. (Better late than never in regard to the GBS advice, the corporation was now on the point of vacating its premises for a new Town Hall.) I noted one vast, former Non-Conformist chapel which had become 'Home-Style Furnishers', with a large range of bargain sofas and beds. A few relics of Merthyr's great age persisted: a row of restored 1825 cottages, built by the Cyfartha Iron Company for skilled workers and their families; the red-and-yellow brick engine house of the Dowlais ironworks, complete with classical cast-iron portico; and the Guest Memorial Hall, modelled on ancient Greek lines by Sir Charles Barry (architect of the Houses of Parliament) and now a social club.

In a quiet street called Lancaster Villas, with substantial semi-detached red-brick houses overpainted with red paint as if to emphasise that they were in a house-proud part of town, I found 'San Mari', which did bed-and-breakfast. I was let in by a short, stocky elderly man called Tom, who made me a cup of coffee while we waited for his niece Astrid to turn up. Astrid, who ran San Mari, was out shopping.

'Merthyr's cheap for some things,' Tom said. ''specially clothing. I expect London's dear, isn't it?'

Tom walked with difficulty. He told me that he had been in a motor-cycle accident and after that a car crash, which had broken his pelvis in two places. He had taken early retirement last year from a job with the Council. He wore a tweed cap indoors and told me about his cat. We were on our second cup of instant when Astrid arrived and showed me a spacious, nicely decorated room with a firm bed. She was an attractive woman in her late forties with a retroussé nose and good-humoured eyes. She had been named Astrid, she said, after the pre-war Queen of the Belgians. She was on the medical staff of the Hoover washing machine factory just outside Merthyr. Before joining Hoover, she had been a nurse for some years at a hospital in the Persian Gulf. 'The work was fine and I liked the expatriate life, the sun, the water-skiing, but I couldn't stand the way those states are ruled or how women are treated out there.' Astrid didn't speak Welsh. 'I'm not a nationalist. I don't see the need for it.' She added that my room had been booked by a man who met 'a lady friend' in Merthyr once a month, but had called that morning to cancel. 'It sounded as though they'd had words. I told him I'd keep his deposit till next month – I'm sure they'll be on good terms again by then.'

In The Lantern, a pub in Bethesda Street to which – because of its proximity – I repaired for dinner, I read the local *Merthyr Express* while sipping a pint of Felin Foel pressurised keg bitter. 'It's pronounced like "feeling foul",' said my host, who had recently moved here from Folkestone, in Kent, 'but it's not bad.' I didn't think it was particularly good, either – though perhaps no worse than most English beers stored under pressure and brought into the glass by gas. The Lantern had no real ale and what its menu called 'beef stew' seemed, when it came, to be made from canned minced meat. Work had begun repanelling the lounge bar but evidently for some time had been suspended; the feeling seemed to be that the customers probably wouldn't notice exposed brickwork and plaster dust. I took comfort in the *Express*, which had a story about the chairman of a Merthyr social club (not the converted Guest Memorial Hall), who had been having an affair with his ex-wife and had been brought before the local magistrates accused of causing her grievous bodily harm. 'He caught me by the hair and dragged me up the stairs,' ex-wife Marilyn Morgan said of former hubby John Roger Price. 'He started taking the bedclothes off the bed to see if there was anybody in there. He punched me and I fell to the floor.'

The Merthyr magistrates fined Mr Price £75 and ordered him to pay his ex-wife – and now presumably ex-girlfriend – £150 compensation. I hope the good people of Merthyr will forgive me for the conclusion I had by now jumped to, that their town was a hotbed of scandalous goings-on.

HILLTOPS AND HEADWATERS

'YOU'LL BE WANTING a hot breakfast before setting off on your walk,' Astrid said, as I approached the kitchen next morning. I didn't disagree. Ahead of me this day I had what would be, if I got to my destination, my longest walk so far, and over the toughest terrain. And so it was 'the full breakfast' with thick but tender rashers of bacon, mushrooms, tomatoes, a sausage, fried eggs, and fried bread that got me started. Over a second cup of coffee, toast, and marmalade, Astrid and I talked about the importance of marmalade – hard to understand how in some countries they managed to begin their days without it! She made me a substantial-looking packed lunch. Then, with a thanks and goodbye, I was off. There was sunshine and a light north-westerly breeze. A street-sweeper working his way along Lancaster Villas returned my greeting with a sunny 'Good morning.'

On my way out of Merthyr I passed Cyfartha Castle, a mock-medieval seventy-two room edifice, built in 1825 for one of the Crawshays, and now a museum and gallery. But it felt too early for exhibits and photographs of Merthyr's iron age, and I kept going past the castle and its man-made ornamental lake which – waste not, want not – had also served as a feeder pond for the Crawshays' ironworks in the Taff valley below. Here the Taff was formed from two rivers, the Taf Fawr and Taf Fechan, Big Taf and Little Taf that is, and in the enlarging process gained for no doubt good Welsh reasons a second 'f'. I passed a woman who said 'Hello', a man in a blue anorak who ignored my 'Good Morning', and another man who – after my 'Good Day' – exclaimed 'That's the life!' Striding along, I felt it was. My route became a bit complicated in the once separate village of Cefn Coed, where the Heads of the Valleys mainroad sliced across the northern edge of the town. But I was still navigating with a Merthyr street map and managed to get to the correct, west side of the river, now the Taf Fechan, and to a footbridge across the Heads of the Valleys road that led me into a strikingly beautiful vale. I switched to a new ordnance map, sheet 160, 'Brecon Beacons' – it was a milestone, a minor accomplishment. I then sat for a few moments on a bench and studied the map, feeling grateful to the surveyors and draftsmen who had brought these sheets of wonderful topographical detail into being.

The Beacons are a forty-mile-long range of what in some parts of the world would be called hills but here are mountains. Daniel Defoe, touring in the 1720s, made the good point that although the Beacons are not absolutely high, like the Alps or Andes, they rise abruptly, 'which makes the height look horrid and frightful'. The geological gist is that they have an east-west backbone of Old Red Sandstone flanked on the southern edge with Carboniferous Limestone and Millstone Grit – and out of them pure water pours in numerous rivers, sometimes brimming over in waterfalls. Their highest peak, and the highest point in South Wales, is Pen-y-Fan (2907 feet; 886 metres). The Beacons are contained within a national park, one of three in Wales, set up in the 1950s. I was making for their central segment and following for the moment the former railbed of the Brecon and Merthyr Railway which opened in 1863, became a part of the Great Western Railway in 1921, and closed in 1962. No rails remained in the grass-banked cutting I walked through below Trefechan village or on Pontsarn viaduct, a massive brick structure with seven tall arches that bridged a

deep gorge, on which I crossed to the east side of the river.
A mile further on, the old track forked – a branch line had
run through a tunnel, whose entrance was closed with a
barred gate. The former main line to Brecon stayed in the
open air on the wooded bank high above the river, with
small hedged fields in the narrow vale and the tower of
Vaynol church rising from the trees on the other side.

At ten o'clock the morning sun had disappeared, grey
clouds were covering the sky, and the wind blew colder
from the Beacons; my nose ran. I began to think apprehen-
sively about the Beacons, whose bleak summits I meant to
walk over. The term 'wind-chill factor' came to mind. I was
already wearing one sweater. I had a spare one but no thick
coat, only my nylon raincoat. Providentially I had brought a
beret, scarf, and gloves. All might be needed on the peaks if
there were rain, sleet, snow, or – a daunting thought – heavy
cloud. Although I was enjoying being astray in Wales,
getting lost was nothing I looked forward to. Not long
before this I'd walked in the New Forest, not far from where
my parents used to live. It was a sunless day. I took a path
I'd never been on, deep into the forest. I was without a map
or compass. I got lost. After an hour I began to mark the
gates I passed through; a few twists and turns later I re-
passed through one of my marked gates. Finally, fortunately,
I managed to make out from the clouds which way the wind
was blowing and decided – assuming it was blowing from
the south-west – to keep walking into it and thus get back to
civilisation. So I did, but the wind was in the north-east, and
I found myself in Lyndhurst, five miles from Brockenhurst
where I meant to be.

Well, now I had a map and compass, and little wildness
was so far in evidence. There was a children's playground
where my track crossed a country road, and yet no houses in
view; the country for the moment felt like a pleasant park.
Alongside my track an actual railway appeared – the single,
narrow-gauge line of the Brecon Mountain Railway, which

runs steam trains on holidays and in the summer over a
slightly more than two-mile long section of the old Brecon
to Merthyr route. My own route was blocked by barbed
wire, where a farmer had adopted part of the old right of
way. I was forced to scramble up an embankment, on hands
and knees at one point, to the mountain railway. I walked
along the sleepers between two-foot gauge rails, assuming
that it was too early in the season for frequent trains or that
I would hear one coming before it ran me over. (Railway
buffs may like to know that there are plans to extend the line
if passenger business allows: laying a mile of track in 1983
cost £30,000. Extending the track northwards along the old
route for three and a half miles would take it through the
highest railway tunnel in the British Isles. Rolling stock for
small railways isn't easy to find. The line's main locomotive
is a 1908 0-6-2 well-tank steam engine which previously
worked for East German State Railways; it is still named
Graf Schwerin-Lowitz. The railway company constructs its
own passenger coaches on chassis and bogies taken from
South African Railway freight wagons.)

My passage along the little railway soon came to an end.
The northern terminus was a faded-cream building that
looked more like a farmhouse than a station. Piles of rusty
rails awaited the line's extension. There were other heaps of
buffers, sleepers, and spare bogies, which looked like giant-
sized weight-lifting equipment. Several old railway cars had
been converted into a stationary café, but this was locked
up. As for the park, it now had a lake – in fact a long
reservoir, formed by a dam across the Little Taf. This body
of water, stretching up into the Beacons, is named after the
nearby village of Pontsticill, which it would probably inun-
date if the dam ever gave way. (Pontsticill is one of those
Welsh names which the English tongue finds embarrassingly
tricky; turning the 'll' into a muted 'f' and putting the stress
on the right syllable isn't easy for a Saxon. Pons-*tis*-iff is a

stab at it, and may get you a smile rather than a frown hereabouts.)

I followed the once-again-railless track along the east side of the reservoir. For an hour or so I saw nobody. There were many sheep on the hillsides – ewes giving suck to some lambs while others baaed loudly for attention. The track, rising gently, ran sometimes over open ground, sometimes on embankments, and sometimes through cuttings – where the going got muddy. In several places the way traversed bridges over sunken lanes. At one of these, a chain of narrow planks resting on elderly iron girders offered passage for those with the requisite sense of balance. At another, *sans* planks, the wayfarer was forced down a bank to the lane and up the other side. For a long stretch I was in woods, my view of the water filtered by tall pines, which also screened me from the increasingly icy wind.

At the head of this reservoir stood a dam for another smaller reservoir called Pentwyn. My map also indicated a Mountain Rescue Post, a name which prompted immediate reflection: People sometimes have to be rescued in these mountains. The rescue post shared the buildings of an outdoor education centre from whose grounds I heard – without seeing – some sort of competition taking place. A man was shouting, 'Are you ready? Get set. *Go!*' Then cheering. Similarly invisible were the ghosts of passengers on the platform of a little station of the dismantled line, waiting for trains long past. The one-storey station building was shut up – windows boarded, doors padlocked. Grass grew on the platform. Then the peaks of the Beacons re-appeared, seeming to get higher as I approached them. The clouds looked thicker and lower, moving fast toward me. I told myself I had passed any feasible point of return. The next safe harbour was further on, not back.

At noon, just beyond the head of Pentwyn reservoir, I halted for lunch. I'd at last seen people: three men of the Forestry Commission heading into Taf Fechan Forest, whose

firs were planted on several square miles of hillside here. I
sat with my raincoat between me and the grass and ate the
sandwich Astrid had made for me. From my backpack
bottle, filled at a San Mari tap, I drank water which had
presumably come from these reservoirs. I watched a hawk
patrolling overhead but didn't leave many crumbs for the
mice that might interest the hawk. As I prepared to get
moving again through the forest I felt big spots of rain and
donned my raincoat, scarf, and beret.

The path left the trees and passed through a gate with a
sign, UNSUITABLE FOR MOTORS. I found myself on the lower
slopes of a hill called Tor Glas, with two small reservoirs
named Neuadd to my left at the very head of the valley
where the Taf Fechan formed. The path climbed at a slant
up the hillside to where Tor Glas abutted the jagged ridge of
the Beacons. I had to lift my gaze to them now, lying in
front of me like a gargantuan dark sharp-spined monster. I
forded a small stream by stepping on well-placed stones and
ascended the red soil bank of the little gorge it had furrowed.
Further on, water ran down the hillside and along the edge
of the path to join the stream, which fed the reservoirs and
the Taf Fechan. It was a case of seeing where one's drinking
water came from – a natural element becoming a factor of
civilisation. It was my introduction to the fact that, even in
times of not much rain, every Welsh hillside seems to ooze
moisture. Little springs well up. Streams form, join others,
and become rivers. Most downhill tracks are in the way of
becoming the beds of torrents when it rains heavily. The .
streams are often channelled in a ditch along one side of a
track but, if not given a clear run, dig into the track, cross
all or part way over, and make their own downhill furrow.
Farmers and highway workers are kept busy laying pipes
and culverts to manage these burgeoning, burrowing streams
in the least damaging way and help them in the direction
they want to go.

For a little while the sun made fitful appearances. Shadows

of the now looser clouds marched toward me down the steep flanks of the Beacons. I had for an hour or so the sort of walking that could only be called exhilarating. It was new ground to me and impressive terrain. Several sheep trotted ahead of me for several hundred yards until it dawned on them they were free to scatter in any direction. One lamb dived for cover under its mum as I approached. On my left, beyond the upper Neuadd reservoir, an imposing line of cliffs named Craig Fan Ddu formed a tall buttress that curved up to the highest peaks of Corn Du, Pen-y-Fan, and Cribyn. (I give the names as my map had them, though the Ordnance Survey's Welsh spellings are erratic and not always as given by other authorities.) The twelfth-century chronicler Archdeacon Gerald, who lived in Brecon, said that Corn Du and Pen-y-Fan had a throne-like form, which was why in his day they were called Cadair Arthur, Arthur's Chair, 'a very lofty spot and most difficult of access'. As it still was. I chose a convenient place – where the path ran below a waist-high shelf of ground – to pause and rest my pack. The clouds were thickening again; the air I took into my heaving lungs was colder.

Restored, I set off again, up to a pass through which the north wind blew strongly, and there turning aside along the saddle which rose to Cribyn and Pen-y-Fan. The path was made of small rocks jumbled together and I picked my way over them from perch to perch, as one might on a stony beach. This brought me to a high ridge between the peak of Cribyn, to the east, and Pen-y-Fan to the west. The ridge sloping up to Cribyn was like the sharp edge of a flint axe-head but the soil was dark, the ground boggy. I kept going westwards until I was half-way up Pen-y-Fan, on drier ground, where I again paused for breath. Here the ascent was steep. I wondered if my grip-sole leather boots, excellent for level walking and boating, were quite the thing for gradients of this kind, with thinly grassed reddish soil that didn't offer a good deal of purchase. Here I noticed that I was by no means alone on the mountain. Five girls with light packs were labouring up the path, occasionally throwing themselves on the ground to catch their breath, make doleful complaints, or shriek with laughter. Another party of hikers was nearing the top. The path itself became a well-worn red-brown groove, and partly for the sake of not adding to the erosion, partly for less steep a climb, I zigzagged uphill, tacking about forty-five degrees to each side of a direct course to the summit. The last stage I negotiated sideways, digging the edges of my boots into the skimpy turf, and hoping I wouldn't have to resort to hands and knees.

I didn't. It was two fifty-five p.m. when I reached the flat summit of Pen-y-Fan. The other party of hikers – two men and two women in serious climbing kit – were already there. It struck me that for most of the day I'd been absolutely on my own and here, on the highest, toughest ground, I was in company. Perhaps those who had worries about possible overuse of a Cambrian Way, taking in all these peaks, had grounds for their concern. In any event, if those of us up there had come for the view, the weather suddenly obliged. On really clear days, so it is said, you can see all the way to Plynlimon, a mountain some forty miles north of here. Now, although nothing like that was possible, the clouds had parted. A hazy sun shone. To the south I had a view over the reservoirs almost to Merthyr. The upper faces of the mountain resembled old light-green velvet, very thin and worn. On the north and east sides Pen-y-Fan fell away in . almost sheer drops. I stood for a few minutes a little way back from the north edge, rocking slightly from the strength of the wind that hit the scarp and came over the top. In *The Mabinogion*, Arthur's knights Kay and Bedevere sat on top of Plynlimon 'in the highest wind in the world'. This wind also felt high, but, as in a sailing boat or open plane, it made you feel as if you were in motion. The air, the wind, was blowing solidly toward Pen-y-Fan, and the earth, the mountain, the summit of Pen-y-Fan, was turning through the wind.

The pleasure of reaching the top of a mountain is not long-lasting. Like other pleasures, it is soon followed by thoughts of what comes next, in this case descent. I went down westwards, along the back of Pen-y-Fan's slightly lower sister, Corn Du; then over a ridge and northwestward to where the steep scarp rises above a small fingerbowl of a lake, Llyn Cwm Llwch. Here stood a rough stone obelisk with an inscription: THIS OBELISK MARKS THE SPOT WHERE THE BODY OF TOMMY JONES AGED 5 WAS FOUND. HE LOST HIS WAY BETWEEN CWMLLWCH FARM AND THE LOGIN ON THE NIGHT OF AUGUST 4TH 1900. AFTER AN ANXIOUS SEARCH OF 29 DAYS HIS REMAINS WERE DISCOVERED SEPT 2. ERECTED BY VOLUNTARY SUBSCRIPTIONS. W. POWELL PRICE, MAYOR OF BRECON 1901.

When I got to Brecon I found out more of this sad story. Tommy had been on a weekend holiday with his father, a Rhondda miner. They came by train to Brecon and then set off to walk four miles to the home of Tommy's grand-parents, who farmed at Cwm Llwch. It was six p.m. when they left Brecon and at eight they arrived at an army training camp at a place known as the Login, only a quarter of a mile from the farm. There they stopped for a drink at the canteen. And there they met Tommy's grandfather and thirteen-year-old cousin, Willie John. Willie John was sent back to the farm to announce the arrival of the visitors and Tommy went with him. About halfway, however, he changed his mind. Perhaps he became nervous in the twilight, among the trees along the stream, crossing the rough planks that served as a bridge. He started to cry and said he was going back to his father. Willie John ran on, delivered his message, and then hastened back to the army camp. It was barely fifteen minutes since he had left it. But Tommy wasn't there.

A search was immediately begun. Tommy's father and grandfather were helped by soldiers. They searched without success till midnight and started again at three a.m. Police and members of the public joined the hunt but no sign of the five-year-old was found. For nearly a month the valley was combed, bracken raked, and undergrowth cut. A suggestion that the little lake a mile or so higher up the valley be dragged was not followed because no one believed the little boy could have climbed that far. The search centred on the wooded country around the army camp and down towards Brecon. Gypsies were interrogated; abduction and murder were considered. Tommy's father searched for several weeks on his own before being persuaded to return home to the Rhondda. But he couldn't stay at home. God knows what his desperate wife had to say. At the farm again, he climbed up into the Beacons, as did a few others. But still no Tommy.

It was on 2 September that a woman named Mrs Hamer, who lived in Castle Madoc, some miles north of Brecon, came to the Beacons with her husband, a gardener. She had dreamt of the spot where Tommy would be found, but Mr Hamer took some persuading. Late in the day, on top of the scarp above Llyn Cwm Llwch, they found what remained of Tommy's body. He had been wearing a sailor suit and had a whistle on a string around his neck that might have saved him if – early on – he had thought of blowing it. It seemed that, running back to his father, he must have veered away from the path to the army camp and on to a track which wound up to a high promontory called Pen Milan. Possibly, not finding the camp, he thought going uphill would take him back to his grandfather's farm. It was soon dark. It had been a long day and a long walk from Brecon for a five-year-old, and yet he climbed 1300 feet and over two miles of difficult ground. He must have then succumbed to exhaustion and exposure.

The stone inscribed to Tommy was hauled up to the ridge on a horse-drawn sled a year later. Standing not quite upright, it still serves its memorial purpose of making walkers in the Beacons think for a minute or two about what it must have been like to be a small boy stumbling alone up here at night ninety years ago.

By three-forty it was clouding up again thickly. I took heed of Tommy's fate, consulted map and compass, and decided on a great circle route offered by a track that led around a south-bound stream, across a Beacon named Y Gwrn, and down to an outdoor education centre at a former pub called The Storey Arms on the A470 main road to Brecon. The track was in places vague and easy to lose. Several times I found myself on extremely boggy ground. Once I stepped in deeply but got my leading boot quickly out before the ooze lapped into it. On another occasion I tripped, going downhill, but fortunately sprawled on soft turf which was relatively dry. I reached The Storey Arms at four-forty, and took off some outer clothing in the comparative warmth of the lower altitude. Pity the place was no longer a pub or even, as it has been in the recent past, a transport café! I had another half-hour of walking northward along the verge of the A470, trucks and cars bustling by. Then, some seventeen miles from San Mari, I climbed a stile and walked across a meadow and through an old orchard to a farmhouse, Llwyn-y-Celyn, built in 1645 and now a Youth Hostel.

Somehow I managed to get through youth without staying in one of these establishments, which were set up in the 1930s in a charitable effort to provide cheap and simple accommodation for young people wanting to enjoy the countryside. I went to several summer camps in the USA, slept under canvas while in the British Boy Scouts, and suffered whatever rigours of enforced gregariousness three years at a boarding school and two years in the army threw my way. Communal life, in other words, was not outside my experience. But it was at some distance. Nevertheless, I had been looking forward to staying at a Youth Hostel, as I knew I surely would on this journey when I ran out of steam

far from town, village, or farmhouse B-and-B. I had therefore joined the Youth Hostel Association, which now accepts
members of all ages and allows them to arrive by foot,
bicycle, or motor vehicle. Most hostels open at five p.m. It
is possible to book in advance or turn up soon after five, as I
did, hoping there would be room. (It was another five miles
along the road into Brecon.) The warden of the Llwyn-y-
Celyn hostel, Charlie Carter, a bulky, bearded man in his
late thirties, took my membership card and £8.20, which
paid for supper, bed, breakfast, and the hire of a sheet
sleeping-bag liner. (Duvets or sleeping bags were provided.)
I was in room three, bunk twenty, he said, and the hostel
was going to be nearly full; two school parties were expected
in an hour or so. As I later realised, this was fair warning.

Meanwhile I took advantage of being an early arrival. I
found my bunk – happily a bottom berth – and read the
instructions posted on a wall about how to leave duvet and
blanket folded in the morning. I tried to turn on the room's
electric heater but it was apparently governed by a time
switch and its time for providing warmth had not yet come.
I had a shower in the chilly washroom. I then repaired to the
empty lounge, whose old ceiling beams had iron hooks on
which meat and vegetables had once hung. There was no
television or radio, but several shelves of books, magazines,
and games, and an ancient range in which logs were burning.
I took a *National Geographic* to a rocking chair by the fire so
that I was well-placed when several vans and mini-buses
turned up and disgorged the school parties.

One school group was co-ed, with boys and girls from a
comprehensive in Bristol. The other was all girls, from a
private school in Putney, London. The Bristol party were
self-catering, opening their cans and packets in a kitchen next
to the dining-room and cooking their own supper. The
Putney girls and their teachers and I ate the supper that was
brought forth from another kitchen by Charlie and his wife.
In a youth hostel, much of the work is shared out. I was

given the job of serving leek and potato soup from a cauldron. The girls fetched plates of cold meat and salad and then cleared away and washed up. Both parties had after-supper activities. The Putney girls were taken for a stroll down to the river in the valley below the hostel. In the dining-room, the comprehensive students were given a lecture on hill-walking and map-reading. 'What is a map?' boomed a teacher – teachers can be as noisy as pupils. No answer. 'A map is like an aerial photograph of the land,' he said, loudly. Yes, I thought, but that isn't all, is it? A map is a picture; it is a representation of the land and what we have put on it, with meaningful colours and all those informative conventional signs – a sort of sunburst for a viewpoint; a wigwam for a campsite; a red triangle for a youth hostel; ye olde-y lettering for ancient features like mottes, earthworks, and standing stones . . .

It was probably just as well that I was sitting by the warm range again or my enthusiasm might have caused me to put my hand in the air. I talked to an Australian woman, middle-aged, who was travelling around the British Isles and lodging only in youth hostels. She had been here for four days. She said, 'The best time to stay in hostels is Monday to Thursday.' This was Friday.

At what seemed to me – after an arduous day – like going-to-bed and getting-to-sleep time, her words came to mind. The room I was in contained a dozen bunks. They were occupied by the male teachers of the Bristol school and some young men who were going to spend the weekend hiking in the Beacons, all soon dormant. The next room, through a doorless doorway, contained the Bristol boys, whose high spirits and as yet underused energies went on being expressed in jokes, pranks, and goonish chatter. The sleeping-bag liners – which had a separate pocket for a pillow – provoked much badinage. One boy whose voice was still unbroken said, piercingly, 'I'll just get into my condom now.' This produced the boyish equivalent of shrieks and giggles all round.

Overhead, the ceiling resounded with thumps and thuds, as the Bristol girls evidently played at jumping off their upper bunks. Letting my mind dim, exasperation evaporate, and reaching a point at which I could ignore the sounds of my fellow hostellers, the talk and jumping eventually replaced by snores and the occasional bang of the door into the toilets – all this proved difficult. Now and then (so it felt), I slept.

Cold underfoot in the morning. Memories again of school and army. I recollected that, in those days, no matter how dreadful you felt, no matter how warm the bed and chill the air, early rising was imperative if you wanted unhindered use of the ablutions and plentiful hot water. Resisting the urge to shout a vengeful 'Wakey-wakey, you lot!' and refraining from singing the hymns of matinal celebration with which I occasionally alleviate the bore of shaving, I quietly entered the washroom, filled a jug with steaming water from an electric water heater, and, at one of the half dozen sinks to which only cold water was piped, scraped away the stubble in splendid solitude. I took a pre-breakfast walk in the old orchard and down into the misty valley bottom. When I went to collect the porridge, Charlie glanced at me and guessed, aloud, that I had not had the best of night's sleep. He agreed with my suggestion that segregation of exhausted adults and the noisy young might be a good thing, but wasn't practicable for most hostels. The YHA needed the business of school groups. It felt bound to be a catholic organisation. However, I was pleased to see that this tolerant attitude hardened slightly after breakfast, when morning chores were handed out. (You don't get your YHA membership card back until you've done a job.) I was given the task of straightening the books and games on the shelves in the lounge – which took me about a minute. Some of those I recognised as the main noise-makers and pranksters

from the night were detailed to vacuum the bunkrooms and
scrub out the washroom and toilets.

I set off at nine-thirty in watery sunshine. I was making
for Brecon, to the north-east, but meant to avoid the direct
route along the A470. I crossed the road and headed over a
north-thrusting spur of the high moorland called Fforest
Fawr, the Great Forest. In time well past, a forest was an
unenclosed woodland area kept for hunting. In time greatly
distant, so the old tales ran, Arthur and his companions
hunted a large boar named Trwyth across these moors and
across South Wales. I followed a track which ran northward
along the flank of a deforested peak called Fan Frynych.
Unlike the Beacons around Pen-y-Fan, which belong to the
National Trust, this was private land, and a sign which
brought this to my attention requested that walkers stick to
the path. Perhaps to ensure compliance with that request,
the sign went on to provide a generous dollop of information
about the terrain. The steep cliffs to my left had been formed
by Ice Age glaciers; the crags and gullies supported Arctic-
Alpine plants at the southern edge of their British range;
ravens, ringouzels, and kestrels bred here. The land was
being managed as a traditional sheep walk, though here and
there the dry-stone walls that divided up the hillsides were
collapsing and barbed wire fences had been set up to keep
the sheep in or out.

As the track came to small streams that poured quietly
down the slopes, there was evidence of different decisions
having been made by those who had used it and formed it..
Generally the track went straight down into the hollow in
which the stream ran and immediately up the other side –
this was often the steepest, muddiest, wettest way. Sometimes it took a jog uphill and went diagonally down the bank
to the stream at a point where there was less depth of water
or a narrower gap to jump. Now and then, however, such a
detour upstream brought the walker to a morass. In these
cases, I was often faced with the need to cross surface run-

off that hadn't quite formed into a proper body of running water, and I would be forced to look for hassocks or little mounds of dry bracken that offered footholds above the wet and spongy peat. Once in a while I was favoured with a lucidly straightforward route: clear water, well-spaced stones, dry banks to descend and climb.

Well below me now, the A470 was screened by the woods of Coed Tymawr. Behind, to the south-east, the ridge of the topmost Beacons – Corn Du, Pen-y-Fan, and Cribyn – made a high, ragged horizon. I crossed the shoulder of the spur and went downhill on a track surfaced with red soil and green oxidised coppery pebbles. This brought me to a lane which turned north-east through hedged fields. I surprised two rabbits drinking from a water-filled ditch. Near a prosperous-looking farm called Forest Lodge, a number of huge worn black tyres had been dumped on the verge of the lane, together with some old timber and iron pipes. I could smell the rubber of the tyres. Farmers have a natural sense of possession in regard to 'their' land that sometimes seems to swell into a bloody-minded arrogance. But some intruders made an equal assault on the senses. I hugged the hedge to let a covey of motorcycles go by – trail bikes, with mudguards set high above their knobbly tyres, fizzing and racketing along the lane. When they had gone and the cloud of two-stroke exhaust had lifted, the Saturday morning calm was broken only by the baa-ing of hundreds of sheep.

The hedged sheep meadows gave way to an expanse of flat here-and-there marshy heath called Traeth Mawr, a not uncommon name in Wales that means literally big beach but is often used for inland areas of bog. The track remained dry and straight. On the edge of a section of the heath known as Mynydd Illtud common, near the village of Libanus, I called in at the Brecon Beacons National Park Mountain Centre, which provides refreshments and information. I browsed in the bookshop – taking as the lighter cargo the names of several books that looked as if I should read them rather than

the books themselves. I sat on the outside terrace with a cup
of coffee and a Welsh Cake, a kind of cold griddle cake, and
a view of the Beacons six miles away. Then I walked on
across the heath toward Brecon, delighted by the springy
ground. It had not long before taken the deep impress of a
horse's hooves but put a bounce into my own steps. The sun
was burning through; no need for gloves, scarf, or hat today.

The track joined a tarmac-surfaced country lane. On one
side of this the hedge had recently been 'laid' – the under-
brush cleared out, the sturdier saplings cut almost through
with billhook or slasher and bent over to an angle of roughly
forty-five degrees, supporting stakes driven in, and then
vigorous upward growths from the laid-over saplings
wound around the stakes and the adjacent saplings. The
object was to fill the gaps and make the hedge stock-proof.
Hedge-laying is one of the old agricultural crafts that seem
to persist in western Britain because of the nature of farming
here, with fewer arable crops, no demand for vast open
fields, and a continuing need for hedges to provide security,
shade, and shelter for animals. This hedge grew out of a
grassy bank. The hedge bottom was rich with primroses and
other wild flowers. I knew I was down from the high hills
because at this altitude it was spring again, and warm. I
stepped inside a field gate, sat under a tree, and, with several
hundred sheep looking at me, turned my socks inside out
(an old soldier's trick, which gives one a brief feeling of
having fresh socks on, perhaps partly because it involves
airing one's feet for a moment or two).

In the course of the next hour, striding toward Brecon, I
encountered no other walkers. One car went by. I passed a
torn leather armchair and a rusting kitchen stove, dumped in
the ditch under the hedge. The lane, going gradually downhill, seemed to sink deeper below field-level. A huge black-
winged beetle crawled across the way. High overhead in an
increasingly blue sky a jet left in its wake an elegant double

white trail – a reminder of people, on other journeys, for
whom 'Wales' was just a momentary green glimpse below.

About Brecon: Defoe, rarely at a loss for words, wrote, 'The
most to be said of this town is . . . that it is very ancient.' Its
older name of Brecknock is derived from the name of the
land, Brycheiniog, ruled by the local fifth-century king or
chieftain, Brychan. It is thought that Brychan, the martyr
Tydfil's father, was himself of Irish descent. In any event,
modern Welsh-speaking inhabitants, who aren't numerous,
call the town Aberhonddu – the place at the mouth of the
Honddu river. (The signs on the edge of town that give both
names also announce that Brecon's twin town is Saline USA,
though there is nothing salty about either the Honddu or the
larger river it here joins, the Usk.) Before Brychan and his
folk, the Romans were hereabouts and before them Iron Age
peoples who had a fort on nearby Pen-y-Crug hill. At the
end of the eleventh century the Normans advanced slowly
westward from Hereford, through the Hay gap, and defeated
the local Welsh ruler. The Normans built a castle near the
junction of the Usk and Honddu, the remains of which are
now part of the Castle Hotel. The chronicler and reforming
cleric Gerald held the post of Archdeacon of Brecon, among
various other livings and titles. The previous archdeacon, an
elderly man named Jordan, was suspended for living with
his mistress, and in 1175 Gerald, then twenty-eight, inherited
the job. He had a small house about a mile north of town in
the hamlet of Llanddew, 'convenient enough for my studies
and my work . . . The house gives me pleasure and . . . is
conducive to thoughts of the next world.'
    Among the notable natives of Brecon are Edward Stafford,
Duke of Buckingham, and Sarah Siddons, actress. Buckingham, hoping to regain feudal powers over his great
landholdings, kept a small private army. But the then
monarch, Henry VIII, wasn't pleased with this – nor with
the claim to the throne Buckingham would have had if

Henry died without a direct heir. Henry had him executed
on a trumped-up charge of treason in 1521. Although the
Duke is not visibly commemorated in the town, 'Sarah
Siddons' is now the name of the inn, once 'The Shoulder of
Mutton', in which the late-eighteenth-century tragedienne
was born, daughter of the actor Richard Kemble. In part of
the town's military barracks, converted into a museum, one
tragic but heroic event recalled is the 1879 Zulu War battle
of Rorke's Drift, where 140 Welsh soldiers faced 4000 Zulu
warriors and won, most often posthumously, a record
number of Victoria Crosses.

Brecon on a Saturday afternoon was lively enough, full of
shoppers, some in smart 'county' clothes. Part of the charm
of the place lay in an irregular pattern of streets, wide and
narrow, joining one another at various angles. A large parish
church stood aslant the High Street on an island which
divided traffic and pedestrians around it. A statue of the
Duke of Wellington, the Iron Duke, stood outside Brecon's
biggest hotel, named after him. I felt I deserved some
comforts after my night at Llwyn-y-Celyn but thought I
hadn't yet walked far enough to go the whole hog. I
therefore booked into the Lansdowne, slightly smaller than
the Wellington, which stood in a broad street called the
Watton, leading down to the barracks and the terminus of
the still navigable Montgomeryshire canal to Avergavenny.
In the residents' lounge I talked to the proprietor, a middle-
aged ex-Londoner who had met his Welsh wife while
working as a management trainee at the Ebbw Vale steel.
works.

'We're all a bit uncertain here about what's going to happen to Brecon,' he said, while the hotel dog, a sleek, ruddy-
chestnut Doberman bitch called Zara, sniffed my trousers.
'The town has done well in the past from wool and the
army. It has the attraction of the Beacons, but the National
Park authorities are cautious about acquiring too many
visitors. There are schemes being pushed for a big hotel and

a marina on the canal, but they haven't got the go-ahead so far. I realise places can't just stay the same. Still, I wouldn't want Brecon to cease to be the place I came for.' He said that his grown-up children had left, not finding enough to hold them here. He was looking forward to a round of golf tomorrow, Sunday. (There was a hint of John Cleese's mercurial Fawlty Towers proprietor about the Lansdowne patron. Next morning, when I handed back my room key – which from the start had been lacking a room-number tag – he snapped, 'Ah, lost its tag, eh?' I said, 'No – or rather, yes,' a bit flustered in my denial of blame for the loss. 'It was like that when I was given it.' Our friendly conversation about Brecon's future seemed to have been forgotten. He didn't believe me.)

I had taken the suggestion of the proprietor's cheerful wife to dine early, as the local Round Table organisation was having its annual get-together at the Lansdowne. (King Arthur's original round table had been intended to ensure that those sitting at it had no precedence over one another.) The members, mostly Brecon businessmen, arrived in dinner-jackets, their wives in flouncy frocks. The proprietor's wife greeted them as they came in. 'What time've you ordered a cab for, then?' she asked one man.

'Ten to twelve.'

'My! You left at quarter to four last year.'

'I'm on good behaviour tonight.'

'I'll believe it when I see it.'

One of the waitresses, putting a big dish of sherry trifle in front of me, told me that four a.m. was indeed a likely time for the Round Table festivities to finish. She said, 'Last year we found one of them in the hotel car park at four-thirty. He hadn't a clue where he was.'

I expected the worst – I thought I might soon be missing the youth hostel. But the only great burst of noise came early on – at ten forty-five – and close at hand. I opened the door of my room to find a dozen of the Round Table ladies formed up in the corridor, laughing. They were now wearing overalls and boiler suits, men's boots, and hard hats. 'We're miners,' one said to me in a loud whisper, nicely ignoring my pyjamas. 'We always do a cabaret and we're just waiting up here so that it's a surprise when we go on.'

I heard no more but at some point dreamed I was in a Castell Coch sort of banqueting room, dining with Arthur and Lancelot, Guinevere and Morgan-le-Fay.

A decision had to be made at Brecon: whether to go due north over the hills to the town of Builth Wells, about fifteen miles away, or proceed westwards along the Usk Valley towards Llandovery, twenty miles or so distant. (An in-between course, north-west, was counted out when I noticed that much of it would be across moorland marked on my map with the legends DANGER AREA and ARTILLERY RANGE. What swayed me was simple. The Usk looked beautiful, limpidly grey on this misty Sunday morning. Several anglers, wearing waders, were standing at a weir below the ruined castle. (Gerald wrote that the Usk was good for trout.) I walked along a minor road on the north bank of the river. On the other side lay the golf course where the Lansdowne proprietor – rather bleary-eyed this morning – intended to play. It was almost raining, a sort of Irish mist, and I draped my raincoat over my pack and shoulders to keep off the moisture without generating heat and condensation underneath. It was a nice walk, if damp, across green fields to a farm called Pennant. The stiles at the hedgerows were solid, my chief complaint being that the added height of hikers with backpacks wasn't considered at these crossing points, where I and my backpack occasionally tangled with overhanging branches. For that matter, the muddiest part of a field tends to be next to a stile, because cattle in their contrary way like congregating there. I would break loose from the snagging hawthorn and step down into squishyness.

I was following a way the Romans had taken to a fort they
had built close to where a stream called the Ysgir joined the
Usk – a road which had been part of their military infrastruc-
ture in Wales, but which at this point was no longer evident.
The field path joined a farm track by no means up to Roman
standards. The Roman engineers had constructed their roads
for all-weather use, laying them out as straight as could be
between prominent landmarks, though not necessarily
straight over great distances, and sometimes following older
tracks. They made their roads by excavating a bed and then
putting down various layers of material: larger stones mixed
with earth, smaller stones with earth, and gravel or flint on
the surface. The road would be edged with kerb stones;
ditches on each side took the run-off from the cambered
surface. This farm track, between hedges, had the ditches
but was less than half the twenty-two foot width of a
standard Roman road. I halted on meeting a tractor, pulling
a cartload of brushwood, that was coming out of a field on
to the track. I opened the gate into the field on the other side
to which the tractor was heading, but the farmer driving it
got down anyway to retrieve a sawn bough which had fallen
off. He had a torn cloth cap and lined, weathered features.
He asked, 'You going up this old Roman road?'

'I am.'

'You've had the best of it. My, it's muddy up there! You
can still turn back.'

I said no, thanks, I would go on. A bit of mud wouldn't
hurt.

He smiled, as if he knew better. 'You're on your own?'

I said I was.

'Aren't you lonely?'

'Not really. I enjoy it.'

'Ah, I can see that. And will you go far?'

'I'm heading towards Llandovery, and then maybe
Aberystwyth.'

'Your legs'll be shorter by the time you get home.'

He was right about the mud. There was first a stream to ford, and water running several inches above the stepping-stones. There was a bog, with mud, and barbed wire to duck under while attempting not to sink in the mud, meanwhile cursing the friendly farmer who had strung the wire. On one small island in the bog I paused and tardily tucked the bottoms of my trousers into my socks. I scrambled through entangling brambles. It was clearly a long time since the orderly Romans had come this way. In the drier places under the trees bluebells were just about to come out. There were lots of rabbits. I felt the wet mud soaking through my socks. And then, *eureka!* An asphalted drive appeared with several cottages on my right beside a pond, on my left a wooded hill. I was so pleased with the hard dry surface that I missed the overgrown entrance to the track along the hillside that led to the Roman fort, and I had to scramble up to the track a few hundred yards further on, through brambles and rotting wood. I was thinking, while I puffed and stumbled, that the Beacons were sissy stuff compared to this nature-reclaimed and farmer-fenced Roman 'road'. Having regained my way, I expressed my feelings of well-being by singing a snatch from the 1950s musical *Salad Days*: 'Remind me, to remind you, we said we'd never look back.'

I came out of the woods. The track, paved (possibly by the Romans) with stones that were now set in firm turf, crossed a large field full of sheep and lambs. Away to the south, beyond the Usk, the Beacons were covered in thick grey cloud from their lower slopes to their peaks. A large grey-stone slate-roofed farmhouse stood between me and the fort. I gave a friendly greeting to a corgi and a sheepdog who were guarding the front path as I went to knock on the door. The man who answered – a farmer whose Sunday morning wear was a dark-green army-style sweater with cloth shoulder patches – gave me permission to look at the fort, and hospitably added the necessary directions for how to get there, through the farmyard, a maze of railings and gates, and a cluster of cows.

Y Gaer, the fort or castle, is what the Welsh have come to call the Roman's Cicucium. (*Gaer* or *Caer* derives from the Latin *castrum*.) It is now a raised enclosure, about the size of a football pitch, with an exposed stone wall six to ten feet high running along its north side, overlooking the farm pond. Ducks on the pond, the stones joined by durable Roman cement. A narrow gate next to a bastion at the north-east corner gave access to steps up to the grassy field within, where sheep were grazing. This was one of the largest Roman fortifications in Wales, at a hub of their road system, and even in its present form – the bones of the thing – makes a contrast between firm, right-angled Roman organisation and the flowing Celtic surroundings. Here, from AD 75 to 100, a five-hundred-strong Spanish cavalry regiment was garrisoned to make sure that the Silures, a tribe of British Celts, did not cause trouble. (Caratacus or Caradoc, one of the Silurian leaders, led a resistance movement against the Romans.) When the Roman forces withdrew there remained Roman roads, Roman forts, and Roman words, particularly those to do with building – caer and castell, mur (wall) and ffenestr (window), pont (bridge) and ffos (ditch). And there probably remained Mediterranean blood, from the legionaries who had married local girls and taken early retirement in the Usk valley.

I wandered around the fort, jumped down into the little turf-floored roofless bastions, and climbed up on to the . medieval mound or motte that had been raised in Norman times next to the river. While the Celtic peoples had preferred to live on the windy hilltops, where they could see the enemy coming, the Romans confidently built their bases in more comfortable spots like this, counting on their skills with stone and the use of natural obstacles like water to provide defences.

Leaving the fort, I encountered the helpful farmer again in

his farmyard. He recommended a route I wouldn't have otherwise taken across one of his fields, using a tractor parked on the skyline as a landmark. This brought me to the Afon Ysgir and a bridge, called with Welsh variousness Pont-ar-Yscir. It was an ancient stone structure with twin arches and a peak in the middle of the span that looked as if it would strand any low-slung vehicle. The Ysgir was in good flow. From here it was easy sauntering on a little road which ran along a low hillside above the Usk. On the far side of the river, a pink-grey mansion stood among tall trees – Penpont, built in 1666, and chosen during the Second World War to be a Resistance command post in the event of German invasion. The route of a dismantled railway lay on my side of the Usk but, with most of its bridges down, didn't form a practicable alternative to the road I was on. As it was, I had the road to myself. In the course of passing through several hamlets the only person I met was a farmer in clean blue overalls and a blue cap with the legend MOBIL, coming out of a roadside barn. 'Going far today?' he enquired.

'I was thinking about Sennybridge' – about three miles on. 'Does anyone do B-and-B there?'

'Try the pub, The Usk and Railway.'

This exchange took place on the edge of Trallong, a settlement with a sub-post office and half a dozen houses. Inspired by the sound of the name, I began to sing, 'It's a long, long trail a-winding, to the land of my dreams.' And when very few more words of that song came to me, I switched to 'Keep right on to the end of the road, keep right on to the end.' Possibly the momentum gained from this exhortation to myself was what caused me to miss a turn I should have taken. I realised this after half a mile, and went back. I then took the turning I had missed, on a lane which twisted down toward the Usk. The sheep and lambs in the lush meadows of Park Farm had their ears stuck out and were looking at me warily – no doubt rightly, as I

represented those who would fleece or eat them. I had my
raincoat on now, in drizzle, as I crossed a stream called the
Cilieni, foaming down to join the Usk. I passed the entrance
to a military training depot, headquarters of the extensive
practice ranges, and crossed the Usk into Sennybridge. A
village of four hundred people, it was once a stop on the
Swansea to Brecon railway line – which closed, like many
rural lines in Britain, in 1962. Now the place is defined by
its position at the junction of the A40, the main road through
this part of Wales to the west, with the road which runs
down through Fforest Fawr to the South Wales coast. Apart
from the army base, Sennybridge has a weekly livestock
market, two saw mills, an agricultural machinery dealer, a
farrier-blacksmith, a post office, a shop, and three pubs.

The Usk and Railway looked a bit like a Victorian railway
station. Prominent in the main street, it would have been
hard to miss even if thirst and need of shelter had not given
me reason to stop. However, a sign on the door announced
that the Sunday midday opening times were from 11 a.m. to
3 p.m. Gloom – it was three-fifteen. On the other hand, the
door was still open. The public bar was crowded. Easing my
way through, I glimpsed fake wooden beams and imitation
antique panelling; but the hub-bub was genuine. Several
dogs lay under chairs – and pubs that allow dogs tend to be
good pubs. I took off my pack, wiped the rain from my
face, and acknowledged a few friendly gestures that opened
a way to the counter. The lady in charge gave a slight pout
when I asked for a pint of bitter, so I said 'If time's a ·
problem, a half will do.' She drew me a pint. Encouraged, I
asked, 'Do you do bed-and-breakfast?'

'No, we don't,' she said. I began to consider a wet Sunday
afternoon walking on, seeking accommodation. But she was
looking past me, examining the throng. She said, pointing,
'There they are. Talk to Lyn and Lionel over at that table.'

I did: Lionel Charlwood, in his mid-fifties with curly grey
hair and beard; and Lyn, his wife, somewhat younger, with

a rose-petal complexion; both cheerful, outgoing people. It was quickly established that they would put me up for the night at their house in the nearby village of Crai. Although we were well into 'drinking-up time', a few 'last orders' were being squeezed in. I was introduced to Tony, a spry retired poacher who did odd-jobs; he was presently doing some interior painting here at the pub. While Tony was at the bar, getting a final refill, Lionel said that Tony had been after salmon not long ago in a river on the military training area when all hell broke loose, explosions all round him, guns going off, men in camouflage uniforms with blackened faces charging at him. 'He said he hadn't seen the red warning flags flying. I think he's stuck with decorating since then.' I met a man who bet me twenty pence that he could balance fourteen four-inch nails on top of one four-inch nail driven into a block of wood. (Learning how was well worth twenty pence.) I shook hands with a six-foot-six New Zealander named Paul who was here for the sheep-shearing. As we were leaving, with Lionel telling several people he'd see them that evening, singing broke out, in Welsh, not a tune I recognised, one male voice in the ascendant. 'That's the blacksmith,' said Lyn. 'He always gets them going.'

Crai – Lyn driving – was four miles up the road which ran southwestwards into the Beacons National Park. Cwm Uchaf, 'Highest Valley', the Charlwood's home, was an old farmhouse at the edge of the village where the Charlwoods ran various activities. Lionel introduced me to his mother, recently widowed, and to three dogs – a doberman called Major, a black-and-tan Jack Russell called Minnie, and Lady, a springer spaniel who was a guest while her owner was abroad. Lionel then gave me a tour of the house, which contained several guest rooms, an office, a bunk room, a small gym, and an armoury and storeroom for hunting, camping, and canoeing equipment. Among the Charlwood enterprises were outdoor courses for school groups;

'Management Assessment Services' courses to develop the leadership qualities of executives; and 'Ubique Security Services', which provided training in surveillance and personal and property protection and gave 'Middle-East candidates' pre-Military Academy instruction. Lionel handed me a Ubique brochure which had an illustration showing a newspaper headline – '£11 Million Ransom' – and two blank-faced men apparently protecting from kidnap a pair of black-robed Arabs getting off an executive jet.

For the moment, the only fight was to get Major and Minnie off the couch and an armchair in the living-room, where Lionel and I watched part of an old Clint Eastwood movie – with lots of gunfire – about training US marines. Over dinner (splendid roast lamb; wonderful apple pie), Lionel, after some prodding, talked modestly about his life. He had grown up in Bethnal Green in the East End of London. He had joined the army as a boy soldier at fourteen. 'I never wanted to be anything else,' he said. He was a soldier for eighteen years. He went with the Lancers armoured regiment to Korea for the last few months of the war and then to Malaya and Borneo with the Special Air Services. 'Some things I can't talk about,' he said. 'Still covered by the Official Secrets Act.' On several occasions he came to Sennybridge for training and in free moments visited The Usk and Railway, 'not just to get out of the rain'. He left the army with the rank of Captain in 1967. 'I had several security jobs in Germany. Then I drove Formula Three cars, the smallest racing cars, and managed a motor-racing school. I ran a wine bar and restaurant for ten years and as a hobby used to take scouts and school-kids on survival courses. Sennybridge and the Beacons were always in the back of my mind. We came down on a visit and found Cwm Uchaf and that was that.'

Lyn, who is Lionel's second wife, said to me, 'You did the right thing stopping in Sennybridge today. It's the friendliest place I've been.'

Lionel and I drove back to The Usk and Railway after dinner. He had a rendezvous arranged with another ex-army man who worked with him. 'You really ought to see the pub regulars when they're all in a gambling mood,' he said. 'They'll bet on anything. They've had worm races, with the contestants plucked from an Usk fisherman's bait pail. They had a race for ferrets in lengths of plastic drainpipe snaked around the bar. A lot of them did well on Desert Orchid recently. When the bookie from Ystradgynlais made his weekly visit, to collect bets and pay them their winnings, they had a horse in the bar waiting for him, and a girl dressed as a jockey.'

At The Usk and Railway, the ex-army element had increased. The evening barman, Allan, who had tattooed forearms, was an ex-Guardsman and former Londoner who had married a Sennybridge girl; he delivered local mail in the mornings. Martin, the big friendly square-faced man Lionel had come to meet, had been a Colour-Sergeant in the Greenjackets, a crack infantry regiment. He and Lionel were planning a three-day 'escape and evasion' exercise for a party of part-time Territorial Army men from Berkshire. 'They aren't used to the mountains,' Lionel said. 'I think this is going to stretch them a bit.' The exercises were meant to encourage military skills such as map-reading, field craft, fitness, and leadership – and were also meant to be fun. In this one, dubbed Exercise Nimrod by Lionel and Martin, the Beacons were understood to have been infiltrated by Redland Special Forces. Working in conjunction with the Beacons Liberation Front, the Redland invaders had captured several installations and set up patrol bases. Meanwhile, Friendly Forces were keeping open certain roads. Martin said, 'We might set them the task of blowing up an unmanned radio relay station.'

'A hypothetical radio relay station,' Lionel added, quickly. 'We don't use real weapons or explosives on these exercises.

Just thunderflashes for noise and effect, and to keep the lads on their toes.'

Buying a round at the bar I encountered Paul, the tall New Zealander, who accepted my offer of a drink despite having several full pints of lager lined up. He was the advance man for a dozen Kiwi sheep-shearers who would be here for much of the shearing season, which starts in the lowland areas in mid-April and runs to the end of June on higher ground. Paul told me that his countrymen had been shearing in Britain for the last twenty years and that generally at least 300 came for the work. His own base and girl friend were in Munich, where in quiet times he installed cable television. Most of the year he travelled with his shearing equipment to wherever he was needed – in Germany, Norway, Britain, Canada, the Falklands, and New Zealand. Back home there he had a smallholding and orchard; his parents were looking after it.

'No sheep?' I asked.

'No sheep,' he said. 'When I quit this work – and I've been doing it for six years – I'll never want to see another sheep.'

Paul took a sip from his glass and a good part of a pint of lager went down. I wondered aloud whether his size helped him grasp a sheep firmly as he removed its fleece.

'My height is no advantage. You spend all day bent over, with your head near the floor. It's tough on the back and on the muscles in the back of your legs. It can cripple you for anything else.' The shearer had to hold the sheep on its back, gripped between his knees, with its head poking back through his legs. A skillful shearer could remove the wool from 300 sheep a day; a 'top gun' could shear 500. There were roughly eleven million sheep in Wales – over four to every inhabitant – and Paul didn't think they'd get sheared without Kiwi help. After Sennybridge he would be going to the Lake District and then Scotland. He received thirty to forty pence per sheep here; in Germany the rate was nearer one pound.

Paul introduced me to Brian Davies, a forty-five-year-old
Sennybridge man who some years before had been world
champion sheep-shearer. Now, from a converted chapel just
up the road from The Usk and Railway, he ran a flourishing
business selling shearing equipment, importing a breed of
New Zealand sheepdog called Huntaway, and acting as agent
for the Kiwi sheep-shearers. Davies said, 'I left school at
fourteen having failed every exam and haven't looked back.
I sheared my first sheep when I was nine and before I started
doing it for a living I would do it for nothing, I liked it so
much. I like teaching shearing now. The men who think
they are big strong buggers are the hardest to teach – you
can't just shear through strength. It's a matter of harmonis-
ation – getting the sheep to relax and anticipating how and
when it's going to move.'

Almost all shearing is done with electric shears powered
by diesel generators, and the sheep have to be dry so that
there is less risk of electrocution. Paul said, 'I've been hit by
a few really bad shocks.' He had trouble getting boots that
fitted him – size sixteen – and favoured double-lined Australian denim trousers, thick enough to prevent sheep-fat and
dirt getting into the skin of his legs and possibly infecting
them. Brian Davies added, 'The wool looks soft, but it wears
away at your fingers. Your fingertips get so thin, they bleed
easily. You can tell a sheep-shearer by his worn-out hands,
his bare knuckles.'

A question of honour was bothering me as I set forth from Crai next morning. Should I have asked Lionel or Lyn to drive me the four miles back to Sennybridge so that I could have resumed my walk exactly where I had left off? Instead I was heading under my own steam for Trecastle, which was about two and a half miles west of Sennybridge and also about four miles from Crai. However, I squared my conscience about this slight discontinuity in my walk by telling myself that the way from Crai to Trecastle not only avoided the main road from Sennybridge to Trecastle but was, to boot, longer: I wasn't taking the easy option. I swung my arms high, loosening up. (I had declined an invitation from Lionel to have a pre-breakfast go on the Cwm Uchaf assault course, which had pipes to crawl through, ropes to swing from over muddy ditches, sheer walls to mount.) It was a cool morning, with light northerly airs and high thin cloud – and with the promise of being a fine day. Looking back, I had a view of Fan Gyhirych, the loftiest peak in these parts. My route took me downhill into the valley of the river Crai which flows northward to join the Usk. The thickly hedge-rowed fields were full of sheep, baa-ing and gurgling, perhaps awaiting the short-back-and-sides ministrations of Paul and his colleagues. A Tornado fighter-bomber momentarily drowned out these bucolic sounds, flashing down the valley, a dark dart trying to keep ahead of its own ear-buffeting screech.

At ten o'clock there were hints of blue sky and enough sun to make weak shadows in the lane. White May-blossom was beginning to appear in the hawthorn hedges in the lower parts of the valley, though it was still April. I crossed the river by a little road-bridge and climbed the hillside past Danygraig Farm. Three dogs barked dutifully at me before approaching closer to sniff my boots with friendly curiosity. In the farmyard were parked a Saturno tractor (from Italy) and a Peugeot car (from France). But despite these cosmopolitan indications, and the unseen agricultural subsidies arising from Brussels, many in these parts were – I gathered – dismayed by the flood of foreigners flowing over their land. (My own impression, to date, was that many nooks and crannies of South Wales were filled with Londoners.) Lionel, questioned about this, had agreed that there might be a basic anti-incomer feeling among the local Welsh but he and Lyn hadn't experienced it. In Sennybridge, at least, people were long used to the army, and ex-army folk were warmly received.

I had more zip in my pace than the day before. As I swung along, my view of the country was in quick snaps – a red Royal Mail van passing, the driver-postman waving; a pile of mangels or swedes dumped by a field gate; the rear half of a blue Mini van placed in a field as a feeding station. I crossed the Usk again at Pont Newydd and strolled along the A40 mainroad through Trecastle. The important relic here is the Norman motte, a mound about thirty yards in diameter. The Bayeux Tapestry shows how these looked in their time, capped with a wooden tower, and a defensive ditch around the base. The adjacent stockaded yard or bailey, almost seventy yards long, is protected by a steep earthern rampart. All this was the Norman incomers' way of protecting themselves against the Welsh. Trecastle now is a village of some forty houses, three pubs, and a half-sized rugby field. It had fifteen shops at the turn of the century; I saw one. In mid-morning few inhabitants were about. I exchanged

greetings with a plump red-faced man and kept going. I
turned off the main road and along a lane uphill to the Roman
road which traverses Mynydd Bach Trecastell toward
Llandovery.

The sheep up on the mountain moorland had had their
necks or tails dyed a high visibility orange; one had got out
of its enclosure and – seeing me coming – was pressing
against a wire fence, trying to get back in. The Roman road
was surfaced with stones packed in firm earth; it was straight
without being too straight – a road laid out and built by men
with a human tendency to waver ever so slightly. According
to my map, it ran past a cairn, a tumulus, a bog, two stone
circles, and several Roman camps. More noticeable than any
of these bumps, protrusions and hollows was the fact that
not a single other person was up here. How crowded our
lives are, how hemmed in we are by our fellow creatures in
urban Britain! No wonder Wales attracts Londoners. I could
see the Beacons all the way from Pen-y-Fan in the east to
the various sombre heights to the south of me known as the
Black Mountain (Mynydd Ddu in Welsh). This is at the
western end of the Beacons range. At the far eastern end,
out of sight, were the Black Mountains. The similarity in
the names prompted reflections about the possible lack of
contact between the peoples who had lived near these two
chunks of high ground only thirty miles apart – and about
the conspicuous dark peaty flanks of both that presumably
got them their names.

Where the road became a rutted track I left it and followed
a sheep path. This was a thin line of short green grass across
the generally tussocky, tousled yellow-brown of a rather
boggy hillside. Sheep, it is said, never get caught in bogs;
therefore a safe rule on boggy land is, Follow the sheep
tracks. The sheep which had trodden this path had also been
visiting the largest of the Roman camps, Y Pigwyn. I stood
on the hilltop inside several lines of jumbled earthworks,
like minespoil or mammoth molehills, anciently turfed. I

admired the view the legionaries had enjoyed. A soldier on
guard up here would have been able to send signals to one of
his mates in the fort a mile to the west. Any sign of the
troublesome Silures? Here I lunched, reclining Roman-
fashion on my raincoat on the turf. Together with a sandwich and a Cox's Orange Pippin, Lyn had provided me with
a small chocolate bar named Balisto, coincidentally close to
the Roman *ballista*. According to the map, the camp was on
the border between the counties of Dyfed and Powys –
clearly an old border. Between the camp and the Black
Mountain were the headwaters of the Usk and a large
reservoir framed by a dark forest. Overhead, a lark twittered.
Lying on my back, I let my thoughts spiral up, as they easily
do on lonely hilltops where one feels closer to immensity:
thoughts of aeons, of time then and time now, and of such
haphazard manifestations of creation as the turf, the sheep,
the lark, and me.

Just before one I set off, happy to go down out of a rising
raw north wind into more sheltered ground. I walked
through a small forest of larch. Even some coniferous trees
renew their needles, which were bright green at this time of
year. Several miles, all downhill, brought me past a big
Edwardian house (that – a sign of the times – called itself a
Management Training Centre) and into Llandovery.

Llandovery is a partial Englishing of Llanymddyfri which
(to quote George Borrow) 'signifies the church surrounded
by water'. The town sits in a vale where three rivers join
together: the Bran, the Gwydderig, and the Tywi or Towy.
After two nights and a day here Borrow called Llandovery
'about the pleasantest little town in which I have halted in
the course of my wanderings'. Having seen Brecon (as
Borrow had not), and with a number of little towns yet to
come, I was slightly more hesitant with my praise than my
distinguished predecessor – but I also had no difficulty in
pausing here for several nights. I stayed at The Castle Hotel,

where Borrow had lodged. Mrs Moore, the lady of the house, showed me the Borrow Room, which had a four-poster bed, and the Nelson Room, with a grand mahogany bedstead in which the naval hero slept while staying here. Nelson toured South Wales with seventy-three-year-old Sir William Hamilton and his wife Emma in the summer of 1802, during the peaceful interlude that followed the Treaty of Amiens. The travelling ménage à trois was heading for Milford Haven, to take part in celebrations for the anniversary of Nelson's victory at the Battle of the Nile. In Merthyr Tydfil the ironmaster Richard Crawshay had entertained them. In Brecon, a deputation of farmers greeted them, some overcome, and weeping at the sight of the slight-figured, one-eyed, one-armed Admiral. Here in Llandovery Nelson signed a portrait of himself for the landlord of The Castle – a picture no longer at the hotel, said Mrs Moore. Quite where Sir William slept is not known, or whether Emma was with her husband or her lover or treading the creaking floorboards of the corridor between their rooms. I at any rate decided to forgo the pleasures of association afforded by the Borrow and Nelson rooms (at sixty pounds per night). I took instead a simpler chamber which cost eighteen.

It was sprinkling with snow as I walked around the town in the late afternoon. Llandovery, population 1700, is soon seen. A small square, just off the main road, is dominated by an old market hall, the post office, and several banks. There are a few streets of well-maintained houses. The narrow main road, squeezing past The Castle Hotel, causes the drivers of big trucks to be polite to one another. Llandovery's largest church is still on the edge of town, as are its railway station and new market buildings. The castle itself, close to the hotel, is a ruined stone tower standing on a rocky tump – a mound which looks as if it was the result of a huge bucket of earth and stones being turned out upside down. The castle overlooks the municipal car park which was full not only of cars but tractors, Land-Rovers pulling double-decked trailers crammed with bleating sheep, and various vehicles which were mobile shops: one van, back doors open, offered fresh fish. The town has an excellent bookshop – with many books in Welsh as well as English – and a well-known boys' school, Llandovery College, three of whose pupils I saw walking along in dark-blue blazers, novel only in that they were all Chinese and eating jam doughnuts.

The most famous sons of Llandovery and vicinity are both clergymen. William Williams of Pantycelyn (1717–1791) was a Church of England deacon who became a Methodist preacher and wrote many notable poems and hymns, particularly the stirring 'Lead me, O thou great Jehovah', which the crowds at Cardiff Arms Park often break out with when encouraging the home side. An earlier cleric, Rees Pritchard, who was born in the late sixteenth century, became vicar of Llandovery and was the author of a long and much read poem 'The Candle of the Welsh' that attacked immorality. The behaviour of the Reverend Pritchard – known affectionately as 'the old vicar' – may have helped the popularity of his poem. According to Borrow, the vicar himself was 'in the habit of spending the greater part of his time in the public house, from which he was generally trundled home in a wheelbarrow in a state of utter insensibility'. His parishioners used to say, 'Bad as we may be, we are not half so bad as the parson.' He is said to have finally given up drink after the tavern goat – which he had got intoxicated the night before – refused a brimming tankard of beer. 'My God!' said the vicar, 'is this poor dumb creature wiser than I?' Borrow adds, 'He left his tankard untasted on the table, went home, and became an altered man.'

In the Market Bar of The Castle, no goats in sight, I had a pre-dinner pint. The Market Bar is the hotel's public bar, and at six p.m. the customers included a middle-aged man with clear blue eyes, wearing a cloth cap, who said he had been a farmer but now worked on the railway. He began to

tell me about sheep – their life-cycle and the importance of
teeth – but he spoke with a Welsh accent much thickened by
drink. He said that I must go to a competition in the mid-
Wales town of Llanwrtyd Wells where men on foot raced
men on horses over a twenty-mile course. 'Man versus
horse!' he said, and kept on repeating this. 'Man versus
horse!' We were joined by an old man of elfin physique
named Bill, also drunk, who gathered his residual jauntiness
together and asked the barmaid (a handsome woman) for a
drink on tick. She refused. Bill went off in a huff but
returned in a few minutes with enough cash for half a pint of
lager. With this in hand he began to pester the barmaid for a
date. She had earlier been talking to another man at the bar
about her impending divorce but fended off this unwelcome
attention with, 'Sorry, I'm a one-man woman.' Three men
at a nearby table were talking in educated English accents
about local rock formations and Bristol Channel tides. Bill,
once again disconsolate, began to sing, 'Now the day is
over, night is drawing nigh . . .' A glass was broken. The
barmaid said, 'That's it, Bill. No more. Time to go home.'
Bill replied, 'Are you going with me, then?'

I retired to the saloon bar, deeper within the hotel, where
I was the only customer and Mr Moore, the proprietor,
served me a drink. He told me that he had been born in
Monmouth, a border town just in Wales, and that he and his
wife had recently come here from running a country inn in
the Wye valley. 'It's lovely here, but things are changing
fast. What has really made a difference to this part of Wales
is the M4 motorway from London. Once that was built,
people in England realised how easily they could escape to
the West. We've got a lot of elderly English people retiring
here. But I can't complain about business. We're already
booked up for most of the summer.'

I made several excursions from Llandovery. I was aware
now of being in Welsh-speaking Wales; here Welsh was the

native tongue. Coming west from Brecon, past Sennybridge, the balance had shifted. In the market, in the shops,
in the banks ('Banc National Westminster Bank' said the
sign of one, the Welsh term coming first), I felt a slight
timidity, embarking on a question in English – though
assuming that I would get an answer in English. The
presumption – and I was aware of it as such – was that even
if I knew no more than a few words of Welsh, every Welsh
person spoke English.

The Moores gave me a ride to Llandeilo, a town about
twelve miles south-west of Llandovery, where I had
arranged to meet an American woman who I'd been told
spoke fluent Welsh. Leigh Verrill Rhys was in her thirties, a
native of Maine, and ran a distribution business for Welsh
books, magazines, and recordings; she had just returned
from a sales trip in 'foreign parts', that is England and
Scotland. Over lunch in a Llandeilo cafe, she said that she'd
first come to Wales after graduating from university in San
Francisco. 'The first Welsh I ever heard was while I was
waiting at a bus-stop in North Wales.' Her serious features
softened with the memory of what clearly had been a life-
changing experience. 'Until then it hadn't occurred to me
that there was a spoken Welsh language. I bought a
dictionary and a teach-yourself book but didn't make much
progress. It *is* a difficult language. Back in San Francisco, I
started writing a novel set in Wales. I took a course in Welsh.
I soon realised that to get anywhere with it you have to
throw yourself into it with reckless abandon. What I didn't
realise was that one of my instructors was later to become
my husband. We visited Wales together. A year later, in
1981, I decided that my future was in Wales. I abandoned
the novel, quit my California teaching job, took out a bank
loan, and came to Wales to learn Welsh for real. I was
absolutely taken with the language and felt my life depended
on it.'

Leigh Rhys's husband Dulais Rhys now teaches music in a

school in Carmarthen, twelve miles west of Llandeilo. They
have three small boys: Gwion, Iestyn, and Osian. She went
on, 'Dulais was exceptional in that he grew up in Wales
speaking Welsh first. He couldn't speak English at all until
he was seven. Welsh *is* the language of Wales. It may not be
spoken by all the people but it is their language. Even the
non-Welsh-speaking Welsh are surrounded by it, though
they may not acknowledge it. But we have to make a push
to counter the influence of London and of the English media.
Take the BBC – they try hard with the pronunciation of
other languages, why can't they get it right with Welsh? We
need more statutory government support for the language
and more money particularly for adult education in Welsh.
The problem is acute right now because of large-scale
English immigration. They used to come in twos and threes
but now it's a flood.'

Leigh Rhys said that she fervently supported the effort
that was being made by a society called Pont, or Bridge,
founded by Gwynfor Evans, the patriarch of the Welsh
Nationalist party Plaid Cymru. This aimed to bridge the gap
between Welsh-speakers and new settlers who did not speak
the language. She had written a leaflet for distribution to all
newcomers in this county of Dyfed, encouraging them to
commit themselves to their new home by learning Welsh.
She sternly put me right for my pronunciation and indeed
use of the name Llandovery – which naturally should be
Llanymddyfri, with its 'l's and 'd's puffed forth like 'f's.

I asked if she ever missed the USA.

'Once in a while. I think heaven must be a small town in
Maine, with tree-shaded streets. But you know I've found
so many of what I used to think were the best qualities of
American society here in Wales. Maybe more so. This
country is relatively classless, open in terms of opportunity,
and full of people who delight in personal contact, in making
connections with you. I met someone yesterday, a complete
stranger, who when they found I lived in Carmarthen told

me "Oh, I have a cousin there," and pretty soon we'd exchanged all sorts of family history. The Welsh are passionate about education and they have a genuine belief in equality. No one here is too important to speak to. I've never met anyone in Wales, however famous or successful, I couldn't approach in the street and start talking to. Thomas Jefferson said "Never bow to anyone." He would have approved of the Welsh, I think.'

Later I sat in an elegant little coffee shop in a street facing Llandeilo's largest church and cemetery, which formed a sort of green in the town centre. Some well-dressed mourners were drinking coffee and eating patisseries after a funeral, talking for the most part in Welsh but breaking into English for figures. ('. . . one hundred and fifty thousand pounds . . .' said a lady, amid a flow of Welsh words, possibly referring to a bequest of the departed.) The café owner, a tall middle-aged man who spoke English with what sounded like a German accent, told me that one could live in Llandeilo for thirty years and still not be regarded as 'from these parts'. Incomers might need not only the commitment Leigh Rhys called for and some of her initial 'reckless abandon', but perseverance.

I took the train back to Llandovery. 'Please knock,' it said on the ticket window in the station. I knocked, bought a ticket from the friendly railman who appeared, and traded remarks on the afternoon weather. 'Lovely sun.' 'Biting wind, though.' Flowers in pots on the platform, a touch of railway-station care as we no longer often find it in southeast England. The train was a two-car affair, diesel-powered, like a country bus, carrying parcels, children going home from school, women and their shopping. This was 'The Heart of Wales Line', Swansea to Shrewsbury. The driver had to stop to collect a token which gave him right of passage over a long stretch of single track.

★   ★   ★

I went up into the foothills of the Black Mountain and visited a family of Londoners who had bought an old mill and farmhouse as a vacation retreat: a youngish architect; his young wife, an editor in a publishing house; their three small girls. It was a pretty spot, at the foot of a steep hill, the mill stream running down through a valley where sheep pastures were interspersed with woods, the old buildings nicely restored. They loved the place and the land around, appreciated the space and isolation, so different from the city. But they were in two minds about the local Welsh. Although a number in the vicinity were very friendly, those they had met in the course of buying and doing-up the place had not given them confidence. The architect said, 'The title deeds were all bizarrely deficient. The solicitors seemed to be inept, inebriated, and in cahoots with one another. The builders were determined to give us what they wanted, not what we wanted.' Eventually the family found a highly competent builder who was, by chance, an ex-Londoner. It occurred to me that the Welsh were in many ways in the same situation as the Sicilians, a people who for centuries have had to put up with invaders and intruders, who take the business and money provided by newcomers, and who find it hard not to resent the process.

A few miles up amid the bare hills is a lake called Llyn-y-fan-fach. This has a legend attached to it: a story of a beautiful girl who rises from the lake, marries a young man who has brought his herds there, has three sons by him, but eventually – when he breaks a vow – returns to the lake, though she sometimes surfaces again to teach her sons the secrets of fairy medicine. Richard Sale, one of many writers who has re-told the tale, believes it may be based on folk memories of the encounter between the Celts when they first moved into Wales in the final millennium BC and the incumbent people, who were skilful with herbal remedies. If this is so, says Sale, 'the implication of the story is that the culture shock was minimal and that the Celts mingled with the original settlers rather than destroying them out of hand'.

Not far away from the London family's farmhouse and mill was a trekking centre where the three girls went for riding lessons. Here many of the incomers who had homes in the area met as they brought their children for exposure to animals and outdoors activity; here they talked about their journeys between London and Wales, about schools, about property problems. And here was Ginny Hajdukiewicz, who ran the centre, also an incomer. She told me, 'When the Royals moved in to my part of Gloucestershire, I knew I could no longer afford it.' So – in the early 1980s – she moved to Beili Bedw Farm, near Llanddeusant, and began to annoy many of the local farmers by fiercely attacking the way they treated their horses and ponies. Ginny's husband, a Polish engineer, worked in Gloucester and came to the centre at weekends. Ginny was pale, straight-haired, with a nun-like calm under which, I soon realised, great passion seethed. In old wellingtons and a shabby raincoat she led me around the stalls in a large shed, introducing me to various beasts she had rescued and quietly delivering tales of atrocity and victory. Most of the animals were now looking plump and well cared-for though they had been skin and bones when she found them. She talked of the ailments and diseases horses and ponies can suffer: laminitis (a painful disease affecting their feet), sweet itch (an allergic reaction to midge bites), worms, lice, grass sickness, spasmodic colic, broken bones, poor teeth, arthritis. Some mares, she said, were treated by their farmer-owners almost like foal factories.

I asked where she acquired the animals.

'At sales, where they are generally being sold for slaughter,' she said. 'They fetch from twenty-five to fifty pounds. Sometimes I have to pay more.' She showed me a thin grey stallion which she had recently bought at Llandovery market for £200. 'A vet's bill for treating him might be £150 – only our vet is chairman of the trust we've set up to provide a

haven for horses and ponies, and he'll give me a break.' She
took me to a stable. As we entered, two ponies edged away
nervously to the far end of their stall. 'These are almost wild
still,' she said. 'And they're in grim shape, with very bad
cases of worms.' She closely examined a pile of droppings.
'The worm count in that is at least a thousand.' Left on the
mountainsides, where they had been put for cheap grazing,
the ponies would have died. If Ginny hadn't bought them,
they would have gone to a slaughterhouse. Her trust has
supporters in towns and villages in various parts of Britain;
they raise money by cake sales, jumble sales, odd jobs,
sponsored events. Ginny takes photos at markets of mal-
nourished and mistreated animals and arouses the fury of
their owners. One farmer not long ago took a stick to a
recalcitrant pony he had just sold to Ginny. Ginny snatched
the stick from him and told him that if he did that again she
would ram it up his rear end. The word of this incident
spread fast. Ginny is single-minded, and the condition of
horses and ponies being sold in the area is said to have
improved since she has been in action.

'The hardest thing about this job is not the hours of
mucking out and struggling with bales of hay, but having to
accept that there are hundreds of horses and ponies who need
help and can't be given it,' she said, closing the stable door.
'Farmers make all sorts of excuses, one being "He wouldn't
enjoy retirement." That may be true of a few horses but
most do like it, if they're properly looked after. They need
their feet trimmed and extra feed sometimes and shelter in
wet weather. They like being groomed and they enjoy being
ridden by young children.'

Four small ponies with four small girls aboard were led
into a paddock by a teenage assistant of Ginny's and several
parents. Ginny went to take charge of the lesson. The little
girls looked happily apprehensive and the ponies – if not
visibly enjoying themselves – looked not at all distressed.
Ginny carried a riding whip, her badge of office, but it hung

limply from her hand, as from long disuse, as she set the
young riders in motion with the call 'Ride on!'

In the new hangar-like buildings of Llandovery market, near
the water-meadows of the Bran, no ponies or horses were
being sold next day. From the pastures and moorlands the
sheep had been brought in vans and trailers, unloaded,
chivvied into pens where they were weighed, graded, and
marked, and then sorted again and driven into other pens by
flat-capped farmers and their sons and daughters. Small
farms, family concerns. The sheep were prodded and
pushed, whistled and yelled at with strange cries. The market
floors were concrete, with open drains. The pens were
divided by galvanised-steel tubular railings and gates. No
longer hedges, stone walls, or turf. The sheep clustered
together, expecting the worst. The life blood of Wales.
Meanwhile little clumps of men formed and re-formed,
standing alongside the pens, chatting together, comparing
their own sheep to those of others, looking at the sheep with
the cool eyes of connoisseurs. What are you worth? Do I
really want you? What condition are you in? What are your
long-term prospects, the cost of keeping you? What are you
worth? I soon gathered that a number of the men were here
not because they had sheep to sell or wanted to buy but
simply out of habit, a by-now ingrained curiosity as to what
the sheep were like today, what prices would be got; and
also to talk to old friends and breathe the sheep-scented air.
Now and then a man who was clearly serious about buying
would break away from a huddle with his colleagues and go
and brood over a pen-full of sheep. In a while he would join
the small crowd which stood below the auctioneer. From
this white-coated worthy came an imam-like chant, a ritual
sing-song of numbers – 'twenty-eight, twenty-eight,
twenty-nine, thirty, thirty . . .' – interspersed with rattled-
off phrases like 'What-am-I-bid-now?', 'Any-more-bids-
now?', and 'What-am-I-offered?' An elderly farmer near me

identified a man in a blue overall coat as a buyer for a large meat wholesalers. Though the actual mechanics of bidding remained mysterious, perhaps as at art auctions a matter of winks, nods, and written bids, I got the impression there were several active buyers. The price for a sheep weighing about eighteen kilos averaged thirty pounds. 'They're selling well today,' said my informant. 'They've got quite a lot of belly on them.'

NORTH-WEST TO THE SEA

NEXT DAY CAME clear and cold; sleet or snow were forecast for later. I got going after a full Castle breakfast, glad to be footing it once more. There was frost melting into dew on the handrails of the bridge over the Towy and the river beneath running fast and transparent. I was looking for the Roman road called Sarn Helen that ran north-west, but for several miles I found myself on lanes which behaved most unRomanly, winding uphill and downdale, around fields and along hillsides, sometimes almost doubling back, as if the intent was to take the least direct route. Even more strangely, I wasn't offered the usual, more-to-the-point alternative of a cross-country footpath. But not to worry – the cool air tasted sweet. I saw two chaffinch and not a single car. I was grateful for life. I passed tiny hamlets named Talog, Siloh, Ysgrafell. The landscape was nicely mixed: in one place, in the foreground a sort of parkland with a grassy sward, a bank out of which rose old trees, and grass dappled with sun and shadow; then in the middle ground a thick copse; and in the distance a line of bare hills. In one lane I passed a chapel which shared the same roof as the cottage attached to it but had no neighbouring habitation. Plain pebbledash relieved by bright orange doors and a sign: CWMSARNDDU BAPTIST CHAPEL. ERECTED 1814. REBUILT 1858. REBUILT 1876. In the small well-tended graveyard the stones were mostly inscribed in Welsh. Among the names of the departed: Richards. Morgan. Owen. Harries. Prickett. Jones.

A congregation. From here there was a lovely helpful view down into a little valley. I saw my way of saving a quarter of a mile of roundabout roadwork by cutting across a large meadow. This brought me to Siloh, five houses and another small chapel and graveyard. Did they have a different preacher down here? What doctrinal differences drove these tiny congregations to build and support two chapels so close together, so far out in the country? Local pride? Other questions were prompted by the next isolated building I came to half a mile further on: two houses, semi-detached, sharing a party wall, and giving two households for better or worse great propinquity.

Between Ysgrafell and Bwlch-tre-Banau I passed a meadow with some sheep and two ponies. On a roadside tree a handpainted sign had been nailed, the words arranged to fit the tall, skinny board:

> THESE PONIES HAVE
> 37 ACRES RUN
> AMPLE SHELTER
> RUNNING WATER
> HAY/SILAGE GIVEN DAILY
> MINERAL BLOCKS
> SYSTEMATIC WORMING
> PROPER VET CARE WHEN NECESSARY.
> PEDLARS IN CALUMNY
> PLEASE NOTE
> PARTICULARLY
> ENGLISH TRASH.

I wondered if Ginnie had been out this way. Certainly xenophobia seemed to have been aroused (perhaps Roman trash faced the same abuse). A little further on, another sign had been written by someone with less command of the foreign tongue: TRESSPASERS WILL BE BROSECUTEED. Or was this posted by a person with a keen sense of irony and a knowledge of Shakespeare? Several of the Bard's Welsh characters – like Sir Hugh Evans, the 'Welsh priest' in *The Merry Wives of Windsor*, and Fluellen in *Henry V* – pronounce many of their 'b's as 'p's, so why not vice versa? (I leave to one side the possibility that Shakespeare knew about these things because he was a Welshman, noting only Owen Dudley Edwards's remark: 'Shakespeare's Welshness makes excellent sense to otherwise dispassionate and scholarly Welsh persons.')

I found the Roman road beyond the village of Porthyrhyd – a small asphalted side-road which became a stone-surfaced lane which became a grassy track over the hills. A young black horse was being led down into the village by a tall man with a jet-black moustache and checked cap. The horse shied when it saw me, and the man held tightly to the horse's bit. I said, apologetically, 'I must have surprised him.' The man said with a friendly smile, 'That's all right. He's never met anyone hiking before. That's a good way to see the country.' Up on the crest of the hill Pen-y-Fan was just visible, a faint grey shape, far astern. Several vehicles had been left up here – a rusty truck, with grass growing above its long deflated tyres; and a roofless railway wagon, now a sheep-feed store. A hundred sheep and their lambs approached me, loudly baa-ing, possibly hoping for a hand-out. I took note of gates: those which were well-made and easy to open, with galvanised spring-loaded bolts to keep them closed; those which were older, held shut with a loop of orange baling rope; and several which were recalcitrant, which needed to be lifted off their hinges and then re-hung after I had slipped through. A few narrow gates made things easy by having weights on wires which pulled them shut again. At some, of course, the simplest method of passage was by climbing over. The modest lesson learned was that these barriers to my progress provided challenges that were varied and never insuperable. Going down to Aberbowlan, a hamlet of one and a half houses, I saw a dead lamb caught in a fence, a live rabbit hopping away, violets flowering in a hedge bottom, and a nine-inch diameter lump of shiny white rock, like opaque fused glass, which I supposed was quartz.

Once again the letters PH had appeared on the map to encourage me. I hastened downhill past a farm called Albert Mount and into the village of Caio. For the last mile or so my route had been along not only a Roman road but a droveway, on which for centuries cattle had been driven out of Wales into England to be marketed. Caio had been a centre at which herds of cattle were collected from the surrounding country and had been the home port of many notable drovers. One eighteenth-century drover named Dafydd Jones was also a hymn writer, and in one of his compositions he compared the throngs appearing before the Lord on Judgment Day to cattle arriving in Caio. However, the noise the drovers made as the herds moved had nothing heavenly about it. According to one person who remembered the sound, it was 'something out of the common, neither shouting, calling, crying, singing, halloing or anything else, but a noise of itself, apparently made to carry and capable of arresting the countryside'. Farmers, hearing a drove approach, made sure their own herds and flocks were secure in case their animals were entangled with the passing drove and drawn along with it.

In the high days of droving in the eighteenth century some fifty or sixty thousand head of Welsh black cattle were driven every year into England. Up in the north-west, cattle and sheep began their journey from Anglesey by having to swim the Menai Strait. The droving season generally went on from midsummer to Michaelmas and the droves moved from dawn to dusk, making about twenty miles a day. The droveways were often deeply-trodden, soft-surfaced, sunken lanes; the treading and grazing of the animals has left some ways bracken-free to this day. The droveways enabled the drovers to avoid the traffic and tolls of the turnpikes, though sometimes the turnpikes were used for speed of travel and consequently higher prices at market. The drovers, as travellers, had other uses. They returned with salt, cloth, and news of the world beyond Wales which they carried from village to village – such as reports of the battle of Waterloo. Other people used the droveways, like the hosiers of the mid-Wales town of Tregaron, carrying their goods for sale elsewhere, or those who were going to England for jobs or education. Some went along with the droves for protection against robbers, wolves, or the danger of getting lost. Most drovers rode ponies. Some went on droving to a great age, the way Edward Morus, also a poet, did; he died in Essex in 1689 aged eighty-two. The drovers were of course accompanied by their dogs, often corgis, though on the return trip, with no cattle or sheep to chivvy, the dogs sometimes made faster progress than their masters. When the dogs showed up, the women knew their men would be home in a few days' time.

The drovers handled a great deal of money. Vicar Pritchard, in his poem 'The Candle of the Welsh', exhorted the drover 'to be honest in his dealings . . . to refrain from imbibing too freely, and to drop the habit of absconding with his employer's money to Ireland and the Low Countries'. A more affable point of view was that of John Williams, a Welshman and Archbishop of York, who in 1645 compared the Welsh drovers to the ships of the Spanish treasure fleets, in that they brought to Wales 'what little gold we possess'. The drovers acted as agents for Welsh people, paying bills in England out of the sums they received for the sale of livestock and being repaid when they returned home. Eventually these repayments took the form of deposits in Welsh banks, called into existence by the droving business and lack of confidence in the Bank of England (which in 1797, during the French Wars, suspended the redemption of its notes in cash). In Tregaron there was a Bank of the Black Sheep, and in Llandovery a Bank of the Black Ox. The latter was founded in 1799 by another David Jones, a farmer's son, who had worked in The King's Head Inn where cattle dealers often asked him to take care of their money. The bank went on issuing cheques bearing the black ox until early this century, when it became part of a larger British bank.

At that point, too, cattle droving was just about finished – though sheep droving continued into more recent times. The growth of railways – and then road motor transport – made for speedy shipment of livestock over great distances. It was the end of an occupation and it diminished the need for many ancillary services and many inns. It was in such an establishment on Anglesey that George Borrow met a drover named Bos. Borrow suggested that 'droving was rather a low-life occupation'. Mr Bos, taking Borrow for a pig dealer, said proudly that it was 'not half as low-lifed as pig-jobbing'. And he went on to claim that 'there is not a public house between here and Worcester at which I am not known'. Inns flourished along the droveways, providing beds for the leading drovers and homebrew beer and cider for both the leaders and their helpers – who generally had to guard the animals overnight and sleep alongside them. The herds and flocks were usually lodged in the village's Halfpenny Field, a ha'penny per beast per night being the common charge. Many villages also provided a shoeing forge where cattle were shod for the long journey ahead. (Other animals apart from cattle and sheep were taken along the droveways: pigs were provided with leather-soled socks and geese had their feet dipped in a mixture of tar and sand.)

In Caio, a pretty village allegedly named after a Roman General Caius who once commanded in the area, I stopped in at The Brunant Arms, opposite the church. I appeared to be the first customer of the day. The proprietor, an affable, bearded man in his mid-forties named Stuart Landen, recommended the Marstons Pedigree bitter, and – after going into the cellar to take a cork out of the barrel – drew me a pint of it. He said that Caio in droving days had had five inns; The Brunant Arms was the sole survivor. The Marstons

was the best beer I'd so far imbibed in Wales and I compli-
mented Mr Landen.

'It's an English beer,' he said, 'from Burton-on-Trent. But
there aren't many real Welsh beers, and I haven't yet found
one I feel strongly about.' In the age of conglomerates not
many independent breweries remain in Wales; among those
that do are Brains of Cardiff, Buckleys of Llanelli, and
Felinfoel, also of Llanelli. Welsh Brewers, so-called, with a
base in the former Hancocks Brewery in Cardiff, is now a
division of the British brewers Bass. In many parts of Wales
it is hard to avoid English beer – whether Ansells of
Birmingham or Banks of Wolverhampton, neither (to my
taste) brews of serious character. In the last year or two a
small brewery in Penarth has begun to fight this English
domination with a beer called Bullmastiff, which Mr Landen
said he had heard good reports of but not yet sampled.

Once again, I'd encountered a transplanted Londoner.
After making me a ham sandwich, Mr Landen told me that
until a year before this he had been a commercial photographer in Islington; his wife was a solicitor. They had bought
a house in Caio as a holiday home. He said, 'Then the pub
came on the market. We took the plunge and threw up
London altogether.'

Caio has a population of thirty-five, barely enough to
support one pub, but many people drive in from the surrounding country. Caio also has a friendly general store and
a primary school, with three teachers and roughly thirty
children. A bus to and from Lampeter, eight miles away,
runs once a week. 'You need a car,' said Mr Landen, 'but
there are no traffic jams out here, even at the height of
summer. If you say you're going to be somewhere at a
certain time, you can be sure you will be – which is no
longer the case in many parts of south-east England.' His
wife drives several days a week to Llandovery, where she
does part-time legal work. In August the Landens help run a
drovers' fair – that in 1989 was the first to be held in Caio in

seventy years – with craft stalls, stands with flowers, fruit, and vegetables, and a sheep and cattle sale. During the winter they attend a Welsh language class in Pumsaint, the next village to the west, with a dozen or so other adults. 'It's not as difficult as I feared it might be,' said Mr Landen, serving a motorist who had just arrived. 'I wouldn't claim I'm anywhere near fluent, but some of the locals are now coming in and ordering their drinks in Welsh – and I can understand them.'

As I set off again, I felt a touch reluctant: Caio would be a good place to come back to. I took a lane that wound over a hill toward Pumsaint. One car passed, then stopped – it was the other customer from The Brunant Arms. He asked, 'Would you like a lift?' Then, before I had time to speak, he said, 'I didn't think so.' My words of reply were framed in my mind, but I'd been waiting for more than a week to use them and was slow off the mark. How I was walking through Wales and – except for side trips – wanted to walk all the way, but thank you anyway. I got out the 'But thanks,' and he was off again, the sound of his car soon blotted out by the more staccato noise of a four-wheel Honda all-terrain vehicle on which a farm worker was rounding up sheep in a nearby field. He had the help of a dog to which he now and then whistled over the racket of his machine.

A mile of noise-free walking brought me to a sylvan hillside overlooking the Cothi river. A roadside stile gave access to a path which meandered around the birch- and oak-wooded slopes, belonging to the National Trust, that have been mined for gold since at least Roman times. Here and there small signs indicated the mouths of pits, shafts, and adits providing ways into underground workings. Little quarries remained from open-cast mining. I'd been prospecting the area for half an hour before I came on a visitor centre and realised that I'd come into the mines by a back way. However, I paid the entrance fee and bought a scholarly booklet, from whose ore I extracted a good deal about the gold of Dolaucothi.

The mines here are mentioned in the 1695 edition of the antiquarian gazetteer *Britannia*, revised by Edmund Gibson from William Camden's original (1586) account of his tours in search of Roman remains. In the early nineteenth century antiquarians who visited the site were told of local tradition that the Romans had worked the mines, and finds of Roman jewellery in the area supported this. But what metal or mineral the Romans had been extracting was not rediscovered until 1844, when a Geological Survey team found a speck of gold in a piece of quartz. This encouraged a renewal of mining at Dolaucothi, which went on intermittently until 1938, and brought very little profit to the companies involved. The basic problem with the gold here was that it was too finely disseminated among troublesome waste. Separation was difficult and the Romans may have made it pay only because they had cheap slave or convict labour. The host rock is shale, about 438 million years old; but the gold ore is not in a dominant vein. The Romans generally obtained the ore from open pits which were gradually extended underground in tunnels. They built watercourses or leets, which brought river-water from as much as seven miles away to 'hush' the ore, washing away soil and rock and leaving the gold exposed on gorse branches. Water was also used to crack fire-heated rock. It may have been used to power mills for crushing ore, though this was often accomplished by hand. The Roman workers are thought to have removed half a million tonnes of rock and ore from the pits here and to have extracted from this about 800 kilogrammes or 1760 pounds of gold. This doesn't seem a lot – it would have formed a cube with sides of about forty-five centimetres or eighteen inches; but at today's gold prices it would have been worth more than eleven million dollars.

The mines are now an asset for University of Wales students of mineral exploitation and archeology. There are many visitors in summer (according to a lady in the National Trust visitor centre), although the underground workings aren't open to them. What you can see of the shafts and pits is a bit clean and tidy, and doesn't help you to imagine the hard work that went on in them. The Romans presumably were glad that Phoenician accounts of Britain's mineral wealth had proved true, and somewhat justified their invasion of the island. However, the iron, lead, silver, and copper found elsewhere in England and Wales may have pleased them more than the difficult gold of Dolaucothi.

It was a short walk to the main road – the A482 to Lampeter, once part of Sarn Helen – and across the river Cothi into Pumsaint. Pum or plyn (as in Plynlimon) means five in Welsh, and the five saints connected with the place are Ceitho, Celynnen, Gwyn, Gwynog, and Gwynaro. Some accounts say they were born here. They are associated with five pools in the river, which attracted pilgrims seeking cures for various aches and ailments. The saints are said to be sleeping in a cave not far away, ready to awaken on the arrival of 'a virtuous bishop'. (Perhaps there are more of those about now than there were then?) The saints are also thought to have miraculously left their marks or footprints on a stone, the Carreg Pumsaint, to be seen near the mines – though modern experts think more prosaically that the stone's bumps and hollows came about from its use in ore-crushing.

There were scarcely five of anything to be seen in Pumsaint on this particular afternoon. A few houses; an inn, The Dolaucothi Arms, in whose car park the foundations of a small Roman fort have been uncovered; a car-repair garage which was once a forge where cattle were shod as the droves moved through; and a chapel, where one plaque commemorates a local woman, Joan Evans, who went along with a drove into England in order to go to the Crimea, where she served as an army nurse with Florence Nightingale. I strode on for another mile until I reached a small hexagonal house

built right at the roadside – a good landmark for the
driveway opposite leading to Llstroiddyn Home Farm, if
you missed the sign advertising bed and breakfast. The little
house was a former turnpike tollbooth. In previous times I
would have had to pay a toll to the proprietors of the road.
In the eighteenth century Parliament set up trusts to improve
and maintain roads in return for tolls, but many 'tollgate
farmers' simply erected tollgates, with ditches and chains to
prevent travellers evading them, and did little about the
roads. In Wales in the 1840s resentment against English
landowners was already high among the tenantry, and the
ever-increasing turnpike tolls were a prime cause of an
outbreak of violence known as the Rebecca Riots. In the
course of these disturbances, bands of angry men, disguised
as women, pulled down many Welsh tollgates. (They were
otherwise God-fearing men who knew their Bible, particularly Genesis xxiv. 60: 'And they blessed Rebecca and said
unto her, let thy seed possess the gates of them that hate
thee.') Although two Rebecca leaders were arrested and
transported, a commission of inquiry resulted in the abolition
of the road trusts and in county boards being set up to ensure
better roads and fair tolls.

At Llstroiddyn Home Farm the lady of the house, Mrs
Sian O'Shea, was Welsh and Welsh-speaking, despite her
Irish name. Her husband, of Irish descent, came from
London and worked in Llandovery as an insurance broker.
Most of their land was rented out to neighbouring farmers;
the O'Sheas kept only chickens and peacocks. They had four
children, the youngest at Caio primary school. 'We lived in
London for a while,' said Mrs O'Shea, stoking the big solid-
fuel stove in the kitchen. 'I was loth to come back here, but
for the children's education it has turned out to be the best
thing.' I had a bedroom with a view over a field of sheep.

It was drizzling by evening. Mrs O'Shea drove me down
to The Dolaucothi Arms, where I planned to eat dinner. It
was not the liveliest of nights at the Pumsaint inn. I was the

only customer. The landlord explained that his wife was away but he could rustle up some gammon, chips, and peas. While I was eating, he told me that the local Roman commandant's quarters had been directly under this bar where I was sitting. The inn had also sheltered two of the most notable walkers in Wales. George Borrow stopped here on his way south and found it 'a good specimen of an ancient Welsh hostelry', with people who were kind and attentive. He praised his bed, in which he dreamed indistinctly of what had happened to him during the day, and he woke once to hear the murmuring of the river Cothi – 'the stream of the immortal Cothi'. This was a reference to Lewis Glyn Cothi, a fifteenth-century poet whom Borrow regarded as one of Wales's greatest and who wrote among other things a most moving poem after the death of his son Sion y Glyn.

The poet (and walker) I connected with The Dolaucothi Arms was Edward Thomas, who stopped at the inn in 1913. Thomas sat here and penned a dedication for a book he had just finished, *The Icknield Way* – dedicating it to a walking companion, Harry Hooton. He wrote that although he had 'become a writing animal, and could write something or other about a broomstick, I do not write with ease: so let that difficulty give the dedication its value'. Thomas's father was Welsh, and though he himself claimed always to feel 'in the profoundest sense, at home' in Wales, much of his own writing about Wales – particularly a book called *Beautiful Wales*, published in 1905 – seems to lack buoyancy. Certainly one wouldn't take it to be the work of the man who, encouraged by Robert Frost, produced some of the finest English poetry between 1914 and his death on the Western Front at Arras in 1917.

On the day he stayed here in 1913, Thomas had been walking on the old Roman road and had been reflecting on the origin of its name Sarn Helen – which is generally taken to mean Helen's Highway. One of the tales of *The Mabinogion*, 'The Dream of Macsen Wledig', came to his mind.

Macsen Wledig was what the Welsh called the Roman General Magnus Maximus, by birth a Spaniard, who was raised to the purple by the legions in Britain in 383, established himself at Treves, and was defeated and killed at Aquileia in 388; in Welsh mythology he was not a usurper but 'the Emperor of Rome'. In Thomas's paraphrase of *The Mabinogion* story, as recounted in *The Icknield Way*, Macsen 'dreamed that he was journeying along a river valley toward its source, and up over the highest mountain in the world until he saw mighty rivers descending to the sea, and one of them he followed to a great city at its mouth and a vast castle in the city. At the end of the journey the dreaming Emperor found a girl so beautiful that when he awoke he could think of naught else, while years went by, except her beauty.' The Emperor sent out messengers to discover the road of his dream. 'At last they brought him to the castle and the same girl Helen sitting in the hall of it. She became his bride, and he gave her three castles – one at Arvon in North Wales, one at Caerleon, and one at Carmarthen in the south. Then, says the tale, "Helen bethought her to make high roads from one castle to another throughout the Island of Britain. And the roads were made. And for this cause are they called the roads of Helen Luyddawc"' – that is, Helen of the Hosts.

Another Anglo-Welsh poet to brood about Helen (or Elen, as she is also called) was David Jones, who fought like Thomas in the First World War but survived to write his masterwork, *In Parenthesis*, about it. In an essay, 'The Myth of Arthur', Jones quoted *The Mabinogion* lines describing Helen's charms: 'Not more easy to gaze upon the sun when brightest, was it to look upon her by reason of her beauty . . . A frontlet of red gold was upon her head, and rubies and gems were in the frontlet, alternating with pearls and imperial stones . . . She was the fairest sight that ever man saw.' Jones felt, however, that there might have been more to this Helen than simply the wife of Magnus Maximus. 'I think we have to posit some kind of archetypal "Elen" from remote Celtic antiquity to wholly account for the numinous power and splendour attaching to Elen Luyddog after whom the *viae* were called the Roads of Helen of the Hosts.' Other authorities suggest that the name may have gained further resonance by 'conflation' with that of St Helena, mother of Constantine the Great. A thoroughly downbeat explanation for Sarn Helen is that it is a corruption of *sarn-y-lleng*, the legion's road.

I walked back to the O'Sheas' farmhouse along the verge of the dark highway, the drizzle now only a thick wet mist. Was I walking the road of *my* dream? Mrs O'Shea and her youngest daughter Teleri were watching *Dallas* (in English) and now and then chatting (in Welsh) about the plot of *Dallas* and Teleri's homework which she had to finish before she went to bed. I slept without memorable dreams though waking once I heard the peacocks.

It wasn't quite raining when I set out next day, along the main Lampeter road for half a mile, across the Fanafas river, and then turning on to the straight minor road that now carried Sarn Helen due north. Dodging the morning puddles I strode along at a pace no centurion ought to have complained about. The only knowledge I could recall of the legions' marching practice was that when they camped, the men slept in big hide tents; each held eight men and was called a *papilio*, presumably because it folded up like the wings of a butterfly. The first settlement I came to was Ffarmers – a village with an English name which has been simply and quaintly Welshed. (The name apparently derived from The Farmers' Inn, which is now the post office and shop.) At the crossroads in the centre of the place The Drovers' Inn still stands. Here droves paused or formed, and eloquent, well-lubricated transactions no doubt took place between farmers and drovers.

The road climbed, gradually narrowing. I passed a pony-trekking centre, with several old caravans being slowly subsumed into the undergrowth – its name, Cae Iago, made me wonder why Shakespeare favoured one of his chief villains with a Welsh name. I crossed the river Twrch. This was at a ford where the road surface lay six inches under the clear flowing water but a rickety mossy wooden footbridge had been provided for pedestrians – for me! A long, slow climb began; there were snowdrops and bluebells under the roadside hedges; I heard myself grunting like a tennis player. Then I was up on the hilltop and the road was neither hedged nor fenced. To one side lay a once-standing stone in a little earthwork and on the other a cairn constructed with small stones; behind was a splendid view south down the Twrch valley, which the erectors of the stone and cairn had long ago enjoyed. Here and there the rock in the ground broke through the turf, slate-coloured but rougher and chunkier than slate. For a mile or so after this the road resumed its Roman straightforwardness, through the edge of a vast and dense Forestry Commission conifer plantation. These modern plantations are usually straight-edged, with long, flat flanks that seem to have little to do with the contours, the lie of the land. They cover a great deal of Wales. However helpful they are to Britain's balance of payments – providing home-grown pit-props, fence posts, and pulp for newsprint – they make a deadening, baleful sight. It also hurts to think that the Forestry Commission's obsession has been supported in recent years by tax breaks given to wealthy folk who have invested in private forests of these depressing trees. But prejudice against them is not new. In 1822, long before the pines, firs, spruce, and larches became as ubiquitous as they are now, William Cobbett wrote happily after his ride to High Wycombe in Buckinghamshire: 'No villainous things of the *fir-tribe* offend the eye here.'

I turned off Sarn Helen (here coincident with a drovers' way) at a point where it descended into the Teifi valley and the village of Llanfair Clydogau. The lane I followed rambled around in a way that made it seem much older than Roman. I crossed a stream by a roadbridge and didn't have to use the separate footbridge which was four feet higher, presumably for use in time of torrents. Then I was again on the heights, this time an extensive plateau, with assorted white, black, and cinnamon-brown sheep for company. It had begun to rain and the sheep were clustering in the lee of a stone wall. If I'd had similar foresight I would have taken shelter, too,

for in a few minutes the rain turned abruptly to hail. I stood
– stockstill – in the middle of the lane and since there was no
other cover turned my back to the weather. Heavy hailstones
– the size of lumps of crystallised sugar – bounced off my
raincoat and off the surface of the lane. The storm lasted for
ten minutes; then the hail turned back to rain and I walked
on, the wet running down my face, a few miles more into
Llanddewi Brefi.

In this little place, named for St David, my first port of
call should perhaps have been at the church of the good saint,
but, close to the church gate, The Foelallt Arms hove into
view. It was ten to one, time for beer, lunch, and drying
out. Half an hour later, I picked a moment when the rain
had eased to dart in through the church gate and hasten up
on to the little hill on which the church stands. To one side
of the mound the river Brefi rustles down towards the Teifi.
On the mound's summit is a crowded old graveyard.
Borrow called here, but, here as elsewhere, is not an exact
authority for ecclesiastical history, and I have turned to other
sources for what follows. David or Dewi was an early-sixth-
century bishop and theologian who had founded a dozen
monasteries; at his principal monastery in what is now called
St David's in Pembrokeshire he led a very strict community
and was known as 'the Waterman', presumably because he
was a teetotaller. David came to Brefi for a synod or council
around 519 with the object of denouncing the Pelagian
heresy. This – in the words of the chronicler Gerald, who
stopped here in 1188 – 'long before had been put to an end
in Britain by Saint Germanus, Bishop of Auxerre, but . . .
had then started up again in those parts like some recurrent
plague'. The traditional story of the synod, followed by
Gerald, was that Bishop David, a small man, had difficulty
in making himself heard by the large throng gathered on the
flat ground. So he placed his handkerchief on the earth and –
mirabile dictu! – the ground rose, lifting David with it. He
could be heard easily at the edges of the crowd. 'His voice

was as a trumpet,' runs the legend, 'and the Holy Spirit in the form of a dove came and stood on his shoulder.' He was recognised as primate of Wales. In 1120, he was canonised. The church – one of more than fifty in Wales that are dedicated to him – of course stands on the mound which rose that day.

A word about Pelagius, the object of St David's attack. He was a Briton, a native of North Wales, to whom Borrow gives the name of Morgan. He repaired to Italy and concluded that there was no such thing as original sin – that man could lead a good life (in Borrow's words) 'by obeying the dictates of his own reason without any assistance from the grace of God'. This doctrine was evidently ahead of its time. Even Borrow felt that it was 'certainly to the last degree delusive and dangerous'. But it had found much support among those discontented with the current civil and ecclesiastical administration. David seems to have done an effective job of condemning the Pelagian position and of rallying the Welsh faithful. A leaflet I bought in the church suggests that the synod was held here because of the proximity of Sarn Helen and because people in this part of Wales had close connections with Irish supporters of Pelagius and needed an extra-strong talking-to.

St David's church is a simple stone structure of nave and chancel, much rebuilt in the nineteenth century, and with a stocky late-twelfth-century central tower. Within, a 1960's statue of the saint presents him with staff in one hand, bell in the other, and a dove on his right shoulder. The importance of burials in furnishing evidence of the past is made clear in several items. A fragment of an early-seventh-century inscribed memorial provides the first written reference to Saint David. A mutilated stone, inscribed in the Irish writing known as Ogham, is thought to have been the tombstone of a Pelagian Christian. Built into an outside wall of the church is a fragment of a Roman soldier's burial stone, showing the letters MIBV . . . TAST. Present burials mostly take place in a new cemetery off the Tregaron road, on the edge of the village, and a sign on the parish noticeboard near The Foelallt Arms gives the applicable charges. This is the 'Table of Burial Fees and Payments as from 1st January 1988':

a) the exclusive rights of burial in a grave 9′ by 4′ £25
b) for interment in a single grave £60
c) for interment in a double grave £90
d) for interment in a grave for three £100
e) for each subsequent interment:
      first opening £90
      second opening £60
f) for interment of a child up to 12 years of age – to be discussed by the Council at the time of burial.
g) for interment of cremated remains £18
(note: b) to g) the cost of materials to be in addition to those charges.)
h) for the right to erect a memorial (including wooden cross) £18

The rules of the cemetery, also posted, specified a three foot depth from ground level to the top of coffins; gravestones and crosses to be no more than three and a half feet high; no artificial wreaths or flowers; graves to be finished level with the ground; and approved vases to be placed in line with headstones.

As I walked out of Llanddewi Brefi past the meticulous cemetery that resulted from these regulations, with too many shiny dark marble gravestones for my taste, I had a vision of the ground rising less uniformly than it had done for St David, the last trump blowing, doves descending, and – Stanley Spencer's painting of the Resurrection in Cookham Churchyard perhaps playing a part in my vision – the dead generations of Llanddewi Brefi resurrecting, absolutely free of charge, and in a way that created havoc with the trim neatness of their resting spot.

★ ★ ★

In the early afternoon the sun appeared. I walked up the lovely Teifi valley toward Tregaron, water-meadows on my left, hills rising on my right, and my head passing through an occasional cloud of gnats, which I took for a portent of better weather. This was a B-road and the traffic amounted to about ten vehicles an hour. I reached Tregaron just before three and made at once for The Talbot Hotel, the most prominent building on the lopsided market square which forms the centre of the little town. Five roads from various points of the compass come into Tregaron in a disjointed fashion, as if they hadn't quite meant to arrive there at all. A tributary of the Teifi called the Berwyn streams right through the middle of the town. Houses are set alongside one another but with an irregular frontage, some on the street, some back from it. I'd been told in Llandovery that the Talbot bar was where the local hill-farmers went after (and during) the market to talk of prices and swap tales. I'd heard the tale of one farmer, who went to an agricultural show in London and told an English questioner that he came from near Tregaron. Asked next, 'Where's Tregaron?' the farmer answered, 'Outside The Talbot Hotel'. As I walked across the empty market square a solitary hen was parading in front of the hotel.

Borrow was told by a man he fell in with on the road north of here that at The Talbot 'they are always glad to see English gentlemans'. (Borrow was fortunate that in his day there were far more people walking the Welsh roads, but he tended to burden his accounts of them with this sort of Darkie speech.) He was pleased with his entertainment at The Talbot, 'had an excellent supper and a very comfortable bed'. I had less initial joy. 'Sorry, we're full,' said the young woman at the reception desk. And when I pressed for an explanation – suspicious that it might be my backpack and somewhat unkempt appearance after sixteen miles and a hailstorm that was creating a difficulty – she said, apologetically, 'It's Harlech Television. They're filming a meeting at the school tonight about Welsh-language teaching. They've got a big crew, all staying here. It takes a lot of them to make a TV film.'

Miffed, the lone representative of an older reportorial craft, I hied over the bridge spanning the Berwyn to The Sunnyhill Hotel, a pub with accommodation above. The lady behind the bar, whose name was Pauline, said she couldn't tell me right away if there was a room available. She was minding the place for the husband-and-wife owners. He was at his regular job at a nearby quarry; she had gone shopping in Lampeter; they'd be back about five. Meanwhile, why didn't I take off my pack? After doing so, I sat at the bar with a beer. On the wall was pinned a letter from Welsh Brewers advising their customers – i.e. pub landlords – of a threat to blow up British pubs that had been received from Islamic fundamentalists. Suspicious characters and packages should be looked out for. The three men already at the bar were all known to Pauline. The one sitting nearest me, Michael, was in his mid-fifties. He told me that he hailed from England, where he had been a teacher in Essex; he had also taught in Saudi Arabia but had been caught making moonshine in that dry land and spent six months in jail. Islam! He and his invalid wife had moved to Tregaron because his sister lived here; the sister was now moving to France, but he and his wife would be staying on.

The two men beyond Michael, a jobbing builder and his younger mate, were in the midst of a serious afternoon drinking session. Between three and six o'clock, they each put away about ten pints of beer. In pubs, drink often prompts confessional talk, but the kind of outspokenness in front of a stranger I encountered here seemed to me possibly the reverse face of the secretiveness you also come across in Wales. The younger man, his wife, and three children had apparently been thrown out of their council house for non-payment of rent and were all living with the builder, the younger man's boss. The builder, who did most of the talking, was a show-off. He went on about cars he had driven – Austin-Healeys, Alfas, Maseratis, XJs, TSRs, GTIs – in what I self-consciously began to think might be an unconscious reaction to me, a carless walker. Then he boasted about women. He was particularly proud of a current conquest whom he called 'my toy-girl'. She was – he led us to believe – 'under age'. He immodestly described several recent rendezvous he had had with her.

'What will this man think of us?' said his less braggartly mate, looking over at me.

'I think it's a shame if you ask me,' said Pauline. 'You men are dreadful.' She refilled a glass with a thoughtful look on her face. Then she said, 'In fact I wouldn't mind a toy-boy of my own.'

I judged it the right moment to take a walk around Tregaron. I looked at the church, which like that at Llanddewi Brefi is next to a river and stands on a hillock – this, however, has no tradition of being miraculously raised to improve a saint's speaking range. The church's most notable relic is an inscribed stone, set in an outside wall, that came from the Roman fort of Bremia a few miles away. The church bells are reputed to be those of the abbey of Strata Florida, five miles north-east of Tregaron, removed during Henry VIII's Dissolution of the Monasteries. The best-known speaker Tregaron has brought forth is honoured by a statue in the square outside The Talbot. Henry Richard (1812–88), a strenuous defender of the Rebecca rioters in the English press, became Radical MP for Merthyr Tydfil. Although the statue presents him as a bearded, argumentative-looking figure, he was a proponent of pacifism and international disarmament. Tregaron lacks a statue of its best-known rogue, Twm Sion Catti, or Tom Jones, son of Catti. Born in the late sixteenth century, Twm was said to be the illegitimate son of Sir John Wynn, an energetic and scholarly landowner from North Wales, and one Catherine or Catti Jones of Tregaron. After a humble start as a farm worker and drover, Twm turned to theft and mischief. Borrow described many of his disguises, tricks, and sometimes altruistic robberies, borrowing a great deal from an early-nineteenth-century book about Twm. The author of this work – as Borrow noticed – had in turn either invented many of Twm's exploits or had borrowed them from tales of other Robin Hood-type robbers. What is reasonably sure about Twm's buoyant career is that he eventually married an heiress from Brecon and became the mayor of that town and a justice of the peace there. The latter post brought little satisfaction to the area's miscreants, for Twm's own experience in the thieving trade had given him great insight into their devious ways.

The Sunnyhill's landlord, John, was there when I returned to the pub. He had a room for me. John had been a printer on a Yorkshire newspaper, the *Bradford Argus*; his wife came from Bradford, too. He now worked as an explosives expert at a stone and aggregates quarry. Both his past and present professions were noisy, I suggested. 'Yes, but Tregaron is quiet,' he said. 'Very little crime. Sometimes after a rugby game a few of the lads may walk over the roofs of the parked cars – but there's not much of that.' The other Sunnyhill guests were three young men, steel erectors staying in Tregaron while they set up the framework of a new warehouse, who arrived with their belongings in Adidas sports bags.

I took advantage of the fact that the Harlech TV team would be at the school meeting and dined at The Talbot. The dining-room was welcoming, the food was good, and one of the waitresses – Welsh-speaking, with a punk hair-cut – put on a tape of stirring Welsh folk songs, to which she hummed as she served my salmon. I asked the name of the singer. 'Dafydd Iwan,' she said. 'He's a Welsh nationalist.' From the way she spoke, proudly, I gathered so was she. For a moment, in a muted, less theatrical manner, it was like the occasion in *Casablanca* when the Free French *habitués* of

Rick's café sing the Marseillaise in the face of the German officers. I felt like the representative of an occupying power.

I thought about Borrow again before going to sleep. I was unsure whether I would cross his route and, as it were, run into him again. Six foot three, a powerful swimmer as well as a walker, he was fifty-three years old when he came through Wales in 1854, sometimes covering thirty miles a day and the last five miles of it in an hour. He carried an umbrella, a purse at the start of his trip holding twenty sovereigns, and a leather satchel containing a change of linen, a pair of worsted stockings, a razor, and the *Book of Common Prayer*. He was a great linguist by all accounts – especially his own – and he matched the loquacious Welshmen who talked to him in their own language word for word. His book *Wild Wales* was published in three volumes in 1862 and was a flop; it was forty years before Borrow on Wales was widely read.

April, coming toward its end, did so with a flourish. There was bright dew on the morning grass and a warm sun – the best of days. My start was slightly held up by a wait for the Tregaron branch of the National Westminster Bank to open, so that I could cash a cheque for fifty pounds. I took the road north, then north-east, as it was forced to bend around the edge of Cors Caron, the great Tregaron bog. This lies in a broad valley through which the Teifi wanders. On my right hand the hills, rising into the central uplands of Wales, were higher than those across the valley. A pair of red-and-white training jets streaked loudly south a few hundred feet up and three minutes later screamed back again, as if they'd run out of land to annoy. It occurred to me that the only way not to be deafened by these planes in Wales is to fly one. The sedgy bog was the colour of a sandy beach, though this was a seasonal hue; it would be red in winter. I overtook an elderly man, short, plump, wearing a cloth cap and carrying binoculars, who was walking along with a King Charles spaniel. We exchanged good mornings. He introduced his dog, Chassie. He and Chassie walked here nearly every day, he said. He was from Birmingham but had retired to a bungalow in Tregaron to be close to a married daughter.

The binoculars were prominent because he was a keen birdwatcher. The bog was full of interest. He pointed out to me the old railway right of way, which furnished a route along the edge of the bog and – for a short distance – into it.

He said, 'It used to be the Manchester to Milford Haven line – opened in 1866. The ground was so soft they built the line on bales of wool topped with wooden faggots. There was a halt right here where trains stopped to load farm produce. They closed the line in 1965 and took the tracks away a year later.'

Much of the bog is now a nature reserve. In five minutes, with the loan of the observant old gentleman's binoculars and with the aid of his knowledge, I'd seen grey herons, a woodpecker, a rare hen harrier, a crow attacking a buzzard, a merlin (which is a small falcon), and sundry warblers, robins, magpies, and wrens. I was just about to say farewell and walk on when he thrust the binoculars at me again and pointed – 'Up there!' A large cinnamon-coloured bird with a long forked tail and ragged ends to its wings was drifting over the bog, gliding in wide circles around and around, all the time looking down, waiting to swoop on mice, voles, moles, or any visible carrion.

'You're in luck,' said my informant. 'That's an uncommon one, a red kite.' He told me that the red kite, a bird with a four- to six-foot wingspan, was near extinction. There were only some fifty pairs left in Britain; they breed only in mid-Wales; and despite efforts to preserve them and keep their nesting sites secret several have recently been found dead, apparently killed by poisoned bait put out by farmers to get rid of foxes and crows. Farmers care more for the safety of their newborn lambs than they do for red kites.

I followed the old railway track for a mile into the bog, which is the largest peat bog in Wales. Cors Caron interests natural history students because it is a 'raised bog', where a shallow lake resulting from the last Ice Age has been slowly filled in until peat and plants have risen above the surrounding fens. In time past it has provided peat as fuel, rushes for animal bedding, and grazing for livestock. Wildfowl have enjoyed its pools. Various insects, frogs, lizards, toads, adders, polecats, stoats, weasels, shrews, woodmice, water-voles, and mink have made a home here. The elusive otter, a mostly nocturnal beast of the weasel family, is known to haunt the Teifi where it runs through the bog, since its footprints and droppings, which are called 'spraints', are occasionally seen in the mud. Once hunted, it is now protected by law. The best time to see an otter is the hour after sunset, when it sets out from its holt in a riverbank or tree roots to catch eels or coarse fish. Because of this, and because the railway track did not allow more than a glimpse of Afon Fflur, which runs into the Teifi, I didn't expect to see an otter, and did not.

I retraced my steps back to the road. It was warm enough today for sweaterless walking. In a field next to the road a ewe sat over a newly born lamb, a small white heap, licking it, making a soft purring baa. I looked up for the kite but it was no longer to be seen. Just before noon I came to the village of Pontrhydfendigaid – not the longest place-name in Wales but the longest I'd had to hold in my head as I tried to pronounce it (it means the Bridge over the Blessed Ford). I turned off the road and followed a lane eastward, parallel with the Teifi, to the remains of Strata Florida Abbey: stone foundations, low grey stone walls, and a large Celtic-Romanesque doorway which had once formed the west entrance to the Abbey church. The outlines of cloister and chapter-house are to be seen on the ground and what was once the Abbey's outer court is now a formal garden.

The monastery acquired its name, so it seems, because at its founding in 1164 it was sited two miles away on the Afon Fflur, next to the present Tregaron road. Ystrad Fflur, the valley of the Fflur, was Latinised as Strata Florida or flowery road, and the name followed the monks when they moved to this even more sheltered spot in the vale of the upper Teifi. In April 1188, four years after the move, Gerald and Archbishop Baldwin called here, though the chronicler had curiously little to say about their stay at the Abbey. (Gerald was also somewhat confused when he came to write up his

Journey, recording his visit here before that at Llanddewi
Brefi, though he clearly went to St David's church before-
hand, on the way to Strata Florida.) The Abbot of Strata
Florida, who had joined the Archbishop and Gerald in
Lampeter, rode on with them into North Wales.

I walked around the ruins and gardens, which radiate
repose. There was a prospect eastward up the Teifi valley
into the gaunt hills. Daisies flourished in the thick lawns and
finely decorated tiles covered what had once been chapel
floors. My feeling for the Normans has never been amiable
– they often arrived sword in hand – but there's no doubt
they partly made up for their belligerence by encouraging
monastic orders from the Continent to settle in Britain. The
Cistercians who founded Strata Florida and several sister
abbeys in Wales were vowed to a strict rule that honoured
poverty, simplicity, and toil. They were a papal order, not
controlled from Canterbury. They were not considered a
threat by the natives. Although Rhys ap Gryffydd, the Lord
of Deheubarth, had attacked the Norman intruders and taken
prisoner Robert Fitzstephen, who had provided land for the
monks, Rhys soon became the abbey's patron. He supported
its rebuilding on the new site and granted it grazing rights
over huge areas of the country. The abbey was built with
stone from Somerset, brought by sea to Aberarth on the
coast twelve miles away. Construction took half a century.
By the time the Chapter House was completed in 1235, the
abbey had begun to generate trade and culture, its monks
had evidently become Welsh loyalists, and the local princes
were strongly attached to Strata Florida. One of Rhys's
grandsons was buried here in 1222, as a number of other
minor princes were to be. In 1238, during Edward I's reign,
all the Welsh princes assembled at the abbey when summoned by Llywelyn the Great – then in failing health – to
swear allegiance to his son and successor, Dafydd, as sover-
eign Prince of Wales.

In the mid-thirteenth century this was one of the most

influential and productive places in Wales. The monks – white-robed like their great flocks of sheep – were intelligent farmers. They exported much wool. They caught trout and eels in the Teifi, herring and mackerel off the coast. They mined lead and iron, owned ships, built roads and bridges, and ran fairs and markets. They accommodated travellers and pilgrims, some of whom came to Strata Florida to drink from an ancient wooden cup which was venerated as either a piece of the Cross or the chalice used at the Last Supper. Some visitors believed their ills could be cured by drinking from it. The monks also worked as scribes and artists on illuminated manuscripts. The important Welsh medieval document, The Chronicle of the Princes – *Brut y Tywysogion* – is thought to have been written here, the culmination of a series of annals that were worked on in other Welsh religious houses.

The writer who is particularly associated with Strata Florida is the not very monk-like poet Dafydd ap Gwilym (fl. 1340–70). The ancient yew in the abbey graveyard is said to have been planted over his grave. Dafydd was born not far from Aberystwyth and was celebrated for his love poems and the sometimes sad, sometimes comic amatory adventures that gave rise to them. A recent editor of his verse, Tony Conran, quotes one of Dafydd's contemporaries who remarked on the glibness with which Dafydd threatened to die for any girl he sang to: 'It was a wonder the poor man hadn't died already, twenty times over.' However, Dafydd often made fun of himself, as in his poem 'Trouble at a Tavern', where his efforts to organise a midnight assignation with a girl – 'that bright-as-dawn sweetheart' – lead to trouble, furniture noisily knocked over, everyone in the tavern woken, and Dafydd cowering in the dark, praying:

> And such power has prayer for us,
> Such the true grace of Jesus,
> I found my own bed safe and sure

Though without sleep or treasure,
Thank the Saints, freed of distress.
I ask now God's forgiveness.

No wonder the good (and good-humoured) Cistercians
allowed the Welsh troubadour to find his last bed in the
abbey graveyard.

Strata Florida was not always a fortunate place. The abbey
was struck by lightning and burnt in 1286 and was damaged
in the Welsh rebellion of 1295. During Owain Glyndŵr's
insurgency, in 1401, the much harried army of King Henry
IV took out its frustrations here, murdering the monks and
looting. The horses of the knights were tethered to the high
altar; the abbey wine-cellars were drunk dry. Although the
abbey was rebuilt after this, it did not in its final years hold
its old place in the economy of mid-Wales; its moral power
had also evaporated. Documents have been found that reveal
an attempt to make counterfeit coinage at the abbey in 1534.
A monk, Richard Smith, met a weaver, Evan ap Howell, at
a local inn. After a few drinks they returned to the monk's
chamber at the abbey and there, over a fire, melted down a
tin spoon and poured it into a mould to make groats. Both
parties were caught red-handed. The abbot clapped them in
irons. In court hearings at Shrewsbury, the monk Smith said
that he hadn't known what the weaver had intended to do; it
was he, the monk, who had called the abbot. The weaver
disputed this. He said the monk had known exactly what
was proposed – they had planned it two weeks before.

But being a monk still seemed to help. Richard Smith was
believed, Evan ap Howell was not. Smith was later recorded,
after the Dissolution, as receiving a pension of £3 a year.
Nothing more was heard of Evan. The account of the case
that can be read in the little abbey museum says that the
weaver was presumably hanged at Shrewsbury, 'the usual
punishment in such cases'. At the Dissolution the abbey was
manned by the abbot and a mere six monks. Their income

from rents had been by then reduced to a paltry £150. They were rumoured to have been putting more towards food and drink than towards charity. As with the other abbeys of the kingdom, the monks were pensioned off, the lands were sold, and the royal treasury raked in the cash. Strata Florida lost the lead and tiles of its roofs and the stones from its walls, which found their way to local farms and houses. As noted, its bells are thought to ring now from Tregaron church.

The Welsh Historic Monuments custodian I talked to in the museum recommended The Black Lion rather than The Red Lion as a hostelry to make for in Pontrhydfendigaid. I sauntered back along the lane and over the Bridge of the Blessed Ford which spans the tumbling Teifi, anticipating lunch and a pint. Lackaday! Both the Lions, Black and Red, were shut – doors locked, not even bothering with a CLOSED sign; possibly they only opened in the evenings. Any passing lunchtime trade was so sparse as to be not worth considering. Blasting both establishments with a fearsome Anglo-Saxon curse on those who fail to give succour to hungry and thirsty walkers, I proceeded through the village, feeling fortunate to find a small store where I bought a pork-pie and a chocolate bar. Nothing else of a ready-to-eat sort looked edible. I sat on the edge of the stark village playing-field and ate these items, washing them down with water from my bottle. So much for Pontrhydfendigaid – surely time to shorten its name to match its benefactions.

Had I but known it, this was an indication of the possibilities of the country to come. I walked on, steering more or less north-west on the B4340 toward the Ystwyth valley and through the hamlets of Ystrad Meurig and Tynygraig. The afternoon remained sunny. I noted a seagull, the first I'd seen in Wales, flapping low over a meadow of grazing sheep. Tomorrow, perhaps, the sea! At a bridge over the little river Meurig I rested on the parapet and watched four ducks float downstream in the direction of the Teifi, looking alert while letting the water get them where they wanted to go. A farmer at Tynygraig had found a new use for car hubcaps fallen at the roadside, as caps to protect the tops of his wooden gate-posts. From there it was steeply downhill to Pen-y-Bont, where the Ystwyth emerges from the uplands to the east and runs through a bosky valley toward the sea.

I was glad to leave the road here and turn off on a track which ran, south of the river, below a thickly wooded escarpment. The track was used for Forestry Commission logging machinery. There were piles of damp sawdust, sundry log-ends, and deep ruts full of water. Here and there muddy puddles spanned the track and I was forced to detour through the entangling brush and brambles alongside. (Definitely not the Cambrian Way but possibly Bailey's Way.) When I stopped for a moment to pass water, I felt the modest pleasure of doing so in the open air, in private, with the splash of steaming pee upon the ground: one of those inevitable activities we don't think about until – as then – it suddenly reminds us of our animal nature and part in a great circle of creation.

A mile or so further on, after some twisty roadwork, I stopped at a picnic spot the Forestry Commission had kindly made in a small plantation beside the Ystwyth. I took off my boots and socks and bathed my feet in the cold river water. The little wood was full of bluebells and a sign told me it was a butterfly reserve. As my feet dried, I saw a large White and a small Tortoiseshell, but missed the Wall, Orange Tip, and Speckled Wood, the sight of which was said to be also . possible.

From here what the map called a dismantled railway ran across pastureland near the river, but was not marked as a footpath and seemed to promise problems with unbridged streams and gateless fences. I stuck to the road westwards – warm walking, though there were few vehicles competing with me for the tarmac. At five to five I came into the village of Llanilar, roughly nineteen miles out of Tregaron, feeling that I had done a good day's tramping and ready to doff my pack in a friendly B-and-B. But the white-washed village pub, The Falcons, was shut until five-thirty. In the local shop, where several women and children were clustered around the single cash register, the male proprietor told me that the pub didn't accommodate guests. When he had taken payment from one woman for a can of rice pudding and two ice lollies, he held a conference with another of his customers. Mrs Evans did B-and-B, didn't she? – but she was away for two weeks. What about Mrs Williams, then? He rang her on the phone; no reply. 'It's a bit early in the season, you see,' he said. 'Most of them haven't opened up yet.' He was sure I would find a bed at The Royal Oak in Llanfarian, three miles or so further on. I bought a small carton of orange drink to recompense him for his help and to help me get there. The women and children looked at me wryly, with interest, but without pity.

There was quite a lot of late-afternoon traffic on what was now an A-road. Most of it was coming at me from the direction of Aberystwyth as I trudged along at the edge of the highway. My feet felt hot, hard, aching, soft. My legs were tight, stiff, cramped, and throbbing. I suspected several blisters were forming. I sang snatches of 'Bojangles of Harlem', a Fred Astaire number, as if it might bring lightness to my feet. I didn't watch the cars directly, but in the way an animal might, with an innate sidelong caution, ready to spring into the hedge if one of them looked like running me down. (Ragged Robin was growing at the base of the hedge, which was otherwise prickly.) I tried to encourage myself with thoughts of other walkers: Borrow striding along, swinging his umbrella, at five miles an hour; miners plodding home from their long day in the pits; men and women from remote farms walking cheerfully over the dark hills to Sunday church and chapel; and the drovers ordering their slow-moving flocks and herds eastward into England. I recalled the exhortatory words of other walker-writers:

Belloc remarking that walking was a primitive act, 'natural
to man', and Edward Thomas suggesting that walking
restored us to 'a pristine majesty'. (The message from my
feet had little to do with pristine majesty.) I remembered the
remedy proposed by Frederick Olmsted, the American
farmer-turned-journalist-turned-landscape architect, who
walked from Liverpool to the Isle of Wight in 1850. He
recommended that, when exhausted, you should pour a
wineglassful of spirits into your shoes. This – with a cup of
tea and a bit of toast or biscuit taken internally – would make
you fit 'for another hour or so of hard tramping'.

I had a flask of whisky in my pack but thought this a
desperate, even ultimate measure. What would it do to my
boots? What would the combined effect of Teachers, hot
leather, and sweat have on those who opened their doors to
the knock of a stranger seeking a bed? I made do with the
orange drink and poured none of it in my boots. And at last
Llanfarian arrived, at the junction where my road joined the
main road along the coast, although a sight of the Irish Sea
itself was precluded by an intervening hill. Here was The
Royal Oak – and a Bed-and-Breakfast sign! The pub premises were low and unprepossessing, with a narrow doorway
through which I and my pack just effected an entry. At an
equally cramped bar the landlord stood with a single customer, who turned to stare at me. For an instant, seeing a
pint glass on the landlord's bar-top, I considered asking for a
beer before raising the matter of B-and-B, but some instinct
prompted me to reverse the order of questioning.

'No,' said the landlord, whose hand had in fact strayed
toward the flip-lever for the keg-bitter spigot. 'No, we're
not doing B-and-B anymore. Yes, I know the sign's still up.
We'll have to take it down. You'll find other places about a
mile from here.' He smiled. 'Or maybe a bit more than a
mile.'

On and on. Down into a valley and along a municipal
footpath which had appeared at the road edge. And a twilight

view of the sea through a broad gap in the coastal cliffs that
allowed the Ystwyth to twist its way toward salt water. The
sea as always gave me a Thallasic sense of achievement and
gratitude for having reached it. My spirits revived enough to
impel me past a sign announcing the town boundary and up
a final hill at whose summit I found a large 'private hotel'.
This had an available room and bath, and a severe landlady
who said she could make me a 'bar meal' of chicken, chips,
and peas in the next ten minutes but not thereafter. A similar
Hobson's choice met me in the bar itself, where the slightly
more affable man of the house apologised: the draft beer was
'off'. I made do with a bottle of Bass. I was in any event
grateful for the microwaved food and non-draft beer, for the
tub of hot water and the bed – and for the fact that I was not
benighted somewhere in mid-Wales under a roadside hedge.
By nine-thirty heavy rain was beating against the windows
of my room. By nine-thirty-five I was no longer aware of it.

LAND OF MY FATHERS

MORNING CAME WITH the sound of tyres squelching on wet
roads. My first chore was to deal with a blister which
yesterday's twenty-five miles had raised on my left heel and
which I washed, punctured, and washed again, leaving the
deflated skin in place. A clean pair of wool socks was donned;
yesterday's pair, worn thin, was thrown away. I tied my
boots extra tightly against further chafe. I then set off,
hobbling only slightly, to find a hostelry for several nights
that was closer to the centre of Aberystwyth.

It was no longer raining as I walked in from the southern
edge of town. I was reminded of other small British seaside
resorts on a damp spring morning, slightly tatty, waiting for
the sun and summer holiday makers. At first sight, this
might have been Littlehampton or Clacton or Broadstairs;
Freeman, Hardy and Willis were selling shoes; W. H. Smith
and Boots were doing their thing. But it was – as I had
forgotten – the Saturday of a Bank Holiday weekend. All
the boarding houses and hotels I tried were full. 'It's the .
Welsh motor rally,' one receptionist told me. 'They're
coming through tonight. They generally don't stay for more
than a short kip and a change of clothes but all their friends
and followers come too and have to be accommodated.'
Morris dancers were entertaining a small crowd in a central
street called North Parade. I was asked for a donation by an
elderly man collecting for Save the Children and for my
signature by a young woman with an anti-Poll Tax petition;

she thanked me for it in Welsh before seeing my name and home address, when she thanked me in English. Most of the street-corner conversations seemed to be in Welsh; most seemed to have the animation and ease that one associates with villages – the feeling that there is always time for a good long gossip with whomever you run into. Aberystwyth's population is 11,000, so it is town-size. That it is a cosmopolitan university town was made evident by the high proportion of young people and numbers of Africans, Asians, and Near-Easterners of student age.

In the Tourist Information Office a brochure offered a free night in Aberystwyth to anyone who had been evacuated to the town as a child at the start of the Second World War. Five hundred children came from Liverpool, many from south London, and some took to the place and didn't go home again. This is the first occasion on which I haven't found it an advantage to have been evacuated to Dayton, Ohio, in 1940. 'Any discounts for evacuees to anywhere else?' I asked a woman making hotel bookings. She shook her head, smiling – a game try. After several unsuccessful phone calls on my behalf, she found me a room at The Groves Hotel, one of the best in town (judging by the price). I put aside my puritan mid-walk reluctance to dabble in costly comforts; clearly non-motor rallyers shouldn't be choosy.

After leaving my pack at The Groves in North Parade and making a few phone calls to people I hoped to meet, I walked the seafront from end to end. The promenade runs along a shallowly indented bay. At the north end a cog railway takes trippers up the cliff-face of Constitution Hill to a Camera Obscura which, on clear days, provides a projected image of the sixty-mile view. (In the age of television, this presumably does well from those who prefer to pay for their prospects to be packaged.) At the southern end of the promenade, on a lower but more pronounced promontory, stand the ruins of a castle. This was founded in 1277 by Edward I, in the course of a campaign to conquer Wales; was savaged by

Owain Glyndŵr and his men; and was finally devastated by Parliamentary troops during the Civil War. Between Castle and Camera a long line of pastel-stucco four-storey Victorian hotels overlook the beach. A stumpy little pier, with café and 'amusements', pokes tentatively out to sea. The most striking building on the front is a large neo-Gothic structure, closely akin to St Pancras station in London, which was put up as a hotel at the peak of the railway age and was later adapted for use as the first college of the University of Wales (which also has homes in Cardiff, Swansea, Lampeter, and Bangor). Most of the Aberystwyth campus is now on Penglais Hill, a mile back from the sea, together with the National Library of Wales.

The most densely populated building on the front seemed to be Alexandra Hall. A sign on this grey stone block offered self-catering rooms at modest prices. Milk bottles stood on window-sills. Many of the residents – who looked as if they were living on welfare benefits and would otherwise be homeless – were smoking on the front steps or helping move furniture in and out. One young man, sitting on the prom-enade outside the Hall in the hazy afternoon sun, appeared so content that I stopped and asked what it was like to live in Aberystwyth. He told me that it was better being on the dole here than in Liverpool, his home. 'The sea helps,' he said.

Bank holiday weekend or not, the summer season had not begun. Piles of folded deckchairs were still covered with yellow tarpaulins. Yet many families were picnicking in the wooden shelters on the promenade, while a few hardy children paddled in the chilly sea. One small girl was being loudly summoned by her mum: 'Beryl! Beryl!' Beryl – skirt held up, the water over her knees – did not come. Graffiti scrawled on various walls showed undergraduate and national-ist interests: 'I am, therefore I think.' 'Welsh Water for Wales.' I walked south of the castle to Aberystwyth's small tidal harbour, sheltered by solid jetties or moles, where the

Ystwyth and Rheidol rivers debouch. I like harbours of this kind: the sheds of crab fishermen; the lobster boats and yachts; the gulls stepping over the black mooring chains that lie outstretched on the mud; the collecting-box for the lifeboat; and the big-windowed Customs and Excise lookout post. In the car park that capped the widest section of the north mole sat a yellow Mercedes with German plates and a puzzled-looking driver, consulting a map. I read his expression less as 'Where am I?' than as 'What am I doing here?' Waves from the Irish Sea were breaking over a rocky ledge in front of the Castle – ragged, inclined strata of rock against whose sharp edges the grey-green water shattered in bright explosions.

On 8 September 1866, *The Times* in London ran an editorial which remains famous in Wales. It declared: 'The Welsh language is the curse of Wales. Its prevalence and the ignorance of English have excluded and even now exclude the Welsh people from the civilisation, the improvement and the material prosperity of their English neighbours. Their antiquated and semi-barbarous language . . . shrouds them in darkness.' Thirty years earlier, after an excursion in North Wales, the traveller Thomas Roscoe reflected on the 'equanimity of the modern Welsh – so inconsistent with their old hot spirit'. It was a calmness, he thought, which 'resulted from fair and equal laws, a real adaptation and union of interests with those of the incorporating state'. He believed that 'Welsh loyalty had its origin in a noble and lofty sentiment – the gratitude of an entire nation, and the still grateful recollection of receiving justice from their former oppressor . . . Hence the inactive spirit, the quiet, patriarchal simplicity, the devotion to monarchy, and the passive obedience.'

Times change! In Aberystwyth during the next few days I failed to run into any English expatriates, as I had done elsewhere, but instead encountered a number of highly articulate men and women who spoke Welsh and English with equal vigour; who were keenly but not ill-humouredly concerned with Wales and Welshness; and for whom the epithets 'passive', 'inactive', and 'antiquated' would be utterly wrong. Hot or at any rate vibrant spirits were still to be found. I had a drink with Ned Thomas, at that point a teacher of twentieth-century literature at the university, an editor of a serious magazine called *Planet*, and a member of the European Community's Bureau of Lesser-Used Languages. Thomas – a stocky, energetic man in his early fifties – was also writing a column for the newspaper *Wales on Sunday* and taking evening classes in Basque. He was born in Lancashire of Welsh parents, brought up in Wales, England, and Germany, went to Oxford, learnt Russian while a National Service conscript, and worked for *The Times*. In 1969 he and his wife moved back to Wales, the country to which he now realised he owed the greatest allegiance. He reacquired fluency in Welsh – the language he speaks with his children at home in Llandre, a village five miles northeast of Aberystwyth. (He generally speaks English with his wife, Sara, who is Scots Canadian.) In 1971 Thomas published a short study entitled *The Welsh Extremist*. It was an attempt to convey aspects of contemporary Welsh nationalism to readers Thomas thought of as ordinary, tolerant English people, who sympathised with minorities elsewhere but were unaware of and hence unconcerned about the depth of resentment felt by Welsh-speaking people in Wales. Ten years later, Thomas himself felt sufficiently resentful and frustrated to drop words in favour of action. The Conservative Party, coming to power, had reneged on its election promise to set up a Welsh-language television channel. Accompanied by the principal of a theological college, a former BBC executive, and several sympathetic students who were experienced in this sort of extra-curricular activity, Thomas set off to shut down a television transmitter on a hill near Lampeter.

'We remembered the wirecutters,' Thomas said, 'but as we left the house of a friendly bank manager who'd given us tea, I realised we had forgotten to write a press release – a prime necessity of modern insurgency. We went back to the house and I quickly hammered one out. Then we set forth again. We climbed the hill and our helpful students cut through the surrounding fence before disappearing into the night. We walked into the unmanned facility and pulled the switch. It was prime time in the evening and we had blacked out all BBC programmes over a large part of south-west Wales. Some viewers, in the middle of their favourite soap-operas, were very cross. We stayed put. Twenty minutes passed and authority at last arrived in the shape of a young police constable. He quickly decided that we weren't your usual criminals or vandals, and that someone more senior ought to be involved. He called his sergeant. The sergeant came and asked us to accompany him to the police station.'

There they faced another long delay. The Post Office, which ran the transmitter, was unsure what charges to press. But after nearly a year, during which they achieved considerable publicity, they were charged with breaking and entering. At their trial, they were found guilty and the Judge fined them several hundred pounds apiece plus costs.

'It was cheap coverage at the price,' Thomas said. 'I was continuously interviewed as a leading insurgent. The fines were paid with money collected in one week from visitors to the National Eisteddfod. And when Gwynfor Evans, the venerated leader of Plaid Cymru, the Welsh nationalist party, and its first member of parliament, threatened to go on hunger strike for the cause, the government decided that it was less of a nuisance to have a separate Welsh TV channel than put Welsh-language programmes on the other channels and annoy the viewers who were monolingual in English. We won that one.'

I went for Sunday lunch at the Thomases. Beforehand, I rehearsed what I knew about Welsh political arrangements,

aware that I probably fell into Ned Thomas's category of
tolerant but not overly knowledgeable English. (This category, by the way, might not be as considerable as Thomas
generously assumed. I've met a number of Englishmen who
distrust and even dislike the Welsh, will happily tell you this,
and even assume that you share their prejudice. The English
verb 'to welsh' is still in common if unthinking use as a
description for not paying debts.) As part of my cognisance
of Welsh matters I knew that the administration of Wales
was now led by a cabinet minister – a Secretary of State –
and that the then holder of that office, Peter Walker, was one
of the more sympathetic Tories. He had forcefully attracted
to Wales industrial investment and European Community
funds. I knew that a demand for devolved government and a
separate assembly had foundered in 1979 when, in a referendum, the people of Wales voted roughly two to one against
the proposal. On that occasion, the English-speaking Welsh
had been resisting what they saw as possible domination by
the Welsh-speakers; the south of Wales had been worried by
the dominance of the north. Labour politicians with safe
South Wales seats in the House of Commons had cam-
paigned against devolution, declaring that only through the
Westminster parliament could Wales succeed. So it seemed
that Welsh nationalism had become a movement of the
middle-class in the west and north; most of the Welsh
working class, which lived in South Wales, voted Labour.
Yet I knew also that part of the curious equation was that
many Welsh had done well as individuals in English society. .
The Tewdyr family helped provide a line of English kings;
what one historian called 'the Tudor job-rush' followed, as
the Welsh clamoured for and received patronage at the court
in London. Without Welsh archers, would Henry V have
won at Agincourt? In more recent times, Wales has furnished
a disproportionate number of exceptional writers, artists,
statesmen, legal authorities, engineers, opera singers, and
sportsmen. And I understood that nevertheless many Welsh

retained a sense of injustice, of playing second fiddle to their haughty neighbour (the most oft-cited example of English condescension is the reference in a mid-nineteenth-century edition of the *Encyclopedia Britannica*, 'For *Wales*: see England.') Along with this feeling of being aggrieved went an annoyance with their own frequent servility, with the kow-towing to English wealth and influence.* Sometimes the annoyance became intemperate, even explosive.

The Thomases lived in a large rectory-like Victorian house. Lunch (cooked by Ned Thomas) was salmon, new potatoes, leeks, and aubergines accompanied by a fine lesser-known wine from the Süd-Tirol. Talk was widely allusive. Mostly, out of politeness to the English guest, it was in English, but occasionally there were snatches of Welsh between Ned Thomas, his wife Sara (an educational consult-ant and teacher), their daughter Casi (a graduate student of theology), and a young woman named Marion from New York who was studying Welsh and doing research on the oral traditions that lay behind the Arthurian legend. In English, too, we talked about Welsh. Gerald in the twelfth century noted of the people of Wales: 'Nature has endowed them with great boldness in speaking.' Those who know the Welsh language claim it is capable of conveying nuance and precision in ways that English lacks – perhaps, as Ernest Rhys thought, 'because the Anglo-Saxon mind has no con-ception of the ideas these linguistic hair-splittings represent'. (Rhys, the editor of the Everyman series of classics, learnt Welsh in middle-age 'with the utmost difficulty'.) Sara Thomas said that there were many ways in Welsh of saying

---

* As an example of this inferiority complex, one Welsh farmer told me of a man who worked for him, an excellent craftsman. But asked one day to repair a diesel generator, he said, 'Oh, you'll need an Englishman to fix that.' Borrow put it well – 'All conquered people are suspicious of their conquerors. The English have forgot that they ever conquered the Welsh, but some ages will elapse before the Welsh forget that the English conquered them.'

'I am', which could be expressed in a literary way, a demotic way, and in several dialect ways dependent on which part of Wales you were in.

We came to Arthur. He is thought to have lived at the end of the fifth and beginning of the sixth centuries, but his name is not recorded until several centuries later, in histories and chronicles believed to be based on earlier sources. Arthur was slowly transfigured from a provincial British military chieftain, who led a defence against the Saxon invaders, into a medieval emperor with a court full of knights and ladies. Various Welsh poems refer to him as a valorous hero, but it was the twelfth-century cleric and chronicler Geoffrey of Monmouth, in his *History of the Kings of Britain*, who put Arthur on the literary map. Marion said that many of the old stories Geoffrey had used were in a sense supplanted and forgotten once he had built them into his best-selling concoction. We talked about whether legends necessarily needed real persons at their source. Were the bards capable of inventing heroic tales from whole cloth? The young American, quite persuasive, thought not. The poems and stories began with people who had lived. Arthur, *dux bellorum*, had in fact once wielded a sword.

As Casi Thomas dished up an apple strudel, I raised a question that I felt needed an answer. Gerald, travelling around Wales, had believed – or affected to believe – in miracles. Would it take a miracle to save the Welsh language now? It seemed to me that despite local victories, the war was being lost. Despite the Welsh TV channel, Welsh language schools, bilingual road signs and official forms, the total number of people in Wales speaking the Welsh language was continuing to decline. The figure was now half a million, one person in five. Breton has just about died out in Britanny. Gaelic has almost gone in Ireland and Scotland. The other Celtic languages, Manx and Cornish, disappeared as working tongues in the last few centuries. I gathered that the exceptional survival into the present of Welsh – the senior language of this island, as Tolkien pointed out – was due to translations of the Bible into Welsh in the sixteenth century, the industrial prosperity of South Wales in the nineteenth century (which had kept Welshmen from emigrating), and the persistence into the twentieth century of a rural way of life in the west and north of the principality. But small farms, the basis of that way of life, were also under threat. I had read that Saunders Lewis, the eminent Welsh writer and political activist, had predicted that Welsh would cease to be a living language in the early years of the twenty-first century. Could anything save Welsh now?

Ned Thomas refilled our wine glasses. He said, 'Saunders Lewis also declared that he would remain committed to Wales even if he was certain that within ten years Wales would be finished. I feel just as strongly about it. Of course, it may be that we cling to the language as a way of holding on to an identity. And if Welsh identity could flourish through other means, through political institutions for instance, we wouldn't demand so much from the language.* Certainly as a symbol it carries a high charge for us. For me, the only way to perpetuate Welsh culture is by way of the Welsh language. I know how absorbing and frustrating the effort to save it can be – so much of life seems to go in fighting for Welsh nursery schools or road registration documents!'

The effort was also exhilarating – or so the Thomases made it seem. The possibly mortal struggle of Welsh made for a vitality that suffused the lives of those who cared about it. I remembered meeting a Welsh civil servant years before who had stressed the unfairness of history: 'Scotland had a king, and different laws. Ireland had Catholicism and Rome to help preserve it. Wales had nothing but its language.' And

---

* John Cowper Powys expressed a similar thought in 1939 when answering a questionnaire about his attitude to Wales. He said that he felt 'the Welsh national spirit has had to bank itself up in the Welsh language for want of being able to express itself politically . . .' (*Obstinate Cymric*, 1947)

even that, in some eyes, may not be enough. The historian
Gwyn A. Williams writes: 'Whom the Gods wish to destroy,
they first afflict with a language problem.' However, lunch
at the Thomases left me with the impression that some of
those so afflicted were facing the possibility of destruction
cheerfully, with a confidence that the Gods could be persuaded otherwise, even now.

I took a late afternoon walk along the grey sand and shingle
beach. In the north-western distance, the Llŷn peninsula
thrust itself from the mountains of Snowdonia into the sea
haze between Wales and Ireland. People from Lancashire,
London, Botswana, and Wales sat by the shore. I thought
about the difficulty of being one hundred per cent Welsh in
a country where so much of the machinery and paraphernalia
of daily existence was non-Welsh: national newspapers; most
radio and TV programming; international brands of food;
cars; electricity from the national grid; sweaters from Italy;
wines from France and Bulgaria; coins of the Realm.
Occasionally the stamps you buy in Wales have the Queen's
head slightly reduced to make room for a heraldic dragon,
but most often at the post-office counters you are sold the
standard British issue.

How would I react if I were Welsh? An immediate
response might be to pour scorn on some cherished, almost
holy aspect of Welsh life, in the way the writer Caradoc
Evans did. Another might be not to take this Welshness
thing too seriously – maybe, even, to make fun of it. Moving
with the times, deciding that what mattered to you was in
London or New York rather than Cardiff or Aberystwyth,
you would find most expressions of Welshness altogether
too nostalgic, sentimental, or phoney. The novelist Kingsley
Amis, who taught for some years in Swansea, seems to have
developed a very low tolerance for Cymric enthusiasm. A
great deal of the comedy in his novel *The Old Devils* is at the
expense of the stagier manifestations of Welshness, like ye

olde Welsh items on restaurant menus. These, he tells us, are 'pretty nasty, unless you happen to have a taste for chicken in honey', and they are put there, not because people order them but because they enjoy seeing Welsh words on the menus – 'same with the signposts'. (For all this, the reader of the book is all the time conscious of 'Wales' and 'Welsh-ness'. Not a chapter passes without a mention of Wales and the Welsh. It is as if Mr Amis has perversely acquired a Welsh need to flaunt nation and nationality.)

Another response would involve fury rather than fun. I've lived in a village and I know how one reacts to tourists, incomers, property investors. One wants one's own place. One doesn't wish to be seen as part of a picturesque attraction. Here, by the happenstance of history, forced back to the periphery of an island that was once largely theirs, the Welsh might well be frustrated, desperate, and extreme. Now and then someone feels that the only way to make an effective protest against the tide in which their identity is drowning is a violent way: *no one seems to pay any attention to anything else.*

It may be a tribute to the humanity of the Welsh and the absence among them of the sort of murderous fanaticism seen in Ireland in this century that there has been so little violence in recent years in Wales. In 1936, Saunders Lewis and two friends, D. J. Williams and the Reverend Lewis Valentine, set fire to some hangars at a Royal Air Force bombing instruction school on the Llŷn peninsula. A North Wales jury failed to arrive at a verdict; Lewis, Williams, and Valentine were re-tried at the Old Bailey in London where, having refused to give evidence in English, they were found guilty and sentenced to nine months. Lewis said later that he thought public violence was 'a necessary weapon'. It was particularly necessary when used against the irresponsible violence meted out by the 'English parliament' and 'English corporations' against Wales and its land – for example, by valleys being drowned to provide water for English cities. But when he was asked if the means he talked of included the shedding of blood, Lewis replied, 'So long as it is Welsh blood and not English blood.'

It was in fact Welsh blood that was spilt on the North Wales coast in 1969, just before the ceremonial investiture at Caernarfon of Prince Charles as Prince of Wales. Two young Welshmen were blown up while laying an explosive device at government offices at Abergele, near Rhyl. At the time, an apparently short-lived group called the Free Wales Army was believed to be fomenting violence. In the last few years another shady organisation called the Sons of Glyndŵr have gained a great deal of publicity by fire-bombing holiday homes in Wales owned by English people and by arson attacks on English property agents. So far the police have failed to nab any of the perpetrators. One reason for this may be that there are no long-term, hard-core practitioners of violence; people are angry one moment and ambivalent the next; they feel at odds with themselves, swinging between confident commitment and despondent detachment. Ned Thomas wrote in *The Welsh Extremist*, 'No group is absolutely stable; people are always moving at the edges of such groups, and everyone can understand, sometimes sympathise with the motives of people whose actions they cannot approve.'

I had difficulty getting in touch with John Davies, historian of Wales, Cardiff, and the Bute family, and a teacher at the University in Aberystwyth. A telephone call to the department of Welsh history first connected me with another John Davies, who was perfectly understanding about it. When I finally met John Davies the Bute authority, in the bar-restaurant on the pier, I asked him about this apparent shortage of Welsh names.

'You have to live in Cardiff to appreciate the scale of the problem,' said Davies – an affable, grey-moustached man in his late fifties. 'There are three and a half pages of John Davies in the phone book there. You call the coal merchant and say, "What happened to the two tons of house coal we ordered?" but you already know the answer. It has gone to the wrong John Davies. You learn to be absolutely specific. Give your address and occupation. Perhaps even give your age. Certainly in historical research birth-dates are essential. You may need to distinguish between say the John Davies born in Swansea in 1806 and the one born there in 1807. Place names are sometimes tacked on to help, with or without the permission of the person concerned, as in William Williams Pantycelyn. The historian Gwyn Williams, Trefenter, is thus able to be distinguished from historian Gwyn A. Williams from Cardiff. Most Welshmen for centuries made do with the patronymic system, like Rhys ap Gryffydd, Rhys the son of Gryffydd. Most of the surnames that are current in Wales are the result of the fact that John, William, Robert, Hugh, and Lewis were popular Christian names at the time of surname formation. This seems to have happened among the gentry in the sixteenth century, with the yeomen following a century later.'

(Gwyn A. Williams writes in his *When Was Wales* that Bishop Roland Lee, a sixteenth-century hanging judge as well as a cleric, helped get this process underway. He wearied 'of the long strings of *ap* (son of) in the legal presentments . . . and ordered their deletion'. In the formation of English surnames the *ap* was sometimes embedded, 'so that, say, Enoch ap Hywel would become Enoch Powell'. Richard Sale quotes a traditional verse about Bishop Lee's dictat:

> Take ten, he said, and call them Rice.
> Take another ten and call them Price.
> Now Roberts name some hundred score
> And Williams name a legion more
> And call, he moaned in languid tones,
> Call the other thousands – Jones.)

John Davies went on, 'Paradoxically, it was in the most Anglicised border counties that the inhabitants favoured a greater variety of surnames of Welsh origin. Examples might be Griffith and Wallader. After the eighteenth-century evangelical revival, some families in the Welsh heartland took names from the Old Testament – hence surnames such as Tobias, Moses, Isaacs, and Ebenezer.'

In the nineteenth century, some had adopted their mother's name as well – for example, Parry-Williams. A few who did this possibly were social climbers who thought double-barrelled names counted for more, but according to John Davies it was also the practice of Welsh emigrants in Patagonia, as in the name Jones y Davies. I had seen over a draper's shop in a South Wales town the name J. Haydn Jones, which suggested that uncommon middle names could be handy. The use of nicknames and occupational suffixes –

Davies the Meat, Jones the Fish – was once common. I asked
John Davies if there were any contemporary solutions.

'No mass solution,' he said. 'In Finland in 1906, thousands
of Finns who were fed up with the names Sweden had
imposed on them changed to Finnish names. Here, there's
been a similar impulse in recent years, but the change has
been piecemeal – a Jones will become Iwan, a Williams will
become Llwyd. My own children have had enough of the
inherited confusion. They've decided to change their name
from Davies to Brychan, after Brecon, the town where one
of my wife's ancestors lived.'

We repaired to The Coopers, a pub well placed between
North Parade and the university campus; it was an hour
before closing time and the hostelry was packed, mostly
with students. We met Ned Thomas and a local architect
whose name, in the noise, I caught only as Gareth. Jammed
around a small table, we talked of what Welsh-speakers call
Y Mennlifiad – the Inflow. Roughly fifty thousand English
men and women were moving to Wales every year. The
implications of this for the Welsh language were frightening
enough but were made worse by the outflow of a similar
number of Welsh. Many of the incoming English were able
to sell their homes in England for sums which gave them the
wherewithal to buy property in Wales for more than most
of the locals could afford. The majority of the outgoing
Welsh was made up of young people, looking for skilled
employment and wages to buy houses they couldn't consider
on what they earn at home.

It didn't seem to help that the invasion had been going on
for a long time. The Romans. The Saxons. The Normans.
The Flemings and English who settled in Pembrokeshire in
the eleventh century. I recalled a passage in *Wild Wales* where
Borrow was pretending to be on the look-out for a sheep
farm to rent and aroused the ire of an inn landlord, who
declared furiously that Borrow had come 'to outbid us poor
Welshmen'. Over recent years many incomers have been

agrarian experimenters and self-subsistence enthusiasts, members of religious, artistic, and utopian communities. Cheap land and the dramatic landscape have tempted a number. I said to John and Ned and Gareth that many of the English I'd met here weren't as far as they were concerned invading Wales. Rather they were fleeing filthy streets, overcrowded commuter trains, jammed roads – all the miseries and stress of urban England. Some – like the Lansdowne Hotel proprietor in Brecon and Mr O'Shea in Pumsaint – had Welsh wives who had pulled them in this direction.

'Still, the scale of the inflow is unprecedented and we feel increasingly defenceless,' Ned Thomas said. 'There are Cardiganshire villages where in the last few years all the Welsh-speakers have left or died. The improved A55 road along the North Wales coast enables the English in Lancashire and Cheshire to treat that part of Wales as their own back garden. Small, uneconomic farms are being sold – the land gets amalgamated with larger farms and the old farmhouses are pulled down or sold off as holiday homes. I know this is going on in other parts of the world, too, but the effect is worse here because of the destructive impact on the language. The net result is fewer Welsh speakers. We're angry because there don't seem to be any legal solutions. This is what makes a few think house-burning is an answer. Several councils in North Wales have tried to use planning regulations to prevent houses being used just as holiday homes, but so far higher authorities have overturned these decisions.'

I asked why Welsh politicians were unable to help. Well, it seemed that Welsh members of parliament generally reflected the disinclination of the majority of their constituents to put Wales first. Most Welsh voters are attracted to the major British parties – Conservative, Labour, and Liberal Democrat. Out of the 38 Welsh seats in the House of Commons, only three are currently held by Plaid Cymru,

whose name means 'the Party of Wales'. Plaid Cymru – also
a socialist party – fights no seats outside Wales. Founded by
Saunders Lewis and others in 1925, it seeks a regional
government which would allow Welsh electors to rule Welsh
affairs. Although it has now and then won a number of
council elections – including Merthyr Tydfil on one occasion
– its present strength is in Gwynedd in North Wales, the
bastion of the Welsh language. Many of its supporters are
beginning to look to Brussels rather than Westminster for
the advancement of Welsh interests. As the structures of
European government slowly mature, a good many Welsh
nationalists feel that Wales and other small regions like the
Basque country, Britanny, and Bavaria would be given more
scope within a federal Europe.

Ned Thomas said, 'But we're still up against certain hard
economic facts. Like the importance of the corridor between
Manchester in England and the Ruhr in Germany. The
Channel Tunnel will only emphasise this. Wales remains out
on the edge of a Europe which is actually centralising in
terms of finance and industry. We may be left out.'

It was coming up to closing time. The surrounding noise
was considerable. At the next table, two young men, perhaps
students of literature, were swapping bits of verse. One of
these scholars brought forth the limerick in which Swinburne
met the immense challenge of finding a rhyme for Aberystwyth, not once but twice:

> There was a young girl of Aberystwyth
> Who took grain to the mill to get grist with.
> The miller's son, Jack,
> Laid her flat on her back,
> And united the organs they pissed with.

Many of the other customers of The Coopers were wavering
between serious debate and laughter, between speech and
song. It seemed to me, at least after several pints, that if this
was the edge of Europe it wasn't a bad place to be – so I said

so. 'You're right,' said Gareth, the architect. 'When I worked
in London I earned a large salary and knew no one. Here,
when I step out of the office, I meet dozens of people whom
I know or feel I know.' Compatriots! A homeland. The
good fortune of having a close-at-hand cause to fight for.

From a group near the bar voices were now raised in a
hymn I recognised – though the words were Welsh – as 'All
through the night'. Pretty soon most of the people in the
pub had joined in. Not all were in unison; some did parts
and modulations. Even if they no longer throng to chapel,
the Welsh give voice in pub and club and rugby stand to the
great hymns and anthems like *Calon lan*, Pure heart, and *Hen
Wlad fy Nhadau*, Land of my Fathers. The sound and the
sentiment doesn't appeal to all the Welsh. Saunders Lewis
said in exasperation, 'I violently object to Welsh miners
singing in bloody London streets. It is a humiliation for
every Welshman.' Dylan Thomas's reaction to the by-now
slogan-like phrase Land of my Fathers was a snort of disgust
and 'My fathers can keep it!' In The Coopers, at closing
time, this Englishman felt no such cynicism. I borrow the
figure of speech from Wodehouse: the sound of the Welsh
singing stirred my emotions as with a fifteen foot pole.

I thought it was time to find out about sheep. So far I must have seen several thousand of the eleven million which populate Wales, but, apart from what I'd learnt about shearing and selling them, I didn't know a great deal. I therefore set off early on the first of May to meet two men who, I hoped, would further my education in this respect: Gwyn Jones, a retired hill-farming adviser, and Gwilym Jenkins, a hill-farmer. The northerly weather which had accompanied me to Aberystwyth had changed; for the moment we were back to the more usual damp stuff from the Atlantic. As I walked north-eastward out of town there was a mild south-westerly at my back, hinting of rain. For several miles I was confined to the edge of the main road, with car wing-mirrors seeming to brush my elbow. Although the road would have been the most direct route to my destination, Talybont, about eight miles away, I turned east to get away from the traffic along the valley of a little river called Afon Stewi, and then took a lane which reached Talybont over higher, lonelier ground. I passed a modern establishment which declared itself to be the Welsh Plant Breeding Station. A man was checking weather readings at a beehive-like device in a field planted with different types of grass.

'Humid,' I said to him, by way of greeting.

He looked up from his clipboard. He glanced at the grey scud overhead, which now had a touch of sun breaking through. He said, 'You'll have a nice afternoon, though.'

The village of Penrhyncoch came next – part of Dafydd ap Gwilym's early territory – with a sweet small church. Its little tower, apparently growing out of its roof, had wood-planked upperworks and was capped by a short slate-covered steeple. I shortened my stride uphill to Penycwm on a lane edged with hyacinths. Then, for the first time on this walk, I rolled up my shirt-sleeves. May morning! The lane passed through thin woods out on to open hillside again. At a cross-junction with another lane, a farmer's boy waiting to deflect sheep from one field into another greeted me with a smile and a Welsh hullo which is more like halloo. There was a farm called Elgar ('Holiday Accommodation') and a fine view to the north of the Dovey estuary, with broad sands, and tough-looking mountains beyond. Here the roadside hedge grew from the top of a low dry-stone wall, full of moss, ivy, primroses, and numerous pink, blue, and white wild flowers. Then it was gently downhill to the main road again and Talybont, a long village, with The Black Lion inn set back on a triangular green. Here the hills come down to an expanse of bogs and reclaimed land on the southern shore of the Dovey. On the far side of the village, beside the cemetery, a driveway led to a substantial farmhouse, Tanyrallt, the home of Gwilym Jenkins and his family.

My impression of Welsh farmers had been formed to date by brief encounters. This impression was of some shyness, some suspicion, some kindness, and occasional impatience springing from a need to get on with the work at hand. Their interest in their land and animals appeared to be as great as, if not greater than, their interest in man. I was aware that many were having difficulty making a living out of farming and were driven to sidelines in bed and breakfasts, renting out caravan sites, or running pony trekking holidays. I'd seen signs put up by several farmers indicating charges for driving down their lanes or parking on their land, directed at motorists out looking at Cambrian scenery. Sometimes a box on a fence post had been put up for

payment – fifty pence or a pound. One farmer I had talked
to, near Tregaron, quoted me a price of £20 for half a day
and lunch at his farm. And though my first reaction to this
was shock and a curious embarrassment, *he* wasn't at all
embarrassed – and I soon concluded that he was sensibly
naming a fee which would cover his and his wife's time, and
the food, all required by an inquiring stranger.

My coming to the Jenkinses farm was thanks to Gwyn
Jones, with whom I had talked by telephone, and who met
me there. Jones – a spry, quietly spoken man in his mid-
sixties with straight reddish hair – lived in Bow Street, a
village between Talybont and Aberystwyth; he had retired
in 1984 from the Agricultural Advisory Service but still
enjoyed visiting many of the farms whose land and stock he
had helped improve. He spent a good deal of his remaining
time walking the Welsh hills. Gwilym Jenkins was in his late
fifties, a man of less than medium height with a powerful
nose, good-humoured blue-grey eyes, and deeply lined,
weathered cheeks. He had known Gwyn Jones for thirty
years. Both men were stalwart members of the Welsh
Mountain Sheep Society, Hill Flock Section – an organisation
which has 800 members and of which Jones has been
president, Jenkins chairman. Jenkins's farm is called Tyngraig, the house in the rock, after a farmhouse – presently
rented out – half a mile inland. The farm's 1200 acres stretch
up into the hills to a height of 1300 feet; one hundred acres
are under timber; the rest support about 1500 sheep and a
hundred head of cattle. This is a big farm of its kind – they
are usually around 300 acres – and Gwilym Jones runs it with
the help of his wife and two sons. (He also has a married
daughter.) Welsh is their first language, as it is for Gwyn
Jones.

Mrs Jenkins provided a great spread of food on the kitchen
table and we tucked in. Gwyn Jones said, 'Don't be surprised
by this sort of hospitality. It's a tradition on hill-farms
always to lay an extra place at table for the man who might

arrive from "over the mountain".' But – he went on – times were now hard for many of the smaller hill-farms. Farmers with ninety or so acres were only just surviving. They had to put too many sheep out on their land, with consequent erosion. Hill-farming subsidies, which often amounted to half the annual income of smaller farms, were based on the number of ewes kept, and this encouraged overstocking. Nowadays even on a 300 acre farm one son might make a living from the farm but any other children would have to get jobs elsewhere. Uneconomic farms were being sold and split up into parcels that weren't big enough for practicable sheep-farming use but made attractive sites for holiday homes or small holdings for retired folk.

Gwilym Jenkins felt as strongly as Ned Thomas that the Welsh language wasn't helped by this tendency. One effect was fewer Welsh-speakers in the Welsh countryside. Moreover, the larger farms that remained required bigger machinery, which cost more in real terms than it used to. 'Real terms' for Gwilym Jenkins meant the produce of his land: fifteen years ago it took 200 sheep selling for £4 apiece to pay for a new tractor. Now it took 600 sheep at £30 apiece. (The tractor was necessarily more powerful.) In times like these it was essential to make the land fit to produce not just more sheep but higher quality sheep. This was where Gwyn Jones had been so great a help to Tyngraig – and to many other hill-farmers when they saw the effect of Jones's advice.

'Sheep are grass,' said Jones, by way of introducing his subject. 'The growth rate of lambs is largely dependent on good pasture. To achieve that, we had to improve the land.'

In the Middle Ages, great herds of goats grazed on the Welsh hills. But sheep had also been there since well before Roman times, and they gradually ousted the goats. Sheep are a more valuable animal for their meat and wool and they do wonderfully on poor land as long as it gives them grazing room and isn't too wet. Jones grew up on a farm which was in every sense educational; it was part of the Caernarfonshire

Agricultural College, of which his father was principal. When he came to the Aberystwyth area in 1955 as an agricultural advisor, he noticed that the local hill-farmers were trying to improve their peaty uplands, to make them more fertile (and collect grants for their efforts). But they were doing so by ploughing, which seemed, Jones thought, to interfere with the natural drainage; the higher hill-land traditionally known as 'beyond the mountain wall' soon reverted to heather and rushes.

On his father's college farm, such hill-land had never been ploughed. Slag from steel works, rich with phosphates and trace elements, was spread on the ground together with lime; the rushes were topped and harvested along with grass hay once a year. Jones preached this method here. He worked on other notions aimed at preserving the surface crust of the earth that overlays the peat, discing, harrowing, and spiking it and then seeding the hollowed and ridged crust with rye grass, clover, timothy, and fescue. Great quantities of fertiliser were not needed. An important part of Jones's process was bringing in cattle to graze on the land in early summer; this prevented the young grass from being smothered by heavier vegetation. Sheep were then put on the land to tread in the seedlings. 'My idea was to make a gradual change,' said Jones, 'to graft a nucleus of sown species on the old sward and foster its development by good husbandry – this resulted in a close-knit, productive sward. The improved land made for improved stock.'

Jones's methods were demonstrated with the help of a few farmers though many – over-dependent on the Hill Sheep Subsidy – were reluctant to try his innovations. In the mid-1960s Jones got together with the Jenkinses. Since then, Tyngraig has been the stage for their joint experiment in land improvement. The benefits were not immediate, Jones said, and people who would have expected to see 'instant green hillsides' would have been disappointed. But over twenty years, 'going far by going slowly', the results have

been impressive. The land now provides better keep for an
increased number of ewes and lambs – fifty per cent more in
that time. The lambs also grow faster, reach heavier weights,
and produce eighty per cent more wool – 'a sure sign of
good husbandry'. Other hill-farmers have been persuaded.

Lunch over, we climbed aboard a battered green Land-
Rover, Gwilym Jenkins at the wheel, Jones and I beside him,
and the two Jenkins sons in the canvas-covered back together
with three black-and-white sheepdogs. We drove along the
main road past the chapel where Mr Jenkins served as deacon
and inland, uphill, on a lane that took us past Tyngraig
farmhouse. We stopped once for a ewe which had got out of
a fenced pasture into the lane. The two young men caught it
with the help of one of the dogs and bundled it into the back
of the Land-Rover, to be dropped off in half a mile over a
gate of the field where it belonged. On the lane we stopped
now and then for gates to be opened and closed behind us.
As we passed beneath a cairn and a large stone slab lying on
the hillside, Gwilym Jenkins said to me with a smile, 'One
of your mates is buried up there.'

Gwyn Jones kindly explained: 'Gwilym means another
writer – Taliesin, one of our earliest poets.'

On the map, the place is marked Bedd Taliesin. It is one
of several sites in Wales claimed to be the grave of the sixth-
century bard.

> A strait grave, a man much praised,
> His whetted spear the wings of dawn.

So Taliesin wrote in his 'Death Song for Owain ab Urien',
praising the dead chief. The legend is that Taliesin as a baby
was found in a coracle caught in a fish weir on the coast not
far from here. The person who found him was Elphin, a
local prince. When grown up, Taliesin returned the favour
by rescuing the prince from a dungeon. George Borrow
attributed to Taliesin the famous prophetic lines from 'The

Destiny of the Britons' that Borrow used as an epigraph for his book:

> Their Lord they shall praise,
> Their language they shall keep,
> Their land they shall lose
> Except wild Wales.

According to a work called *Mysterious Wales* by Chris Barber, an attempt was made in the nineteenth century to discover the poet's bones under this cairn and move them to a sanctified spot. 'While the well-meaning persons were digging, they were suddenly startled by a terrible thunderstorm. Lightning flashed and struck the ground with a loud crack. The men fled for their lives, leaving their tools behind, and they never returned to try again.' However, contemporary archaeologists have proved of sterner stuff. Gwyn Jones said that some who had examined it believed that Bedd Taliesin was in fact a Bronze Age burial place, from times far more distant than those of the old Welsh poet.

The lane became a rutted track. At the end of it, well up into the hills, stood a small, disused farmhouse, Caerarglwyddes; it had not been lived in for forty years. We stood at a fence between the house and a shed used for sheepshearing. In the valley below, the thin Afon Cletwr ran westward to the sea. The afternoon was fine as promised and the sun lit the slopes of the hills from green bottoms to bare golden-brown tops; black cattle and tan-and-white sheep were scattered on them. While his sons and the dogs went to move some of the sheep from one area of pasture to another, Gwilym Jenkins résuméd for me his working year.

Lambs arrived in early spring. How early depended on when you put the rams out the previous autumn. Ewes had a five-month gestation period, and you didn't want the lambs born too soon, maybe into severe winter weather. Here the lambing season generally ran three weeks from mid-March – a hectic time. The lambing at Tyngraig was a hundred per cent, for although some ewes were barren and others had lambs stillborn, this was made up for by a number of twins. Only one or two sheep per hundred needed human help at delivery. This might be because the lamb came out backwards or with its feet making an impediment. This month, May, he and the boys would be busy ear-marking, docking tails, castrating most of the male lambs. June was for shearing – later than in the lowlands – and managed here and on neighbouring farms as a cooperative effort. A bit later, when the wool had grown a little, it was time for dipping: immersing the sheep in a chemical dip to prevent scab mites and other parasites that cause irritation and disease. Many of the lambs – perhaps 850 out of 1200 – would be sent to market from July to October. In August the 350 lambs that were being kept for breeding stock would be weaned. In September roughly the same number of elderly ewes were sent to market. In October, the rams were put out, one for every forty-five ewes. A female sheep can go to a ram at one and a half years of age and thus produces her first lamb when she is two; she can go on giving birth until she is five or six. During the winter the ewe lambs – nine months old – are taken to lowland farms – Tyngraig's went to Wiltshire for their winter 'tack'. Extra food supplies have to be provided now and then for the sheep that remain on the hills during the cold months. There were few free moments. Jobs had to be done like haymaking and fencing, for which the Jenkinses used timber they grew on their own land. Gwilym Jenkins particularly enjoyed the actual business of shepherding, of moving sheep, which he generally did on horseback.

The year come full circle, it seemed the moment to ask some questions. Gwilym Jenkins had used several terms that meant little to me, and which I now got him and Gwyn Jones to explain. 'Wethers' are castrated male sheep. Lambs after their first Christmas are called 'Hoggetts'. At the age of a year and a half they are referred to as 'Two-tooths'. Some of the nasty ailments sheep are heir-to are liver-fluke, bloat, louping-ill, pine, scrapie, footrot, and staggers. Buzzards and crows sometimes attack new-born lambs but foxes are the biggest trouble. I knew by now that *hafod* meant the upper farm or summer house and that *hendre* was the main farm, the winter home; but *fridd* and *cynefin* had to be explained to me. The former is 'the land below the mountain wall'; the latter, a word which has no simple equivalent in English, refers to the place on the hills where the lamb was born and reared. Like the German *heimat*, it also suggests the place where a creature feels it ought to live. (In English, farmers speak of animals being 'hoofed' or 'hefted' to a certain piece of ground.) Gwilym Jenkins said that sheep rarely stray from the unfenced hill-land which they sense to be theirs. However, taken to lowland pastures for wintering, lambs sometimes break out.

Welsh Mountain Sheep are one of some forty breeds in Britain. They are thought to be descended from the small Celtic sheep which were here before the Romans came and introduced their own breeds. They are active climbers with a touch of wildness that can make them hard to shepherd. Gwyn Jones said, 'The ewes are excellent mothers. They provide lots of milk and are stubbornly protective. If you approach a Welsh Mountain ewe with your dog in spring when she's with her lamb, she'll stand her ground, stamping a foot at you.'

At the ram sales in Dolgellau in October, Jenkins and his fellow hill-farmers look for a ram or two to buy to invigorate their stock. (A good Welsh Mountain ram might fetch £800–900; an exceptional one £5000.) One thing in the back of the hill-farmers' minds is hardiness – a quality they want to breed into their sheep, and which Gwilym Jenkins defined as an ability to store fat. They look for a ram with good stance, feet well placed, a full and bold head, horns not too thick, and good teeth. The ram's wool is carefully inspected. Jenkins said, 'You want a proper handful, but not so much that with a ewe it would get in the way of milking.' The amount of kemp in the wool is also a matter of interest – the reddish hair that sheds rain but can reduce the sale value of the fleece because it makes the wool less easy to dye. For upland sheep, however, the kemp also means that lambs will be born with a hairier birthcoat that may help it survive a late-winter blizzard. Gwyn Jones thought this inherited ability to survive was one that should be protected and enhanced, and that some Welsh hill-farmers – crossbreeding their Welsh Mountain sheep with, say, Cheviots or Suffolks – weren't concerned enough about it. 'They might get a bit more wool or weight, but their sheep may lose that wonderful hardiness.'

Despite the expansive landscape – the sea in one direction, the peaks of Foel Goch, Moel-y-Garn, and Moel-y-Llyn in the other – I had a sense of a hill-farmer's life being all-enclosing. Gwilym Jenkins said that he had never thought of being anything else. Tyngraig was clearly his *cynefin*. The one thing he complained about was the failure of the government to recognise his Welshness. He was meant to fill up some forms for claiming a grant, given for protecting natural habitat in this area – and the forms were only in English. He refused to sign these. He had had much correspondence with the Welsh Office in Cardiff, which had sent him a Welsh translation of the forms, and though he was prepared to sign this translation, that apparently wouldn't do. It was a question of whether the Welsh language had legal status for the signing of 'statutory instruments'. Well, the last letter from the Welsh Office gave him a fragment of hope that they might be coming round to his way of thinking. 'They want to preserve the wildlife,' he said, 'but they should help preserve our life and our language, too.' To date, refusing to sign the forms had cost him some £6000 in grant.

★ ★ ★

The Land-Rover halted to let me off at the junction of the Caerarglwyddes track with the lane that came up from Talybont past Bedd Taliesin. I said thank you and goodbye, *diolch* and *dda dda*, to Gwyn Jones and Gwilym Jenkins, who would be going back later for his sons and the dogs. Then I set off north-eastwards along a narrow lane. Although the surface had been asphalted, grass and dandelions grew in the middle of it. The walking was uphill and downdale, a small price to pay for backlane solitude. I had ahead of me a meandering twelve miles to Machynlleth, where I hoped to spend the night. I crossed the Afon Cletwr, just below a place where it spurted, brilliantly clear, through a cleft in a hillside, and passed through woods on to open hillside again, dotted with sheep. A few gorse bushes marked the edges of the track. A slippery footpath took me – slithering out of control – down to the main road near the village of Furnace. Twice I sat down hard on the muddy incline. I took this route in order to cross the river Einion, the only bridge being at Furnace where the Einion's waters drive a huge water-wheel which in turn once worked the bellows of a coal-fired furnace for smelting iron-ore: all dependent on an eighteenth-century stone building which has been restored. I had to stick with the road as far as the next village. This also bore the name of its pre-eminent building, though here it was in Welsh, Eglwys Fach – the small church. The church on the west side of the road seemed to me low rather than small, overhung by the wooded hill opposite, the Einion burrowing behind it through water meadows toward the Dovey.

Here at Eglwys Fach the incumbent in recent years was the cleric and poet R. S. Thomas – 'R.S.' as he is familiarly called by many in Wales. I'd been impressed by the interest in writing and particularly in poetry a number of people in Wales had expressed; hill-farmers were not ashamed of knowing of Taliesin or of setting down their own words in stanzas. (A yearbook of the Welsh Mountain Sheep Society's

Hill-Flock Section that Gwyn Jones showed me contained several poems, in Welsh.) But the Reverend Thomas, now living in retirement on the Llŷn peninsula, does not otherwise seem a likely object for familiarity. His flinty verse often conveys as much scorn as affection for his country:

> There is no present in Wales,
> And no future;
> There is only the past,
> Brittle with relics,
> Wind-bitten towers and castles
> With sham ghosts;
> Mouldering quarries and mines;
> And an impotent people,
> Sick with inbreeding,
> Worrying the carcase of an old song.

Although Thomas writes in English, and has had a London publisher, one would hesitate to call his poetry 'Anglo-Welsh' – there might be an explosion on the Llŷn peninsula. He is a committed Welshman, who declines to talk to the press in English, the language he goes on writing in. 'Despite our speech we are not English,' he has written. Elsewhere, identifying with the Welsh who speak Welsh, he writes of 'the English . . . elbowing our language/ Into the grave that we have dug for it.' Occasionally the reader gets an impression that Thomas regards himself as part of a selected core, as when he writes that 'In Wales there are jewels/ To gather . . .' and adds 'Have a care;/ This wealth is for the few/ And chosen. Those who crowd/ A small window dirty it/ With their breathing, though sublime/ And inexhaustible the view.' Even though not all of Thomas's poems are this inhospitable, and his terseness and crabbiness can be immensely moving, one can appreciate the actor Richard Burton's wry judgment: 'R. S. Thomas is a true minor poet but I'd rather share my journey to the other life with someone more congenial. I think the last tight smile that he allowed to grimace his features was at the age of six when he realised with delight that death was inevitable.' The Reverend Thomas has also been one of the few outspoken apologists for fire-bomb attacks on English-owned homes in Wales. He has said that it would be preferable for someone to be killed in such an attack rather than for the Welsh language to die out because of the influx of non-Welsh speakers.

Some people in Wales – happy to accept whatever is particularly Welsh in themselves, in the way you might welcome certain family traits as part of an interesting and not disabling inheritance – suspect that the strength of R. S.'s feelings may arise from a fear on his part that he is not Welsh enough. At any rate, having read much of his work, I thought I should look again at that of the other Anglo-Welsh poet Thomas – Dylan, that is – who didn't speak Welsh, who agonised less about Wales, but whose poems, albeit in English, however romantically self-concerned, are evidently charged with sounds and rhythms springing from a Welsh source. It was enough that Wales was in Dylan's blood; we feel the warmth. With R.S., however sincere the conviction, we feel the chill of desolation.

For an hour or so I walked in country that seemed to compress in the frame of a few square miles bucolic pleasures I had experienced before in a more stretched-out way. A lane took me up from the main road into a wooded vale which was a bird reserve. On a hillside stood a simple stone monument bearing a plaque: TO THE MEMORY OF MAJOR GENERAL LEWIS OWAIN PUGH 1907–81. SUBSCRIBED FOR BY MEMBERS OF THE MID WALES BRANCH OF THE BURMA STAR ASSOCIATION. I passed a farm named Cymerau and – after consulting my map – followed a footpath over the upper slopes of Craig Caerhedyn. In a pasture on the north-facing hillside I saw ahead of me a man, wearing an old felt hat, standing still, the sleeves of his jacket flapping slightly in the south-west breeze. He didn't seem aware of my approach. I

gave him a good berth so as not to startle him and then came
in from the side to say hello and ask about the best way
down into the next valley – the path had become diffused by
sheep tracks. I had got quite close to him before, with a
start, I saw it wasn't a man but a scarecrow, perhaps meant
for the protection of new-born lambs. With no other advice
to take than my own, I got out my compass and oriented
my map. On a downhill heading thus selected I came to a
stone wall, with scuppers at its base to allow rainwater
through and with what could have been a path alongside it.
This ran diagonally down to the Llyfnant river. I smelt a
fox. I saw a tiny bird, presumably a wren. On the bridge
over the Llyfnant I leaned against the parapet, removed my
backpack, and took several long swigs from my water-
bottle. It was one of those simple moments – that may
require all kinds of exertion and plotting to arrive at – when
you feel an overwhelming gratitude for existence. How
good the water tasted!

Another two miles brought me once again to the main
road, the coastal railway, and the broad valley of the Dovey,
all leading to Machynlleth. I arrived there at the end of the
afternoon. In the town information office, just about to
close, a friendly lady found me a bed and breakfast around
the corner: 'Mrs Fleming's. The name of the house is
Brooklyn.'

BRITISH AND FOREIGN

MACHYNLLETH IS ONE of those names that seem to have been especially contrived to divide the Welsh-speaking sheep from the English-speaking goats. 'Machynlleth, pronounced Machuncleth,' says Borrow authoritatively. 135 years later, it sounded on the lips of its inhabitants much like that to me – though perhaps 'Machunfleth' was a closer way of putting it. The little town is still armatured by two main streets, the north-south road and a broad street heading east called Maengwyn Street. The T-junction at which they meet is marked by a tall neo-Gothic clock tower, a smaller version of Westminster's Victoria Tower which houses Big Ben, and commemorating the coming-of-age in 1873 of the son of the local great landowner, the Marquess of Londonderry. In a nearby street the horseshoe doorway of a smithy was built to honour a visit by the Prince of Wales, Queen Victoria's son, in 1896. But despite these manifestations of loyalty to peerage and crown, Machynlleth's most famous connection is with rebellion. Among the mostly Victorian three-storey houses of Maengwyn Street is a low, barn-like stone building called Parliament House – a late medieval structure that may have taken on the name of an earlier building on the site to which Owain Glyndŵr summoned an assembly in 1404. Here, in the presence of representatives from various parts of Wales and envoys from France, Castile, and Scotland, he was crowned Prince of Wales.

Five years before this, in 1399, Glyndŵr had been living

the comfortable life of a well-to-do Welsh landowner. He
was some forty years of age. He had been a law student in
London and a squire to Richard II, the since deposed king.
He may well have been (as Shakespeare, two centuries later,
described him):

> . . . a worthy gentleman,
> Exceedingly well-read, and profited
> In strange concealments; valiant as a lion,
> And wondrous affable . . .

At his estate of Sycharth, on a hill a few miles from the
Shropshire border, a great fortified hall stood atop an earthen
motte, surrounded by houses, shops, and chapel, and ringed
by a rampart and a moat. The poet Iolo Goch appreciated
the honours paid him there and Glyndŵr's largesse:

> Servants to get each job done,
> Supplying all the region,
> Bringing best Shrewsbury beer,
> Bragget, and choicest liquor,
> Every drink, white bread and wine,
> Meat and fire for his kitchen.
> Poets from everywhere gather . . .
> No hunger, disgrace or dearth
> Or ever thirst at Sycharth!

In 1399, however, Glyndŵr fell foul of his neighbour, Sir
Reginald Grey, a supporter of the usurper Henry IV. Grey
seized some of Glyndŵr's land. Glyndŵr went to law but
failed to receive justice; he allegedly received instead from
the English Parliament the response, 'What care we for
barefoot Welsh dogs?' Glyndŵr's outrage was being echoed
at that time in a fury felt throughout Wales. The country had
recently been decimated by the Black Death and the big
landowners were enclosing common land and evicting peas-
ant farmers. Henry IV had imposed new taxes. The attack
Glyndŵr made on Grey in 1400 became a guerrilla war,

which now and then expanded into savage pitched battle. At
Pilleth, on the border with England, a thousand English
soldiers were massacred; according to the horrified report,
'after the batayle ful schamefully the Walsch women cute of
mennes membris and pyt hem in here mouthis'.

For a short while the stars and the weather seemed to be on
the side of the rebels. A comet blazed, surely portending the
victory of the Welsh. Despite having raised a powerful army,
100,000 strong, Henry was compelled to back off in the face
of winter storms and Welsh terrain. In the spring of 1403,
there was more success for that 'strong, lean warrior' – as Iolo
Goch called him – or 'the great magician, damn'd Glendower'
– in the words of Shakespeare's Henry IV. Glyndŵr captured
Sir Reginald Grey and ransomed him for a small fortune. The
rebellion was extended by various family and dynastic quarrels. Jane, one of Glyndŵr's daughters, married Edmund
Mortimer, who had a claim to the English throne. Support
for the Welsh cause came from France and from the Percys of
Northumberland. At Machynlleth, Glyndŵr promised Wales
its own law system, parliaments, and universities.

But already his momentum was failing; the conflict was
scorching Wales. Prince Hal's troops had burned Glyndŵr's
halls at Sycharth and Glynfrdwy. The castles Glyndŵr had
captured were retaken and sacked, his captains killed, his
family taken prisoner, the impoverished Welsh towns that
had supported him forced to surrender. The rebellion petered
out. Henry IV legislated vengefully against the barefoot
dogs: no Welsh person could hold office, marry anyone
English, or live in England. Assemblies for any purpose
were prohibited. The Welsh were not permitted to bear arms
or fortify their houses. No Englishman could be convicted
in Wales by a Welsh jury. An Englishman marrying a
Welshwoman lost all his rights.

Meanwhile, the end of Glyndŵr was shrouded in the mists
of the hills where he and a few companions were believed to
have taken refuge. He is thought to have consulted a seer

when at Carmarthen, 'Merlin's city', and to have been told
that he would be captured under a black flag. But no one is
sure where he was seen last. A royal pardon proferred in
1415 in the name of young Henry V received no answer.
The inconclusive nature of this fading from the scene made
possible a buoyant legend. There was a story that at Valle
Crucis abbey, in the Berwyn Hills in Powys, the abbot was
out on his morning walk when he encountered the great
leader. Glyndŵr said to him, 'You have risen early, Master
Abbot.' The abbot replied, 'Nay, sire, it is you who have
risen early, a hundred years before your time.' The once and
future prince. Whereas in England (as John Cowper Powys
pointed out) you'd travel far to hear mention of King Henry
IV, except in a theatre, here in Wales the Welsh go on about
Glyndŵr as though he were still around. The places and
objects connected with him have a special vibrancy for that
reason. His rebellion remains an essential part of the resistance tradition – a resistance against central power, unjust
laws, and the loss of land and language.

Mrs Fleming, a motherly lady whose first language was
Welsh, made me a cup of tea and brought with it a piece of
buttered Welsh spice-bread. I soaked in a hot bath. Full-
length bathtubs and plenty of hot water! Such tubs seem to
be a strong point of B and Bs – unlike those hotels and inns
which have installed modern 'en suite' facilities, often with
cramped shower cabinets, in which you may get clean but
receive little in the way of recuperation. Mrs Fleming's
thoughtfulness extended to my socks, which I'd washed, and
which she put in her airing cupboard to dry.

The lads of Machynlleth were gathered at the Clock
Tower, evidently their evening meeting place, as I strolled
from 'Brooklyn' to The White Lion Hotel. There I had a bar
meal that warmed and filled but otherwise made no memorable impact. It was still just light at eight-forty-five. After
the day's exertions, I was asleep by ten.

★ ★ ★

I signed Mrs Fleming's visitors' book before leaving. My predecessors were English, Welsh, Dutch, Sri Lankans, Saudis, Canadians, Americans. 'Not so many Americans as before,' said Mrs F. 'Something to do with the exchange rate, perhaps.' Almost everyone had written 'Thank you'. Someone had mentioned 'the lovely bed'. Others wrote, 'I liked my pink-and-lilac room' and 'Great hospitality!' My smattering of Dutch allowed me to recognise a heartfelt expression of gratitude in that tongue. One Californian had scribbled 'The Answer is blown away in the wind.' This seemed self-indulgently evasive. Hadn't he slept well? Hadn't he enjoyed the splendid full breakfast?

It was dull and windless as I walked out of Machynlleth. The Dovey placidly reflected the grey skies as it flowed beneath the stone bridge carrying the main road north to Dolgellau. I followed the Dolgellau road for half a mile and then turned off along a smaller road which ran along the hillside above the main road and the Dulas river. The funnel of the Dulas valley allowed entry into the mass of dense and rugged mountains on the north side of the Dovey. I looked for the peak of the highest of these, Cader Idris, but it was obscured by cloud. After a few miles I took a side lane which twisted up the hillside to a former slate quarry, Llwyngwern, which is now the Centre for Alternative Technology.

Individuals with ideals have in the past frequently come to Wales in order to try to put them into practice. John Ruskin established a branch of his Guild of St George at Barmouth in 1875, in an effort to alleviate the poverty and squalor of Victorian industrialism. Eric Gill, the artist and sculptor, and his family were at the centre of a lay community of craftsmen (one being David Jones) who settled in a former monastery at Capel-y-ffin in the Black Mountains in 1924. Here at Llwyngwern the idea was that of a businessman named Gerard Morgan Grenville. In 1973, he decided to demonstrate ways of using renewable sources of energy. Capital was raised, a charity set up, volunteers mustered, and this out-of-the-way quarry – which hadn't been worked for twenty years – was picked as the place for propagating less wasteful ways of making energy. When the Centre opened in 1975, it had a few working windmills, a couple of water-turbines, one or two solar panels, and the beginnings of an organic garden reclaimed from the quarry waste tip. But visitors soon came. Within a few years, with the help of the Welsh Tourist Board, 50,000 were turning up annually. Full-time staff, modestly paid, were taken on. Courses were run for schools and colleges. At the present time about thirty people work at the Centre: engineers, builders, architects, and teachers. The Centre gets income from admissions and courses, from a bookshop and vegetarian cafeteria, and from a health food shop in Machynlleth. Another offshoot is a firm which does research in energy-saving electronics and manufactures products such as hot-air recirculators, low-energy medical storage cabinets, and portable wind-powered battery systems – sixty of these have been exported to Mongolia to provide nomadic herders with electricity for lights and radios. The cottages that once housed quarry workers have been rehabilitated and new energy-efficient houses built. The Centre's profits are humble, but it remains independent of mains power.

I left my backpack at the admissions booth and climbed the slopes of the old quarry. I looked at various kinds of windmill, water-powered turbine generators, and banks of solar panels. I read a chagrined little sign which said that because of repair work, lack of wind, and lack of rain, a diesel generator was in use today. Most of the time, in standard Welsh weather, it wasn't needed. I visited the kitchen garden, peeked in the compost bins, and observed the posted instructions to respect, please, the privacy of the residents of the nearby houses. I toured one house, open to the public, that had been massively insulated with slate and had heating bills ninety per cent less than normal. I watched some goats browsing on a scrubby hillside and ducks swimming on a fish-filled pond whose water was raised to it by a simple hydraulic ram. I used the toilets. The waste from these, I read, was led to settling tanks and then to composting bunkers where natural processes destroyed harmful bacteria and smells and then, after the addition of straw, produced a nutrient fertiliser. I took note that the quarry railway and its slate wagons, still a hand-and-leg-powered operation, were being used to transport firewood. In the shop, I looked at plans for passive heat-storage units, kits for compostors, and designs for low-energy houses and fruitful gardens. I bought a packet of red campion seeds – the lightest, least-energy consuming purchase possible. From the cafeteria, where a course of students from Imperial College, London, was about to have lunch, I acquired a cup of coffee and a nutritious oatmeal flapjack. These I took to an outside table. For company I had an immensely tame male chaffinch, which enjoyed the crumbiness of the flapjack. No waste at all!

I was befriended by the place. Arriving, I'd felt a slight prickliness, as though in anticipation of strident do-goodery and didactic ecology. But the Centre is not a Green Disneyland or a Mecca whose muezzin blares the call to Schumacher or Thoreau. Diffidence, perhaps, is more productive – particularly when, as here, it seems to co-exist with a determination to bring about change in our attitudes to using, and misusing, the planet. Here, in example and text, are some ways to use up less and reuse more, possibly with a few inconveniences attached but undoubtedly with additional good feeling. The word may not yet have got through to the Powers in government that it is better to *save* energy than build giant new generating plants, but the Centre for Alternative Technology is to be credited with ensuring that three quarters of a million men, women, and school-children have got that message.

★ ★ ★

It was several miles up the Dulas valley to Corris, a village surrounded by abandoned slate quarries. Everything here was slate. Most of the little houses had been built for slate-workers. A pub was called The Slater's Arms. Around the quarries slate waste was piled in great dark grey heaps. Many of the pastures and gardens were fenced with tall thin slabs of slate, stuck in the ground like gravestones, and wired together. Some of the quarry buildings were constructed of two-inch thick blocks of slate, laid on one another without mortar. At the Centre for Alternative Technology I'd learned that from the quarry on the site had come slate which wasn't very reliable: it couldn't be sliced as thin as the roofing slate from quarries further to the north. The slate rocks of Wales are the result of vast compression of the earth about 500 million years ago. Much was quarried, but in some areas it could only be extracted by mining, and the encasing rock had to be blasted loose with gunpowder. It was hard, ill-paid, and often dangerous work. The danger came from rock-falls and blasting, from pneumonia and silicosis. Although the Romans used the North Wales slate for the floors, if not the roof, of their fort near Caernarfon, and the medieval hall of Conwy castle was roofed in slate, the material didn't come into widespread use for roofing until the eighteenth century. Roof slates were split by hand, generally six to ten being obtained from an inch-thick slab, the slate-splitter wielding a mallet against a broad chisel. The slate from this area was mostly used for pig troughs, tombstones, window-sills, fireplaces, and, eventually, in electrical switches. Most British roof-slates are now made of a composition material and the trade in real slates is reduced to that of a few quarries in North Wales, one of which operates with the help of income from visitors to a slate working museum.

I crossed the river at Corris and, having left my backpack at an inn on the main road called The Dulas Valley Hotel, reconnoitred the area unencumbered, at any rate physically.

The omnipresent slate did not lift my spirits. Slate is a mournful stone, with no feeling of sun in it, the way, say, sandstone has. It lacks the inherent fire of coal. Perhaps, too, one associates it with early school days and scratchy blackboards. I walked around the derelict workings of one quarry, a stream running fast through the piles of debris, and worried about an avalanche. How would searchers know where to look? Only the backpack at the inn would recall my visit.

On the lane back down to Corris I came upon a more encouraging sight. A house stood on the hillside here facing up the valley toward Cader Idris, whose summit was still covered with a woolly cap of white-grey cloud. The owner of the property had busied himself – and provided entertainment for the rare passer-by – by creating a number of miniature Italian buildings and monuments which crowded the steep slope below his house. He was clearly a skilled worker in concrete and masonry and refused to take the ordinary outlet of rockeries, crazy-paving, and garden gnomes. The *tour de force* was a small-scale version of a church in Rome, the Trinita dei Monti, with the flight of stone steps leading down to the Fontana della Barcaccia. Into this fountain a dismasted sailing vessel was surrealistically sliding. Its hull was formed of gooseberry-green concrete. Nearby were other churches, castellos, and Palladian palazzos, weirdly juxtaposed, and in differing scales. In the surrounding border, bricks were set so as to show their maker's marks: Huddersfield Brick Co.; Accrington NORI; TIDY; J. C. Edwards RUABON; Mostyn Brickworks. Other decorative insets were Italian road signs, for example ZONA ALPI. The whole thing was a witty shrine to travel in Italy and absolutely unexpected there on that be-firred hillside amid the dead quarries.

George, my host at The Dulas Valley Hotel, was a middle-aged man from Derbyshire. He had been a part-time fireman and had various tales to tell of that profession as I stood at

his bar drinking perforce keg Worthington. He had wit-
nessed tragedies – deaths – dreadful injuries. He had also
been involved in rescues like that at an old peoples' home
where one very elderly woman had said to him, as he
attempted to assist her down a ladder, 'Young fellow, no
man has ever laid hands on me and I will climb down
myself.' He had been at The Dulas Valley for several years;
the inn enjoyed a good passing trade from holidaymakers
driving between the English Midlands and the Welsh coastal
resorts. He thought many commodities were more expensive
here; there was less competition in the sale of consumer
goods; and yet the locals earned less than workers doing
equivalent jobs in England. 'They're also ten years behind
the times,' he said. 'Some of the lads – I mean, they still
wear leathers. They've still got long hair.' In these parts
nicknames persisted and often stuck to a man even when the
condition that had provoked them had gone. One Corris
man went on being called 'Whiskers' long after he had
shaved off his beard. A man who had lived in a cottage built
of corrugated steel was still called 'Tin House' despite now
living in a terraced villa whose walls were pebble-dashed.
Occasionally, George said, there was a bit of trouble at The
Dulas Valley, but that was hard to avoid at any pub. 'Two
lads started a fight in here t'other night but I sent them out
in the road. It was over a woman. After a few minutes it
sounded as if it might be getting serious, so I called "Last
orders please." They came charging back in, each determined
to buy the final round of drinks.'

As he was talking, two young men came in and George
threw one of them a bunch of car keys. They departed in a
car from the car park. 'Wise lads,' said George. 'They walked
home last night. The police are fierce about drinking-and-
driving round here.'

Despite these hints of rambunctious behaviour in the
Corris neighbourhood, it was a quiet night at The Dulas
Valley. I had a conversation with a local contractor who

wanted to know about walking but seemed unable to grasp quite how I got from one place to another. For instance, from Aberystwyth to Machynlleth, he assumed that I would have come the way he always did, by car, along the main road. He failed to see any reason for proceeding by way of farms or hills or hamlets, connected by back lanes and footpaths. My one problem was a strong musty smell in my bedroom. Above the head of the bed wetness glistened on the wall, which apparently backed against the Ordovician hillside. Down this rocky slope a stream ran, sounding like a downpour in the tropics. I opened the window wide to let the smell out and to let in the rumble of the stream and the somewhat less fetid smell of the damp woods. I dreamt of monsters. But at breakfast there was warm milk to add to the coffee.

The apprehensions I have had on a sailing boat when cruising an unfamiliar coast – Will I reach port before nightfall? Will the dangers outweigh the pleasures on this passage? – are not unlike those I have now and then when cross-country walking. On this particular overcast morning, as I set off from Corris, the nagging concern was: Will I successfully get to Barmouth over the hurdle of Cader Idris? Such apprehensions are of course one reason for walking, as they are for sailing, in that they blot out the frets of everyday existence – the unlocatable leak in the roof; the rise in the mortgage payment; the fortunes of one's children. These apprehensions are not necessarily total. Sailing, I continue to take in the sounds of the water, the colours and texture of the sea, the shape of the coast. I feel the wind on my cheek and the sun on my skin. I notice birds and fish traps. But the concern underlying these perceptions is, like Moby Dick, always there. It expands to fill one's mind when observation and perception falter.

Fortunately my senses were kept busy enough as I walked along the edge of the main road, gradually ascending, through Corris Uchaf, or Upper Corris. I was suddenly aware of the weight of my pack, out of balance; a strap had come loose and needed refastening. I walked through a cloud of coal smoke, downdraft from a house chimney, and remembered the smell of London on foggy, smoggy winter days, before Clean Air legislation. I then passed a small

former schoolhouse that was now, a sign said, an Inner
London Education Authority mountain centre; a little further
on, someone had painted in big white letters on a roadside
wall CYMRU AM BYTH, Wales for ever. (It has certainly lasted
longer than the ILEA, which was abolished, a victim of
Thatcherism, in mid-1989.) A dark green Laura Ashley van
went past toward Dolgellau and made me reflect on how one
woman's small Welsh cottage industry had become a successful worldwide business with fabrics and clothing that
answered a pastoral need (or at least the Marie Antoinette
sort of desire of modern women to dress up as shepherd-
esses), although at last mention profits were down and the
company was retrenching – a victim perhaps of fashion's
skittishness, perhaps of overexpansion. (How big is beautiful?) I recalled three of my daughters in Laura Ashley peach-
coloured bridesmaids' dresses at a happy wedding. Then the
road north-westwards up the valley came into a straight
alignment and there was the bulky base of Cader Idris, only
a few miles away.

I paused to make a decision beside a road sign that
announced the southern boundary of the Snowdonia
National Park, which covers about half – the north-western
half – of North Wales. I wanted to climb Cader Idris. A mile
ahead, a path ascended from a spot called Minffordd past
waterfalls, glacial corries, steep crags, and a dark lake to the
summit. I had no desire to test the old saying (said about
other Welsh mountains, too) that those who spent a night
alone on Cader Idris came down either as madmen or poets.
(Having already allowed me a brief fling as poet, the gods
might decide to remove my wits.) But I had been looking
forward to going well aloft. Not since Pen-y-Fan had I been
up to such a height. Cader Idris, 2970 feet high, is said by
the guide-writers to have more glorious views even than
Snowdon, the highest peak in Wales. Although the name
means the chair of Idris, no one is sure who Idris was.
Richard Sale writes that he 'could have been one of the

legion of Welsh giants, though the only giant to have actually
been connected with the mountain was Gwyn ap Nudd,
who hunted the hills with hounds for the souls of those who
had died on the cliffs'. Charles Darwin, who came here as a
Cambridge undergraduate, wrote to a friend: 'Old Cader is
a grand fellow and shows himself superbly with ever changing light. Do come and see him.' An artist who thought
likewise was Richard Wilson, born near Machynlleth in the
early eighteenth century, whose serene Italianate mountain-
scapes are precursors of Turner.

The trouble now was that Cader Idris was socked in. The
ancient volcano was head, shoulders, and torso in thick
cloud. Should I set off up the Minffordd path and count on
the cloud lifting, revealing the glorious views? Or should I
assume that because the day was calm, the sun nowhere in
sight, neither wind nor solar heat was going to stir the cloud
cover? Map and compass might prevent me wandering in
circles around lakes, crags, and corries. But I do not belong
to the Mallory school that says you climb mountains simply
because they are there. I climb for a view, as well, and this
ascent looked as if it would only result in a close-up of dense
moisture suspended in air.

I chose to outflank the chair of Idris. I turned off the road
and walked down a twisting flume of a lane to the water-
meadows at the head of Tal-y-Llyn lake. The valley in which
the lake lies is part of a geological feature known as the Bala
fault. The lake is long and beautiful and lies close beneath
the mountain. I followed a path marked with white posts
across the marshy ground at the head of the lake. Slabs of
slate were placed as little footbridges athwart ditches. The
lake surface appeared to be exactly at the level of the ground
on which I was walking, and presumably sometimes rose
above it. From the direction of Minffordd a cuckoo was
calling. On the north side of the lake I joined a road that
became a track, possibly an old droveway, protected with
turf and stone banked up as a wall, with small trees growing

out of it. Out on the lake there was a skiff and two men
fishing with rods in the heather-coloured water – Welsh
willow-pattern. I passed the yard of a farm called Pentre and
sat for a breather on the parapet of a small bridge. Before
starting again I doffed my pack, took off my sweater and
tied the arms around my waist. For a while I walked on a
bridle-path. Rabbits scampered up the hillside, tails high.

Then it was uphill for me – slanting up through thin
woods until, above the tree-line, I changed course abruptly
and followed a little valley into the folds of high moorland.
Along the lake I had been going west-south-west and was
now going north. My destination was in fact north-west, so
this was once again like sailing, where because of wind and
current you often have to steer a course which is not ideal.
Gazing back across the valley of Tal-y-Llyn lake at the
mountains beyond I could look deeply up a cleft called Glyn
Iago, in which a stream fell down the precipitous face of
Mynydd Cedris – from this distance, the waterfall was
merely a damp gleam. I climbed over a dry-stone wall by
some A-frame steps, generously provided by the landowner.
A dead crow hung on some nearby barbed wire suggested
that he felt less friendly about these aeriel scavengers. I
continued through a gap, where the wind came over the
shoulder of the hill, making my own track, a few sheep
roundabout and much boggy ground, which I did my best
to avoid. An abandoned farmhouse – or rather roofless stone
walls of what had been a house – was called Nant-yr-eira on
my map. An intrepid farmer here had once built dry-stone
walls directly up the hillsides, an immense effort that time
had rendered vain as barriers but had left dramatic. In fact, I
could see now what Richard Wilson and company might
have been stirred by in this landscape. I felt a powerful wish
that I could draw. As aids to memory I'd made a few
sketches in my notebook: the battlements of Caerphilly
Castle, for instance. But the outlines of crenellations and

bastions were one thing, clouds, cloud shadows, distant mountains, and hillside streams another.

I followed a stream down into the next valley. The mossy ground was like a moist green sponge underfoot. Up this valley to the north-east, where a river called the Cadair runs down from Cader Idris, the clouds still hung over the mountain's summit. Down valley, on a rocky and grassy outcrop, stood Castell-y-Bere. Its stone ruins had seen action and ennui, days both better and worse. In origin this was not a Norman or English castle imposed on Wales. Castell-y-Bere was a Welsh fortification, begun c. 1220 by Prince Llywelyn the Great. He was apparently taking advantage of English royal troubles and strengthening the southern frontier of his princedom, Gwynedd. The castle was built with deep ditches, a rectangular keep, three towers, and a triangular barbican. It was manned by the warriors of Gwynedd, renowned for their long spears. But the English kings – demanding feudal respect from their Welsh vassals – were even more skilful with the weapon of Divide and Rule. After Llywelyn's death, rivalry between his son Dafydd and – in English eyes – illegitimate son Gruffydd was encouraged by the English king Henry III. In the next generation, the rulers of Gwynedd were Llywelyn the Last and his brother Dafydd, who have gone down in history as respectively hero and villain.

Wales at that time was still remarkably independent, and Gwynedd was the most powerful of its three principalities. Edward I, heir to Henry III, built new castles, planted colonies, and sent in armies to bring the Welsh to heel. Both Llywelyn and Dafydd wavered in their attitudes toward the royal oppressor. After some years of revolt, Llywelyn made peace with Edward. Dafydd – who had long feuded with his brother and tried to have him murdered – began as a supporter of the English but reverted to being a Welsh insurgent when Edward failed to pay him a due reward. In the revolt Dafydd stirred up against the king, Prince Llywelyn was reluctantly drawn in. He was separated from his men during a skirmish with English troops at Cilmeri, near Builth Wells, in 1282, and killed with a spear. Thus Llywelyn the Last. When his enemies recognised whom they had killed, they cut off his head and sent it to London, where it was borne in triumph through the streets on a pike.

Shortly afterwards, it was Dafydd's turn. He briefly made his headquarters at Castell-y-Bere, but the Welsh resistance faded and after a ten-day siege the castle fell to Edward's forces. Dafydd escaped north to the mountains around Snowdon but by midsummer's day 1283 he had been tracked down and betrayed (according to a chronicler) by 'men of his own tongue'. He was taken to Shrewsbury, dragged by horses through its streets, and there hanged, disembowelled, and quartered. The English quarrelled over which places would have the right to exhibit some of these pieces of their enemy, but there was no argument about Dafydd's head, which joined that of his brother impaled on pikes outside the Tower of London.

This was the end of Welsh political independence. Dafydd's children were taken by the King's men. His three daughters were put into nunneries; his two sons were shut up in Bristol Castle, from which it is thought they didn't emerge alive. Edward's masons came to Castell-y-Bere and improved it for English fighting purposes, adding curtain walls to link the towers and enclosing the courtyard, with an easier defence by crossbowmen in mind. However, in the brief Welsh rising of 1294 Castell-y-Bere was again taken, besieged, and recaptured, and this time destroyed to prevent the Welsh ever using it again.

I walked down into Llanfihangel-y-Pennant, a pretty hamlet. Llanfihangel means St Michael's, and it is to this saint, the archangel, that its church is dedicated. St Michael had a good write-up in Revelations xii. 7–9, where he captained the heavenly host during war in heaven. His cult was strong in the tenth and eleventh centuries when he was prayed to as protector of soldiers and was frequently claimed to have been seen in visions. Chapels and churches were built in his name throughout the Christian world. He was also regarded as the heavenly quartermaster who received the souls of the dead (and is thus thought to be invoked, like Charon, in the spiritual, 'Michael row the boat ashore, alleluia!'). Among other Welsh places with his name are Llanfihangel-yng-Ngwynfa, St Michael's-in-Paradise, in north Powys, where Ann Griffiths, the Methodist hymn-writer, was born, and Llanfihangel Tre'r Beirdd, St Michael's Home of the Poets, in Anglesey, where Lewis Morris was born in 1701, the oldest of the four Morris brothers who became famous antiquaries. Half a mile from the church at Llanfihangel-y-Pennant was the cottage home of a girl named Mary Jones, who achieved another sort of renown. She desperately wanted a Bible in which she could read about St Michael and others in her own Welsh tongue. She saved up her pennies over six years and then in 1800, aged sixteen, walked barefoot to Bala, twenty-five miles away across the mountains, to purchase such a Bible from Thomas Charles, the minister there. But Mr Charles had sold his last – the Welsh Bible was 'out-of-stock'. So he gave Mary his own Bible and a few years later, still impressed by her religious ardour, became involved in the foundation of the British and Foreign Bible Society. This was set up to help make the Bible available in many languages; among other things, it provided the Bibles which George Borrow hawked around Spain for four and a half years in the 1830s.

By St Michael's church I paused to admire the graveyard, crammed with graves, rimmed by old walls. I took note of a sign which told about a crag a mile or so down the valley, known as Craig-yr-Aderyn, Birds' Rock. This rises in an eight hundred foot sheer cliff and is the only inland nesting place in Europe for cormorants, which are of course seabirds. Long ago the sea washed the base of the cliff, and although its level has now dropped sixty feet and the coast has withdrawn five miles, the birds still come here. At this time of year, in April and May, thirty to forty cormorants nest at Craig-yr-Aderyn, impelled by old instincts – and perhaps also because these are the only cliffs to be found for many miles with no human beings close at hand.

I followed a lane across the flat valley floor to the Cadair river. A farm blocked the way. There was no obvious route past it to the river bank and the far side other than through the farmyard. This was full of black Welsh cattle and deep in brown Augean slurry. Muttering to myself adages like 'Nothing ventured, nothing gained', and 'Where there's a will, there's a way,' I tucked my trousers in my socks and swung open the steel gate. I then murmured sweet nothings to the closely assembled cows in case they felt a sudden collective urge to trample on the English interloper. Out safely at the far side, I crossed the Cadair by a simple bridge and washed my boots by dunking them quickly and shallowly in the Cadair's clear waters. The sun was making a fitful appearance. I had a happy lunch on the riverbank opposite Castell-y-Bere and tried to send telepathic thanks to George's wife at The Dulas Valley Hotel for her cheese and pickle sandwich.

The next few hours were walking as it should be – providing variety, exertion, far views, and just enough difficulty and precariousness. The object was to cross the wide shoulder of moorland, some 1600 feet high, that stretches from Cader Idris toward the sea. It was easy at first, along the foot of the steep hillside on the north side of the Cadair; then into a cleft down which ran several converging streams, following a footpath through another farmyard – a smiling young farmer in blue overalls pointing out the exit gate – and then zigzagging up the side of Mynydd Pen-rhiw on an old droveway. The ascent was the steepest I'd encountered since Pen-y-Fan. Now and then I swept an index finger flat across my brow like a windscreen wiper and let globules of sweat run off. Sweat which had preceded this

sweep hung from my eyebrows. I stopped occasionally to
collect my breath and to ask myself great questions, such as
Why does sweat form on the forehead most of all? I also
took the opportunity to look for Cadair Idris's head still in
cloud and at the cliffs of Craig-yr-Aderyn, now below my
height and too far away for spotting the nesting cormorants.
High overhead an interlacing web of three jet trails was
being spun. I was thanking the RAF for confining their day's
manoeuvres to the stratosphere when two other jets came
screaming up the Cadair valley at my altitude, banked over
Llanfihangel-y-Pennant, and disappeared eastwards towards
Tal-y-Llyn and England. We were 700 years from bastions
and spears, curtain walls and crossbows, a distance that could
be measured in the consecutive lives of a dozen men, which
makes it seem short enough. And yet what a distance!

Nearly at the top I became aware of the immediately
overhanging cloud. I could almost punch my hands up into
it. I took some compass bearings as I would have done when
about to be enveloped by fog when coastal sailing. This was
just as well, for – checking my position – I found I had
veered to the west of my proper course, and in a few minutes
the mists were thick around me. Visibility was about twenty
yards. Once I found the track again, no longer well defined,
I kept my compass in hand. It was important not to stray to
the east, where the map showed a close-contoured precipitous escarpment named Craig Cwm Llwyd, over which I
had no wish to tumble. I found myself on boggy ground – a
stream was born – and for a while I had to step from tussock
to tussock to keep the water out of my boots. Moisture,
moisture, everywhere. I was now going gradually downhill
and the clouds thinned. I reached the edge of a forestry
plantation and knew exactly where I was. A track took me
into it, through thousands of small skimpy firs. The effect
was to make me feel in May that exasperation you have in
November on being told by avaricious shopkeepers that
there are so many days left until Christmas. I passed a cairn

that probably predated the first Christmas. (Cairns, standing stones, and earthworks – remains of peoples who once settled these parts – are frequent hereabouts.) At three o'clock I was in older woods, on somewhat lower ground, with a view of the sea and the little beach resort of Fairbourne and the Mawddach estuary. I thought I could hear surf though the beach was a mile away.

On the map, the route down this hillside became fuzzy; the footpath was lost in the contour lines. So it was on the ground. In places the descent was steep enough to induce me to come down facing the hillside, as down a ladder – only the footholds were less evenly spaced and less secure than rungs. There were several isolated small farms to which access must have been difficult for carts and wagons before four-wheel drive, and still tough in winter. I went into an uncontrolled slide at one spot and drew blood from a finger in attempting to grab hold of a dry-stone wall. Then, almost at sea-level, having wiped off mud and blood, I walked out toward the estuary, following a little road which went (so a signpost said) to Morfa Mawddach railway station. One of the cottages scattered along here had a real-estate sign saying AR WERTH, for sale, Welsh-speakers evidently preferred.

At this point near the wide mouth of the Mawddach there is a footway to Barmouth, a single-track railway to Barmouth, but no road to Barmouth. Cars have to detour well inland. A causeway, viaduct, and tollbridge carry pedestrians and trains across the river. The causeway is reached by way of the Morfa Mawddach station platform, where one can pause next to the open-fronted shelter, as if waiting for a coastal train. I looked back at the range I'd come over and the high, apparently-leaning-forward face of Craig Cwm Llwyd which I'd managed to avoid. Equally impressive was the view up the Mawddach. The cool blue river wound inland between sandbanks and deciduous-wooded shores. It came from mountains and was flanked by mountains. Then I set forth along the causeway's sandy path, beside the sandy

single-line railway, to the viaduct, a wooden trestle arrange-
ment. The 500 pilings are greenheart, a tough tropical wood
used here because of past attacks on the viaduct by teredo
worm. (The teredo, in fact a tiny mollusc, bores into the
wood with its shell, digesting the cellulose. In the age of
fibreglass boats, it must be grateful for timber structures, as
long as they aren't built of greenheart.)

The last part of the crossing was on the iron span of a
bridge over the main river channel. The tide was flooding
fast. At the north side I came to a low white cottage which
had an open doorway on the path. In the doorway sat a
buxom red-cheeked lady, babe in arms. She took my twenty
pence toll and gave me a ticket. I asked how many people
walked over the bridge.

'It varies, my dear,' she said. 'On rainy days maybe no
one. But then on others, with the sun out, quite a few.'

I said that I supposed the money she collected went to
British Rail.

'Oh no. The Council looks after the bridge. They have to
replace and renew all the wood, my dear. They work on it
quite hard at least twice a year.'

She and the baby turned back to the violently-coloured
screen of a portable television and I walked on, feeling my
toll money was well spent, into Barmouth.

BARMOUTH, said the between-the-wars railway advertisements, FOR MOUNTAIN, SAND, & SEA. Beneath the slogan, a
picture of happy families on a sunny beach with the mountains behind. The railway reached Barmouth in 1866 and
confirmed it as a resort; since then it has been one of those
little seaside towns that spend a good deal of the year waiting
for the other few months to happen. It exists in anticipation
of summer when – in streets with names such as Marine
Parade and Jubilee Road – the 'private hotels', bed-and-
breakfast places, 'amusements', and little shops selling con-
fectionery, flip-flops, and buckets and spades come alive.
Before the railway Barmouth as a busy small port had
depended on the sea. For several centuries shipyards along
the Mawddach built fishing boats and cargo schooners. From
Barmouth haven there was an overseas trade in timber,
wool, and coarse cloth. Pieces of rough flannel called webs
were shipped to the southern colonies of North America for
clothing slaves. But this trade vanished with the dangers and
embargoes of the War of Independence, and Barmouth ships
moved to carrying slate. Even before the railway arrived
some of the gentry from the English Midlands came to try
the newly fashionable cure of 'sea-bathing', using bottomless
cabins in which they sat, waiting for the tide to rise and get
them wet, and then waiting for it to ebb, so that – properly
dressed – they could clamber back up the beach to their
hotels. By 1880 pleasure craft were running excursion trips

and ferry steamers plied to and from Liverpool. Many of those who chose Barmouth were active people, as they had to be. Barmouth's villas were stacked one above another on the steep ascent which rises immediately behind the seafront. The town attracted Victorian hill-walkers and holidaymakers who roamed the nearby mountains in the care of local guides. Indeed, the town still beckons the energetic. It is surrounded by outdoor pursuits centres where city youth find out about climbing and canoeing. It is where the annual Mid-Wales Marathon begins and ends. It provides the starting point for the Three Peaks Race, which involves competitors in sailing 350 miles to Scotland and running up Snowdon, Scafell Pike, and Ben Nevis along the way.

In a house overlooking the Mawddach in recent years lived the man whose exploits inspired that race, Major H. W. 'Bill' Tilman. At least he lived here between his exploits. Major Tilman fought in both World Wars, cycled across Africa, prospected for gold in Kenya, took part in two early Everest expeditions, and achieved fame of a not too widely sung sort after the Second World War with a series of arduous voyages to remote places in the Arctic and Antarctic, where he then climbed mountains. These jaunts, in a pair of elderly and not very handy Bristol Channel Pilot Cutters, were conducted at an age when most retired soldiers (or civilians) have put their feet up. The Major generally sailed with the help of crews found through newspaper advertisements. Most of those who crewed for him afterwards expressed a stiff upper-lip admiration for their determined skipper but didn't want to sail with him ever again. He was seventy-nine when he disappeared, along with several crew, on an Antarctic voyage in 1977.

I booked into The Lion Hotel in High Street. This small hostelry stands where boats once moored at a medieval quay, but the sea has withdrawn and buildings opposite now obscure a marine view. An elderly man who identified himself as the landlord's father-in-law was in the front courtyard, rebuilding some wooden steps. The keepers of nearby shops and cafés were similarly occupied in pre-season chores, painting the frames of awnings and mending outside tables. Having ditched my pack, I toured the town. For a start, I looked in the former Nonconformist chapel opposite The Lion, one of two of Barmouth's chapels that have been put to commercial use after the praying and hymn-singing finally ceased. This chapel, its pews removed, was now called Discount World. It offered clothes, toys, hardware, and tools at bargain prices in lieu of religious fervour, threats of hellfire, and promises of salvation.

Hard now to conceive what a hold Dissent once had on Wales. It was a hold that lasted from the mid-seventeenth century for several hundred years. The dissenters were Puritans, Calvinists, Quakers, Fifth Monarchy Men, Baptists, Independents, Methodists, and Presbyterians. They ejected the Anglican clergy from their parishes and sent out their own missionaries across Wales. Itinerant preachers like Vavasor Powell covered a hundred miles a week, preaching in several places a day, denouncing wickedness in high places, making converts, dying in jail. Although Methodism in the eighteenth century inspired the poetry and hymns of William Williams and Ann Griffiths, it also embodied a religious enthusiasm that seems curiously alien to many Welsh likings. Gwyn A. Williams notes that 'a Baptist minister was hooted in the streets of Merthyr for trying to *introduce* hymns into chapel'. For many, harp-playing and folk-dancing were now out; religious commitment was total. After travelling through South Wales, Benjamin Malkin wrote in 1803: 'Almost all the exclusively Welsh sects among the lower orders of the people have in truth degenerated into habits of the most pitiable lunacy in their devotion. The various subdivisions of Methodists, jumpers, and I know not what, who meet in fields and houses, prove how low fanaticism may degrade human reason.' But they soon moved out of the fields. Devotional meetings were even held

in pubs until a chapel was built and named Salem or Zion,
Bethel or Tabernacl. Chapel, prayer meetings, and Sunday
school formed the core of many a Welsh community. To
Gladstone, in the mid-nineteenth century, it was evident that
'the Nonconformists of Wales are the people of Wales'.
Nonconformism provided the umbrella for much radical
thought; it helped sustain the Welsh language.

And yet this overpowering impact of Dissent produced a
reaction. Some in Wales actually felt hatred for Nonconformism and all it stood for. In 1916 the writer Caradoc Evans
attacked the claustrophobic hold it had on the Welsh
countryside where you found 'badly-paid farm labourers;
stunted pale-faced children, whose bodies are starved and
whose intellect is stifled at the hands of the village schoolmaster; sexless women whose blood has been robbed by the
soil; little villages hidden in valleys and reeking with malice'.
For writing this sort of thing, Evans was widely reviled in
Wales, but time was on his side. The age was increasingly
secular. Although the Nonconformist sects held out against
the Sunday openings of cinemas and pubs, their congregations dwindled. They resisted merging with one another and
chapels closed. Many are now like Discount World, converted into carpet salerooms and clubs, warehouses and
apartments. Wales now has the lowest average church
attendance of any region in the British Isles. Up Barmouth
High Street, I came to a depressing dark stone chapel, still
apparently functioning, whose notice-board heralded the
coming of Luis Palau, a Filipino evangelist. He was touring .
with a mission called 'Tell Wales'. According to a local
paper, his message was: 'Unless "Tell Wales" and the power
of the Holy Spirit can bring the young people and young
couples back to God, Jesus Christ and conversion, Wales
will become totally secular.' Looking back over some two
hundred years of almost total religious attachment in Wales,
it is easy to think, even to hope, that Mr Palau is backing a
lost cause. But if some in these discarded pulpits preached

narrow-mindedness and joylessness, others fired hearts and souls. Moreover, the devotion was unconfusably Welsh, which means that even today's unreligious Welsh now and then miss it.

I walked down to the little harbour, where an L-shaped breakwater gave some protection for small boats from westerly wind and Irish sea. The Sailors' Institute on the Quay, founded as a Christian haven in 1890 by the local Anglican canon, was closed, as was the lifeboat museum, so I was unable to inspect the ship models, old navigation lamps, sextants, and mussel-rakes on show. (The present lifeboat, *The Princess of Wales*, is launched from a building near the Mawddach viaduct.) Also inaccessible was Ty Crwn, a round stone structure with tiny slits for windows and a low doorway, medieval in appearance but built in 1834 as a pre-court-appearance lock-up for drunks and other offenders. Locked out of these buildings, I climbed up into Old Barmouth by alleyways and narrow flights of stone steps. Here, as the eighteenth-century writer Thomas Pennant noted, the inhabitants of the higher houses have the opportunity to look down the chimneys of their neighbours below. The backdoors of some homes are set in the upper floors, or even in dormers in the rear part of the roofs. These roofs, of course, are always of slate, the houses generally of grey stone and placed on narrow natural ledges or terraces hewn in the cliff-face. Many of the gardens are steep rockeries, with rock plants growing from almost vertical crevices.

Some of these cottages had been the homes and work places of wool weavers, and in 1875 a number were given to John Ruskin by a local lady philanthropist, Mrs G. T. Talbot. Ruskin's activities included writing about art and society, defending Turner, travelling, and drawing, but at this date one of his chief concerns was getting people out of the squalor of industrial cities. To that end he founded the St George's Company, later called the Guild of St George. Its objects, he wrote, 'are the health, wealth, and long life of the

British nation: the Company having thus devoted itself, in the conviction that the British nation is at present unhealthy, poor, and likely to perish'. (Ruskin was fond of sequences of three adjectives or adjectival phrases.) Ruskin gave to the company about £14,000, roughly a tenth of his possessions; however, the company was to be a sort of cooperative, with its property belonging to all its members or companions, 'who have the right at any moment to depose the Master'. The Master, J. R., was in two minds about his position. 'I dislike having power or responsibility; am ashamed to ask for money, and plagued in spending it . . . If I could find anyone able to carry on the plan instead of me, I should never trouble myself about it more.' Ruskin talked a hundred or so people into joining his venture in hopes of a better life on a bit of land. He wrote, 'St George's arrangements . . . are to take the hills, streams, and fields that God has made for us; to keep them as lovely, pure, and orderly as we can; to gather their carefully cultivated fruit in one season . . .' The companions were 'to have *no fellowship* with works of darkness . . . but to walk as Children of Light'. Although he was promoting the agricultural life, it was to have 'as much refinement as I can enforce in it'. Therefore, 'decent behaviour at table will be primarily essential . . . [for example] the neat, patient, and scrupulous use of sugar-tongs instead of fingers'.

The Guild, formerly the Company, bought for allotments land that God had made in Yorkshire, near Sheffield, and established a museum for educational purposes at Walkley, . also in Yorkshire, where Ruskin exhibited his mineral collection. He came to Barmouth by train in 1876. During his visit he made a happy ascent of Cader Idris, but he was dismayed by the leaky roofs of the Guild's Barmouth properties. Although – he was thankful to note – the cottages stood on 'noble crystalline rock', the wind and the rain were making an entry; 'for some time to come, the little rent of these cottages will be spent entirely in the bettering of them, or in extending some garden ground, fenced with furzed hedge against the west wind by the most ingenious of our tenants.'

This was Auguste Guyard, an exiled French teacher, horticulturalist, and friend of Hugo and Dumas, who had been invited to Barmouth by Mrs Talbot. In his own village in France Guyard had tried to establish a model community but had aroused the hostility of the Church. Guyard was tall, with white hair, taken to wearing a grey cloak and red fez. In Barmouth he made a greater impact than the Master of the Guild. For six years – until his death there in 1882 – the Frenchman worked with the poorer cottagers, despite his little English and Welsh, teaching them to read and to make the best use of their resources. He showed them what herbs, plants, and vegetables they should grow. Auguste Guyard is buried on the hillside above the town with a stone inscribed with this epitaph:

> Ci git un Semeur qui
> Sema jusqu'au tombeau
> Le Vrai, le Bien, le Beau.

Here lies a Sower who until death spread the seeds of Truth, Goodness, and Beauty.

And so, before and after death, did Ruskin's and Guyard's patron, Mrs Talbot. One of the founding members of the National Trust, she bequeathed much land above the town to that body, which has done an indispensable job of preserving beautiful places in Britain. Mrs Talbot's land is called Dinas Oleu, the Fortress of Light.

At The Lion there was worried talk in the public bar about a millionaire – clearly no disciple of Ruskin – who was sewing seeds of a different sort of development. This man had applied for planning permission for a 'theme park' at a former gold mine several miles up the Mawddach estuary. Would it be in keeping? Wouldn't it bring in hordes of tourists? One of those in the bar thought it would be good for the local economy; several others put the point that pretty soon all of Wales was going to be a theme park, with coal-mine museums, slate-quarry museums, rural-life museums. Later I read that roughly ninety thousand people in Wales work in jobs related to tourism – twice as many as are in mining and steel-making combined. Although the tourists may seem to swamp the natives, jobs created by the needs of tourists may enable the Welsh to live and work in their own country, and even speak Welsh. What remains difficult, of course, is to ensure that a real life goes on and can be seen alongside the quaint and antique.

My Lion dinner was less interesting: a tough and greasy pork chop, a score of pale peas, a tablespoonful of apple-sauce, and a wet baked potato. But my bed was firm. And after a dog that was kept in the backyard under my window – and sounded as if it was going to yap all night – was let in or otherwise silenced around eleven-thirty, I slept.

While small hotels may provide conversation, they generally lack the more intimate conviviality of bed-and-breakfast places. On the other hand, as a hotel guest, you don't have the same immediate exposure to the owner's taste that you have in most B-and-Bs. In these, you may well get to know the lady of the house's taste in kitsch knick-knacks, particularly in bathrooms where a doll figure with a wide frilly skirt coyly camouflages the waiting replacement roll of toilet paper, or a little plaque catches the eye of the male toilet user as he stands having a pee – 'We aim to please,' it says on the counter-productively offputting plaque. 'Will you aim too – *Please?*' However, breakfasts, as I'd discovered, are one of the great attractions of B-and-Bs: they can be not only full but early enough for those who want to make a bright start. At The Lion, as at other family-run pubs that haven't cleared up before midnight, breakfast the next morning may be a bit tardy.

It was ten-fifteen when I set off, wearing a light shirt and no sweater – a hazy day with a promise of becoming hot. A good beach day, I thought; and here I was presented with a choice to start with of beach or promenade. For the moment I chose the latter. This coast runs north-north-west. The sea was calm and the wooden groins thrust out into it had no work to do holding the beach together. The tide was on the way out, leaving flat sands on which numerous dogs and their elderly owners were being exercised. Soon the terraces

of residential hotels and guest-houses came to an end. I took
deep breaths of the Irish Sea air, which was not very salty. I
kept my eyes peeled for the Barmouth sea-monster, a
serpent-like creature that is said to have been seen on and off
over the past century – most recently by six schoolgirls in
1975. About half a mile out, a lone fishing boat trolled up
the coast. At Llanaber, on the northern outskirts of Barmouth, the beaches narrowed and shelved sharply. A small
headland with its base in the water forced me to cross the
single-line coastal railway and climb up to the main road.

Here stood a big Victorian stone house – with a four-bay
front, a height of four storeys. A sign by the steps to the
door said: THE JESUITS – FRONOLEU TERRACE. Ten rubbish bins
paraded on the path, evidence (it seemed) of numerous
Jesuits. The house had a splendid view of the sea while
behind it the hillside mounted in little eccentric-shaped green
pastures, divided by dry-stone walls as if for a jigsaw. To
Fronoleu Terrace Gerard Manley Hopkins, aged thirty-three,
came for a mid-August holiday while he was a student on a
three-year theological course at St Beuno's, a Jesuit college
in the vale of Clwyd, in North Wales. (This was in 1876, the
same year Ruskin visited Barmouth on St George's business;
but there is no indication the religious and poetic aspirant
met the artist, critic, and social reformer.) Hopkins called his
years in Wales 'my salad days'. They brought into being
much of his splendid if brief crop of mature poetry. In 1876
he wrote 'The Wreck of the Deutschland', and while at St
Beuno's he also wrote such poems as 'God's Grandeur', .
'Spring', 'The Windhover', and 'In the Valley of the Elwy':

> Lovely the woods, waters, meadows, combes, vales,
> All the air things wear that build this world of Wales.

Another St Beuno's poem, 'Hurrahing in Harvest', was 'the
outcome of half an hour of extreme enthusiasm as I walked
home alone one day from fishing in the Elwy. ('And the
azurous hung hills are his world-wielding shoulder . . .')

Hopkins's later poems are often of more sombre mood ('I wake and feel the fell of dark, not day.') but here at Barmouth he was in a sunny state. One morning he rowed up the Mawddach to The George Inn at Penmaen Pool. His poem celebrating that spot is inscribed 'For the Visitors' Book at the Inn' and he evidently tried The George's 'ale like goldy foam'.

> The Mawddach, how she trips! though throttled
> If floodtide teeming thrills her full,
> And mazy sands all water-wattled
> Waylay her at ebb, past Penmaen Pool.

Hopkins learned Welsh, despite some reluctance on the part of his superiors, who told him that he could do so only to facilitate the conversion of Welsh people. But he was fascinated by the language for its own sake, and picked up from Welsh poetry some of its rhythms and devices, like internal rhymes. He later wrote to Robert Bridges that he had learned his 'chiming of consonants' from Welsh and had found in early Welsh poems ways to intensify and make dense sound and meaning. (Dylan Thomas, influenced by Hopkins, seems to have borrowed back again these Welsh elements.) Hopkins flourished in North Wales, which he described to his fellow poet Coventry Patmore as 'the true Arcadia of wild beauty'. He appears to have been happy there even on occasional visits during his wracked forties. He made a Welsh walking tour with a friend in 1886, three years before his death (at the age of forty-five, of enteric fever), and his tormented self-scourging was alleviated for the moment by simple delights like 'the heartiest of breakfasts'.

I saw from the map that in a couple of miles I would have to cross a river that looked as though it would be unfordable where it reached the sea. Therefore I continued to favour the road rather than the beach. The road had an adjacent path for a while, presumably for holiday residents. A steep

meadow of one coastal farm had been made into a caravan
or mobile home park, each metal box on wheels perched on
its own green terrace, as on a golf tee, ready for driving off
or launching. Some of the dry-stone walls along here were
twelve feet thick, perhaps because they had been made
depositories for all the stones from the field within their
limits. The sheep had not yet been shorn, and in their thick
coats were avoiding the sun by lying in the shade of the
walls. When the path ceased, I made do with the road verge,
though its grass was long and wet. I passed an ancient,
roofless 'homestead', as the map called it, built of big, time-
worn, seemingly sea-rounded stones, and with little trees
growing up inside it, their branches windswept where they
rose above the protecting walls. There are old habitations
and prehistoric settlements aplenty in this area. The faint
borders of archaic field systems can be seen on the moorland.
The remains of neolithic burial chambers are numerous: long
cairns, 'portal dolmens', and cromlechs, which are table-like
constructions, often of one stone placed horizontally over
two vertical. It was under the 'grey cromlechs, the only
monuments of Wales', that the painter Augustus John (born
in Tenby, west of Swansea) believed that 'the hidden soul of
Welsh art will be found crouching'. Earlier, Taliesen called
his country Cymru Garneddog, Cairn Wales, because of its
many burial-mounds.

My ambitions for the day were to do with beaches rather
than burials. Just before the village of Dyffryn Ardudwy I
turned down a lane toward the sea. This beach was backed
by dunes: waves of sand from ten to thirty feet high,
momentarily halted with the help of chestnut-paling fences
and dune grass. I walked well below high tide mark on the
damp sand, full of good feelings. The sand made a wonderful
walking surface, letting my heels sink in just so far. Warm
sun and light breeze made a counterpoint of sensations on
my face and forearms. I thought of other dunes I had known
– those near Tema on the Gold Coast, now Ghana, to which

on afternoons away from National Service duty as a nineteen-year-old infantry officer I drove on my motorcycle and
in which – after swimming in the high surf – I lay in absolute
solitude, dozing; and those on the Eastern seaboard of the
United States, out on Long Island near the Hamptons and
on the Outer Banks of North Carolina, where the thrust of
vacation settlement has caused houses to be built (as the
owners may one day discover) too close to the sea. Here
there was no surf today, no houses, and few other people.
The declivities of these dunes sheltered a scattering of
sunbathers, all male, all naked. They lay like creatures which
had just crawled out of the sea for the first time, absorbing
not only the rays of sun but, by full extent of prone contact,
the warmth and energy of the earth – which here was sand.
There was something a bit Nordic, even old-fashioned,
about this display. (Naturism, I recalled, was the almost
obsolete word for the practice.) Hadn't they heard about the
depletion of the ozone layer and consequent skin cancer?

At a point called Shell Island the sandy beach was inter-
rupted. The coast dipped in to an enclosed bay and the tidal
estuary of the river Artro. Shell Island – called Mochras in
Welsh – is in fact a peninsula on which an enterprising owner
has developed camping sites and a small 'leisure centre' of
restaurant, snack bar and games-room for the campers.
Despite this – and not a camper was in evidence this May
day – nature does well here, with hundreds of different wild
flowers including wild violets, wild pansies, various orchids,
sea holly, samphire, wild dwarf roses, and many birds, from
wrens to buzzards. Seals are said to be seen at dawn on calm
mornings. Several hundred kinds of shells are found in
profusion. Naturism is not permitted.

I headed inland from Mochras on a footpath across marshy
reclaimed land. I reached a causeway and had cause to be grateful for the ebbing tide – according to a sign, the causeway
was flooded for an hour or so at high water. Three more
signs in English and Welsh drew attention to other perils:

DANGER – AIRCRAFT LANDING. YOU ARE ADVISED NOT TO LINGER
IN THIS VICINITY; WARNING – KITE FLYING IS PROHIBITED; and,
most intimidatingly, MINISTRY OF DEFENCE. OFFICIAL SECRETS
ACT. PROHIBITED PLACE. PHOTOGRAPHY NOT AUTHORISED.
These measures were on behalf of an airfield, belonging to
the Royal Aerospace Establishment, built on the wide flats
between Shell Island and the village of Llanbedr. Three huge
green-roofed hangars; several runways, the largest of which
ran south inside the dunes almost all the way to Dyffryn
Ardudwy; and several parked jet-aircraft, highly visible
because of their red-and-white paint schemes. Another such
plane, at first a quiet blur in the southern distance, came up
the runway toward me, lifted off, and – I was ready to duck
– passed with a swift scream a hundred feet or so over my
head, banking away inland to the mountains to deafen the
sheep.

I walked alongside the Artro into Llanbedr – the sort of
village that wins tourist-board prizes for being well kept. In
the back of St Peter's Church is an old stone with an incised
spiral figure, like those to be seen in the chambered tombs of
the Boyne Valley in Ireland. It is a figure, says the local
historian Michael Senior, 'which may well represent the
endless cycles of decay and renewal'. At two p.m. – high
time for lunch – I had my own renewal in mind. Fortunately
The Victoria Inn presented itself, a low stone building with
a lawn, thick with daisies, beside the river. I sat in the garden
in the sun with a ploughman's platter and a pint of bitter.
The young barman didn't quite fill the glass; the actual
surface of the keg beer (there was no real ale) stopped three-
quarters of an inch from the top of the glass, the rest being
foam. I asked, politely, 'Is that a real pint?'

'We've got a metered pump,' he said with a Lancashire
accent. 'And they're cheap glasses.'

I apologised for questioning him. Presumably the meter
ensured the correctness of the measure.

'Ooh, don't worry,' he said. 'We get lots of people asking about it.'

It was an afternoon of easy walking. I stayed more or less at sea level on the road to Pensarn, which seemed to be no more than a tidal quay, once for slate shipping, now for small yachts and dinghies. A cheerful young woman scraping last year's anti-fouling from a rudder told me that she worked for a Northamptonshire youth association which ran rock-climbing and sailing activities from this spot – once again, England's young being invigorated by the Welsh outdoors. I stayed with the road to Llanfair – where slate used to be extracted from caverns – and then took the lesser and higher of two roads to Harlech. From the hillside there was an exhilarating northward view over the wide dune-backed beach that runs up past Harlech to Tremadoc Bay and the Glaslyn estuary. Beyond rose the Snowdon range. I whistled the military march 'Men of Harlech', which accompanied the passing-out parade at Eaton Hall, near Chester, when I and my fellow National Service officer-cadets received our commissions. (The words to the march, which I couldn't properly remember, are said to be a tribute to the heroic Welsh defenders of Harlech Castle during the Wars of the Roses, when the forces of the Earl of Pembroke were starving them out.) As I came into the little town, some of the retired men of Harlech were puttering in their trim gardens or sitting in the sun contemplating the results of their puttering.

Before looking at the castle, I dropped into the tourist office and asked about a place to stay. When that was settled – The Nodffa Hotel, at the bottom of the hill from here, across from the golf course – I asked the young woman in charge, whose name was Diana, if she was a native of the town.

'Not really,' she said. 'I grew up near Trawsfynydd – that's to the east from here, over the hills.'

'And has one of Wales's two nuclear power stations,' I said, not meaning to be knowing – but not wanting to be thought ignorant, either. 'Did it bother you?'

'It opened in 1965, before I was born. So it was always there. But I remember as a child getting rashes on my legs after I'd been swimming in a stream, and my father thought it might have been caused by discharge from the power station. He complained. I think they installed some kind of filters after that.'

Gravity took me downhill to The Nodffa, where I left my pack. The hill was almost a cliff, and on my way back up to the castle I was glad of a private path through The Nodffa garden that made my ascent easier. But those who sited Harlech Castle in the late thirteenth century did not do so to facilitate access for strangers. The castle stands on a promontory of rock, sticking out from the shelf of hillside on which the town has been built. The promontory is nearly 200 feet above sea level – and at the time the castle was constructed waves still splashed at the base of the hill. On the landward side of the castle a deep dry moat protects the approach. Each corner of the castle is formed by a round-sided tower, and another higher tower rises above the massive gate-house and keep. The castle was one of a chain of strongholds around Snowdonia by which Edward I – having just beaten Llywelyn and Dafydd – meant to keep a grip on the Welsh. The architect and master of the works was James of St George, a Frenchman who had built other castles for the king; nearly a thousand men laboured on it for six years; and the castle was soon put to the test during the revolt of Madog ap Llywelyn in 1294–5, when it was besieged from the land but successfully resupplied from the sea. However, just over a century later it was seized by Glyndŵr – he had found the royal garrison mutinous and easily bribed to surrender. For a while it was his headquarters and home; his family, including his daughter and son-in-law, Edmund Mortimer, moved in with him. But in 1408 Harlech Castle was besieged, heavily bombarded, and finally taken. Although Glyndŵr apparently escaped, Mortimer died, and Glyndŵr's wife and daughter were captured.

The castle's next role in British history was as a Lancastrian stronghold during the Wars of the Roses. Queen Margaret of Anjou, wife of the incompetent King Henry VI, re-grouped the royal forces here after the Battle of Northampton in 1460. Dafydd ap Einion and his Men of Harlech then held it for seven years against the Yorkist troops of the usurper Edward IV. Thomas Pennant, the eighteenth-century antiquary and traveller, wrote that, when called upon to surrender, Dafydd answered stoutly 'that he had kept a castle in France so long, that he made all the old women in Wales talk of him; and that he would keep this so long, that all the old women in France should talk of him'. But famine subdued him in 1468, and we do not know if the old French women had anything to say. In the seventeenth-century civil war Harlech was held for the king and besieged by Colonel John Jones, brother-in-law of Oliver Cromwell. (Jones lived in the Vale of Nantcol, a few miles east of Llanbedr, and had been one of those who signed Charles I's death warrant.) Although Harlech held out against Colonel Jones, it succumbed to General Mytton and his Parliamentary forces in 1647, bringing an end to the Civil War and its own military career.

I entered Harlech Castle by the land gate – paid my admission, and was told I had about forty minutes till closing time. This was just long enough to climb around this once great defensive structure, now a superb monument to thirteenth-century military engineering and a stunning stage set. Jackdaws nest on the highest battlements. Children run up and down the winding stone stairs. On the water side, visitors gaze down over the walls and cliff to the ground 200 dizzying feet below. You may have to fight the impulse to fly – like the jackdaws or like the gulls, wheeling out over the fairways and bunkers of the links. As you stand framed in a gateway, through which the north breeze is blowing from Anglesey, you may have to resist thinking you are a hero in an opera and breaking into song. I found myself in conversation with a youngish Frenchman, whose wife was sitting on a step, resting her tired feet. Their two children played tag on the grass of the inner courtyard. The Frenchman wanted to know about Mochras – Shell Island – and whether they could go there to camp. He had very little English and my rusty French was called forth to explain that, yes, they could pitch their tent there, the beach and the shells were fine, but they would be at the end of a – how do you say? – runway, *zoom, roar, scream!* My performance clearly didn't impress him. They would go there *demain*, he said.

The horror of medieval war does not attend those who wander around Harlech Castle. It is a stone skeleton, dry old bones on which imagination has to hang the periods of siege, starvation, and bloody assault – and to try to recall, too, that those occurred among long passages of calm, ordinary life. But, outside again, I found on a nearby terrace a piece of sculpture that evoked the deep dreadfulness we now and then fall into. *The Two Kings*, by Ivor Roberts-Jones, the Welsh sculptor who did the statue of Churchill in Parliament Square, depicts in bronze two figures on a stunted horse. One man, sitting astride, is without arms and feet; his eyes are closed from pain or fatigue. The other, a dead hulk, is stretched athwart the horse's rump. The beast's head is twisted down, as if taking advantage of the lack of mastering . hands to go no further.

The subject of the sculpture comes from *The Mabinogion*. I had found these Celtic tales hard to get into. Story lines are unclear; characters come and go without explanation; magic and realism are confusingly interwoven. One moment the characters are in the real world, the next they are acting supernaturally. Things happen in a weird mist, randomly, fantastically. Cei, we are told of one hero, could be as tall as the tallest tree in the forest 'when it pleased him'. There are long sequences of ordeals, which the listeners to the tales evidently enjoyed. There are frequent orgies of death and slaughter, recounted straightforwardly: Peredur slew the knight. Peredur slew the Addanc. Peredur slew the serpent. Peredur slew the witch.

The Two Kings arises from the story called 'Branwen, daughter of Llyr'. Branwen lived at Harlech at the court of her brother Bendigeidfran or Bran, son of Llyr and 'King of the Island of the Mighty'. The King of Ireland, Matholwch, arrives with thirteen ships. He marries Branwen and takes her home, to great joy. Branwen has a son called Gwern. But then things go wrong. Branwen is driven from the chamber she has shared with Matholwch and suffers abuse. She sends a starling to Wales with a message for her brother, asking for help. Bran, with a host, sails for Ireland. ('. . . and in those days the deep water was not wide. He went by wading . . .') In Ireland there is great and strange bloodshed. Gwern – although invested with the kingship of Ireland by his father – is killed. The sculpture affectingly shows Bran bringing home Gwern's body. However, in the tale, after achieving victory over the Irish and the rescue of Branwen, the Welsh King commands his men to strike off his own head, which 'will be as pleasant company to you as ever it was at best when it was on me', and take it back to be buried. Branwen dies of grief on her return to Wales but nevertheless there is feasting at Harlech for seven years, and an Assembly of the Wondrous Head meets for four score years, and eventually Bran's head is buried in London. I don't think it's the moral of the story but it makes clear that the Welsh were in London before the Londoners were in Wales.

The Nodffa ('Place of Safety') was run by Eric Newton Davies and his wife Gillian. My room had a view of Tremadoc Bay and the Llŷn peninsula beyond. In the trees of the hotel garden, birds were singing, possibly descendants of those in the tale of Branwen who sang to the warriors returned from Ireland. It was the loveliest of songs and apparently went on throughout the seven years of eating and drinking. When I turned on the bedside radio, Radio Eireann from Matholwch's country came in loud and clear.

Over a pre-dinner drink, Mr Davies told me that most of the inns in Harlech were run by ex-Londoners; only a pub called The Queen's had a Welsh proprietor. Although his parents had originally come from Wales, he too had been a Londoner for much of his life, working as a banker in the money markets, and eventually commuting from a home in suburban Essex. The stress of dealing with millions and of commuting made him decide to retire early. He was devoted to archery. What better activity in retirement than running a hotel close to a castle where bows and arrows had once been used? He was now a stalwart member of the Harlech Medieval Society, which arranges jousts and tournaments. The walls of The Nodffa's reception rooms were decorated with ancient bows, swords, and shields. A medieval helmet rested on a hall table.

Mrs Davies made poached salmon for my dinner. At ten p.m. an owl had taken the place of the singing birds and its hoots echoed off the cliff beneath the castle.

No day was exactly like any other – in weather, terrain, small incidents, or points of contact. It was fair but hazy as I set off from Harlech. I had a choice of roads northeastward: the straight main road on the flat reclaimed land of Morfa Harlech or the minor road which followed less directly the lower slopes of a wooded hillside, the former coast. This lesser and less-trafficked road was the one for me. I joined it behind the castle and in half an hour my only notable encounter was transient, with a Marston's Ales truck whose driver gave me a thumbs-up sign and got in return a wave. The National Trust owns a section of these woods called Coed Llechwedd and had put up a sign useful for passers-by – like me – whose curiosity about natural history exceeds their ability to retain botanical and ornithological knowledge. I learnt from this sign that the trees in these woods included ash, rowan, and sycamore. Among the plants and flowers were dog's-mercury, red campion, pignut, cuckoo-pint, wood-anenome, and opposite-leaved golden saxifrage. Some of the birds I might see – though I might not identify them – were redstarts, pied flycatchers, and chiffchaffs. I hoped to be able to know the herons, tawny owls, wood-peckers, and warblers if I saw them.

My first problem of the day was a tall gate, chained shut and slanting inconveniently out at the top. This barred access to a track I wanted to take up through the woods. It was the sort of barrier a packless person would have found less trouble than I

did, leaning heavily back about thirty degrees from the
vertical as I hauled myself slowly over it. Although the
footpath beyond was marked on my map, the chained gate
had perhaps deterred recent users; the track uphill became
indistinct. I reached an old wall of moist, moss-covered rocks
– no longer *dry* stone. Which side of the wall did the track go? I
picked wrong, and after several hundred yards had to climb
over the wall, which was about five feet high and bulged out
at the top. It was a feat for which the slanting gate had
somewhat prepared me but also involved digging the toes of
my boots into the cracks and seeking firm handholds on the
slimy and often wobbly stones. The noise I made descending
the far side surprised a furry black-and-white animal, probably a badger, which had been on the point of surfacing from a
hole at the base of a tree. Hearing me, he went down again. I
also sent up a partridge. A few sheep, grazing away from their
colleagues in a nearby clearing, ignored my embarrassment. I
felt I was the first person to have come this way for a long time
– maybe a century. In places trees had fallen over the path,
such as it was. For a stretch the path became a small muddy
stream. I found the most surefooted walking was where the
water was, disclosing stones on which I could step, rather than
alongside the rivulet where the grass hid slippery patches and
boggy depths. Toward the top of the hillside I crossed a field
which – I realised in the last few yards of my passage – had a
black bull in it, his gaze firmly fixed on me.

Midmorning found me above the woods on a narrow
country lane, stone walls on either side. I stepped into a
gateway to let a red Royal Mail van drive past. In the
adjacent meadow bales of hay were being loaded on to
tractor-drawn wagons. I came upon three workmen in
yellow dungarees chatting with a lady at her cottage gate,
and as I approached they began to thrust their spades into
the grass which was encroaching on the tarmac of the lane at
the base of the wall. 'We're widening the road for you,' one
of them said to me with a laugh, as I edged by – he was

probably relieved that I was not a representative of highways'
officialdom. This was near Eisingrug, the Germanic sort of
name for a hamlet of (as far as I could see) two cottages and
a stone house – Maes-y-Neuadd – which had been turned
into a country hotel.

From here I followed the little valley of the Afon-y-Glyn.
The river on the far side from me was flanked by small crags
and cliffs, furry with shrubs growing from them. On the
hillsides roundabout the map showed a profusion of old
settlements and stones, and the lane itself had a well-worn
feeling. Neolithic and Bronze Age feet had walked this way.
Where the lane passed around the top of a pretty pond,
surrounded by natural lawns dotted with fine trees, an
enterprising person had fastened to a tree a sign: PRIVATE
LAND – PARKING 40p. But no sign of anyone to collect the
fee. From this pond, near Llandecwyn, I took an old drovers'
way eastwards around the north end of a range of nobbly
mountains. There were what looked like caves in the hillside
cliffs and several long-abandoned farm buildings. The landscape, benign a mile or so back, suddenly seemed lonely.
Despite the derelict farm buildings, it was as if people hadn't
turned up here yet; the ice age glaciers had only just retreated.
So I started with surprise at the sound of a car engine behind
me. I stepped aside to let a battered Volkswagen labour past,
with a windsurfing sailboard lashed on top. The map indicated that this was a dead-end way for vehicles. But the map
also showed not far from here a lake and reservoir, Llyn
Tecwyn Uchaf, although apparently without road access
from this direction. I didn't see the VW again. No doubt,
having struggled up here, this mountain sailor would not be
put off by the need to make a half-mile portage. If not
exactly what Major Tilman had aspired to, it struck me as
an instance of a similar sporting obsession. Windsurfers do it
standing up on the most remote lakes of Wales.

After that I had the track to myself again, apart from a
herd of Welsh black cattle grazing near a lake named Llyn

Llenyrch. There was no fence or wall between them and me, but the bulls had cows to keep them docile (I hoped). To the north the ground was covered with a recent plantation of firs. To the south were the bare peaks of the Rhinogs, a desolate Cambrian (in a geological sense) range of mountains on which wild goats are occasionally seen, nibbling the heather and bilberries. To the east I could just make out the top end of the huge lake of Trawsfynydd, to which I was heading. I paused for lunch, with a flat rock to sit on, and another upright rock behind me to lean against; the sun was shining; all was well in this particular part of the Welsh world. Or so I thought until the sound of an explosion reverberated from the east. I recalled a sign in the Harlech tourist office Diana had drawn to my attention: a year-old 'Notice to Walkers' warning of possibly hazardous blasting and construction work at the top end of Llyn Trawsfynydd.

I headed on. The track ended at a farm. The way ahead was through a muddy yard that lay between a simple farmhouse and some ramshackle outbuildings from which half a dozen sheepdogs set up a barking chorus when they heard me coming. Beyond the farm, the path forked. I took the right-hand branch toward the construction cranes that now appeared at the north-west corner of the Trawsfynydd lake. The going got difficult. The path, downhill toward some woods, disappeared. I had to negotiate several closely stranded barbed-wire fences. I came down to a stream and crossed it on wide-spaced stones near the place where it joined a river that ran fast in a deep gorge from the lake. From the wooded sides of the gorge a cuckoo called. I was now ascending again and came out of the woods over a stone stile on to open heath. A hundred yards away, men in hard hats were pouring concrete into wooden shuttering for what appeared to be a new dam being built just downstream of another dam. A fence blocked my approach, and I hailed two men who appeared to be surveyors. One gestured that I

should follow the fence around the west end of the construction works. The other shouted, 'Look out for the crocodiles!'

I soon saw what he meant. The way along the fence led
through a morass, soft wet mud that would have swallowed
me knee-deep. There was nothing for it but to retreat. I
made a wide, clod-hopping detour to the west end of the
new dam where I found a footbridge running across it, open
to the public, and a sign: BLASTING IN PROGRESS. DO NOT
PROCEED IF RED FLAG IS IN POSITION. No Red Flag. I walked
out over the works and looked down into the deep and
narrow gorge. I asked a young man coming from the other
side what was happening.

'We're building a new, stronger dam,' he said – the thick
accent was, I decided, Glaswegian. 'Once we've got it
finished, we'll lower the old one.' The old one, behind us,
was holding back the huge lake, created in the 1920s to
supply a hydro-electric plant several miles down the gorge
and well-suited to cool the nuclear power station built beside
the lake in the early 1960s.

I asked him what the working language was on the site.

'Welsh,' he said. 'I'm picking some of it up.' He looked at
my backpack and added, with a smile, 'You should've
brought your fishing-rod. The lake's well stocked.'

I walked back to the end of the dam from which I'd come
and proceeded counter-clockwise around the lake. From the
track along the western shore the huge power station came
into view. Three great boxes of light brown concrete, two
upright, one lying on its side, rose behind a lagoon at the
north-east corner of the lake. Although the generating
authority claims to have made every effort to blend the
buildings with their surroundings, and employed Sir Basil
Spence – the notable architect (of, among other things, the
post-war rebuilding of Coventry Cathedral) – and Sylvia
Crowe, a distinguished landscape architect, the result is still
a confrontation. What is this mammoth plant doing here?
Unlike Harlech Castle, which seems to grow out of its rocky

base, Trawsfynydd power station looks plumped down from the sky. Perhaps it got here by magic, like the Stonehenge stones which Merlin conveyed from Preseli to Wiltshire.

The apparent magic of changing nuclear reaction into electricity is a matter here of transferring the fission-generated heat through carbon dioxide gas to boilers which produce steam to drive turbines which in turn drive alternators. Although the electricity produced at Trawsfynydd is sufficient to power a city of Cardiff's size, the magic has lost some of the allure it might have had when the station went 'on stream' in 1965. Since then there has been the accident at Three Mile Island in Pennsylvania in 1979, and the disaster at Chernobyl in 1986. (The release of radioactivity from the Soviet power station contaminated many square miles of sheep-grazing hillside in northern Britain and North Wales. At this time a number of Snowdonia farms were still producing lambs that had to be marked with indelible dye because they had been tested as having absorbed in the grass they had eaten too much Caesium 137 – a radioactive isotope from the Chernobyl cloud. Then they had either to be taken to safe lowland pastures until the caesium was flushed out of their systems or sold as unfit for human consumption.) In 1988, it was announced that Trawsfynydd power station would have its cooling systems tested, to make sure they were safe. But the Central Electricity Generating Board called off this test in the face of public anxiety. People thought, despite official assurances, that *something would go wrong*. That same year, higher than expected levels of radioactivity were found in the water at the north-east end of the lake, close to the plant. There was a suggestion for a time of a second nuclear plant being built here, but this now looks unlikely, as the real cost of nuclear power – including the cost of decommissioning the reactors and disposing of the nuclear waste – is taken into account. The present power station is now due to be phased out in 1995 and not replaced.

Forty-five minutes of fast walking down to the bottom

end of the lake and across a footbridge brought me to the village of Trawsfynydd, tucked between the south-eastern corner of the lake and the main road north from Dolgellau. In the one street that winds through the village I paused – conscious of my backpack – by a statue of a youngish man striding along with a knapsack on his back. According to a plaque, this was Hedd Wynn, the 'bardic' name of Ellis Evans, a local poet who was killed in Flanders in 1917 and was shortly afterwards posthumously awarded the Chair at the National Eisteddfod. The Great War as always prompts in me a basic grumpy guilt: that by the good fortune of some forty years' difference in dates of birth, men like me died instead of me in those dreadful trenches; and it prompts, too, the chronic reflection that even poets and walkers weren't spared. I walked on past the post office, the health clinic, the Co-op foodstore, and the library, and went into a small shop that sold hardware and garden tools – an 'ironmongers', as was, though nothing made of iron was visible. I bought a battery for my pocket flashlight (carried in my backpack in case of being benighted), replaced the old battery, and clicked it on to make sure it was working.

The woman who served me, a petite blonde in her late thirties, had been talking in English, with an English accent, to a dark-haired pale-faced woman of similar age who spoke with a Welsh accent. As I paid for the battery, I asked what it was like living with the nuclear power station so close by. The lady of the shop said that she and her husband had come here only recently from Devon; the power station had worried them while they were considering whether to buy the shop; but, now that they had done so and were living here, they had ceased to worry about it.

Her other customer, the Welsh woman, said, 'I've lived here for seventeen years and I still don't like it. I think all the time of the children's health and their safety if something happened. The power station has divided families around here. It's like a civil war between those who support it and those who hate it. You see, it employs about six hundred, at good wages, and probably another four hundred jobs in the area depend on it. When Traws closes down it's going to make a big hole in the local economy and our lives. And yet there isn't a farmer around here who won't be glad to see the end of it. You can't look at it without thinking about Chernobyl. There are some that still can't sell the milk of their cows because of that radiation. On our farm, we've had to scan the lambs every time they were to be taken to market. For a while, lots didn't pass. Thank God, they're all being scanned clear again now.'

I joined the main road and walked along the wide verge, buffeted by the bow waves of air from passing trucks. This was both the A470 and Sarn Helen again. Near the top of the lake, close to the power station, which let out a low, dense hum, I turned off on a path which ascended a hillside to the Roman fort of Tomen-y-Mur. The path took me under transmission cables that sizzled and crackled as they carried electricity eastwards from the power station. I stepped quickly beneath the high cables, fearing the lethal pulse of the current – though it didn't seem to bother the sheep grazing on the ground below. The tall steel pylons which carried the cables looked like the skeletons of captive giants, roped together in a procession across the hills. There were not only sheep up here but many rabbits, who scampered away at my approach. I thought about rabbit casserole and wondered how the Romans had caught them.

I reached the remains of the fort and climbed the highest and most steeply banked part of a double mound that was surrounded by a ditch and stone wall. Pennant, my chief authority for the spot, says Tomen-y-Mur means 'the mount within the wall . . . Coins and urns are frequent about this place'. In the ruins of the Roman camp, he adds, an inscription was found indicating that 'thirty-nine feet of the wall was built by the Century of Ardesus'. The present mound is now thought to be a Norman motte set on the old Roman

position. The view from it continues to be extensive: of the
Rhinogs; the lake and the power station; the road in both
directions; and other earthworks which are the remains of an
amphitheatre or cockpit and of exercise grounds. The fort
was part of the communications network set up by Julius
Agricola when he was governor of Britain. It guarded the
junction of the road from the south with the roads that came
from the more important forts in North Wales at Segontium
(near present day Caernarfon) and Canovium (near Conwy.)
In AD 77, the Ordovices, who had been fighting a guerrilla
war from these mountains, slaughtered the best part of a
Roman cavalry regiment. A year later Agricola led an assault
on the Ordovices and in turn annihilated most of the tribe.
Although the post at Tomen-y-Mur was gradually improved
to include such facilities as a bathhouse, what strikes the
visitor – even on a fine May afternoon – is how exposed the
spot is. On a raw, wet winter's day, the soldiers of Ardesus's
Century, in the Twentieth 'Valeria Victrix' Legion, may
well have complained about this particular posting.

The spot had Celtic significance, too. In one of *The
Mabinogion* tales, the young Lord of Gwynedd, Lleu Llaw
Gyffes, established a court here. Unfortunately, he was fool-
ish enough to be tempted by his faithless wife Blodeuwedd
into telling her how, despite his magical powers, he could be
slain. (This involved the use of a poisoned spear, made at the
time of Sunday mass, while our hero was taking a bath from
a river bank.) Sure enough, Lleu was killed by Blodeuwedd's
lover while bathing in the river Cynfael, a mile or so from
Tomen-y-mur. But the tale had, supernaturally, a happy
ending. Lleu flew up in the form of an eagle. The wizard
Gwydion turned Blodeuwedd into an owl and Lleu back
into a human being. Lleu, fully restored, killed Blodeuwedd's boyfriend . . .

Downhill from the fort again I walked along a railway
track which ran close to the main road. A glance at my map
had led me to think this was a disused line, and as I stepped

from tie to tie it was a while before downward observation produced the thought: These are new, recently creosoted sleepers. Moreover, these rails are not as rusty as they would be if no trains ran on them. I stepped quickly off and walked on the stone chippings to one side of the track. The trains that run here must carry materials – nuclear-fuel flasks or nuclear waste, perhaps – to or from the power station; the track connects with the railway network at Blaenau Ffestiniog about six miles to the north.

I rejoined the main road and took the first turning north-westward through the village of Gellilydan, where every dog seemed to be barking. I was hot. The final few miles were the hard ones. But at last the winding back road brought me to Maentwrog, a one-street village full of old dark-stone houses. As I walked down this quiet thorough-fare, a lady exercising her spaniel said to me with arresting familiarity, '*He* doesn't get on with that terrier up there.' She pointed at a nearby garden gate through which a small dog was poking its head, and growling defensively. I said that perhaps the heat was making her dog bad-tempered. 'Well,' she said, an apparent solution making her cheeful, '*he's* getting a haircut next week.'

CLIMBING FOR A VIEW

MAENTWROG! FOR THE first time on this trip, a bit of Wales that had strong associations for me. Thirty-seven years ago – I was twenty-one – I'd come here during my last university summer vacation. The prime object was to do some reading for my final year exams. Plans that I had had to go to Spain with a girl from Vassar had suddenly evaporated when she announced that she was going home to New York to marry an old boyfriend before he went to serve in Korea. Several dons at my college were offering reading parties in attractive country houses, but a disadvantage of these was that one would probably be not only in the constant company of one's tutors but of one's over-industrious contemporaries, who were barely tolerable in the less confined circumstances of college in term-time. A friend named Roger Chadwick, first met during National Service and re-encountered at Oxford, proposed that I join him for a month in a cottage in North Wales, borrowed from a distant relative. There we could have a reading party of our own. We would walk a lot. I could get over the girl from Vassar.

The cottage, named Bron Merion, had once been a hill-farmer's home. It stood on an unpaved track a mile from a back road. It had electricity but no piped water. Running water, however, was in abundance – in a small stream that passed along the edge of the front garden, which we used for washing, and in a spring a few hundred yards uphill behind the house, which we used for drinking. There was an outdoor privy. Bron Merion was high enough up the hillside to be much of the time in cloud. I would open a window and the cloud drifted in like stage-smoke. But now and then the opaque saturated air cleared and we could look out over the descending rugged slopes to the Irish Sea. The remoteness of the spot – about four miles from Maentwrog and two from a hamlet named Rhyd – was emphasised by the single emissary from civilisation who made his way there. This welcome individual combined the duties of postman, milkman, and delivery man for the butcher and grocer, and several times a week he pushed his bicycle up the track with mail and provisions for us.

Roger and I actually did some reading and note-taking at Bron Merion in the mornings and evenings. Afternoons we walked the mountains. The nearest, Cnicht and Foel Ddu, struck me as altogether less comforting than the hills I knew best, the green downs of Hampshire and the Isle of Wight. These North Wales heights were old and worn and on a larger scale. In another age giants or titans might have dwelt in them. They still held mysteries. Here – I felt – be dragons. It was on our return one afternoon from an exploration of the flanks of Cnicht that I met my first Welsh farmer. Roger and I were sauntering back to Bron Merion across some open hillside which did not strike us as anybody's property in particular. A tractor appeared, rumbling toward us. An elderly man driving it brandished a shotgun and shouted 'Devils!' and 'English!' These were apparently the only English words he knew and may have been synonymous. We turned tail.

On Saturday afternoons we walked downhill to Maentwrog. The village sits on the south side of the Vale of Ffestiniog, which Pennant described as 'composed of rich meadows; the sides edged with groves . . . Barren precipitous mountains close this gem, as it were, in a rugged case.' Through the salubrious vale the gentle Dwyryd river runs toward the sea. On the north side of the river is an estate

called Plas Tan-y-Bwlch, once owned by the Oakeley
family, surrounded by great oaks, beeches, and even red-
woods. The Oakeleys – who also ran slate quarries – built
embankments to control the river and reclaim the valley.
They owned Maentwrog. They eventually gave their name
to an old country hotel, formerly The Caen Coed Inn, which
stands near the entrance to Plas Tan-y-Bwlch – The Oakeley
Arms.

Here Roger and I came for our weekly baths. Here we had
our weekly grand meal. We sat in the bar, scrubbed pink and
glowing, and talked with the gentlemen anglers who fished
the river. At closing time, we walked the long walk back to
Bron Merion, singing army songs and snatches of Gilbert and
Sullivan. Now I hummed 'the Ruler of the Queen's Navee'
from *Pinafore* as I walked past The Grapes, a substantial-
looking hostelry in Maentwrog's street, noting it as a fall-
back position should The Oakeley Arms be full or, God
forbid, no longer in business. It was roughly five-thirty
when I crossed the fine stone bridge over the Dwyryd and
saw at the base of a wooded hillside that The Oakeley Arms
was still there.

It was there, but different. Despite the tendency of time to
make things in memory seem larger, I'd remembered it as
smaller, and also as overhung by trees and set right next to
the road rather than well back from it, as it was now.
Perhaps that was because Roger and I had always arrived at
the side, down the lane from Rhyd, and had gone in
promptly without admiring the façade from a distance. But
the road layout had changed as well, the main road having
been widened and moved well away from the front of the
inn, so that one was better able to see all the extensions and
outbuildings. I entered by the front door. No one was
around, so I pushed a buzzer outside a door marked 'Office'.
The same problems of dissociation and awryness persisted.
The interior somehow wasn't as I thought it should be.
Stairs, reception rooms, corridors, all failed to raise a

response in my memory. It was like waking from an
absorbing dream, which one wanted to recall and out of
which one therefore sought to summon up fragments and
images to help one return to; but the clues here seemed to be
for a completely different dream.

'*Noswaith dda.*' The woman who appeared greeted me
brusquely. Not yet middle-aged, she wore her hair in a long
pigtail and looked as though someone had recently made her
cross. However, a room was available, which she showed
me. When I declared the bed was too soft, she led me to
another room whose bed met my fussy criteria. (When I
mentioned my back, there was a hint – the merest twitch of
face muscles – that she might at some point concede a smile.)
The second room was spacious, unmolested by modernisers;
it had period mouldings and old wallpaper, no flimsy par-
titions or plastic shower cabinets. And if the blessed failure
to improve could also have been seen as fading into neglect
(a stubbed-out cigarette remained in a bedside ashtray), I
weighed the neglect as less crucial. I emptied the ashtray in
the toilet along the hall and ran myself a bath. I hoped the
steam and hot water would help me decide whether this
same bathroom had been the scene for my Saturday immer-
sions thirty-seven years before. But they didn't.

It was annoying. Downstairs, in one of the two bars (one
a private 'snug', the other larger and public), the problem
persisted: I remembered only one bar. I pride myself on my
power of recall, my ability to recollect over forty or fifty
years the way rooms fit together in a building I spent some
time in, and to be able to bring to mind where objects were
placed or what the wallpaper looked like. But perhaps four
or five visits to The Oakeley Arms hadn't provided enough
wherewithall for remembrance now. Why then was I so
bothered that the doors of memory refused to swing open
easily? I walked around the ground floor, pondering. There
were dark areas, and I turned some lights on. In the residents'
lounge, a vacuum cleaner had been abandoned in the middle

of the floor, as if news of Pompeian scale had abruptly halted housework.

I made my way to the public bar, where the young long-haired barman served me a pint of Bass and said, 'That's eighty-five pence.'

I gave him the exact change.

'*Eighty-five,*' he said.

'That's right,' I said, pointing to the coins.

'Ah – I mean ninety-five.'

Perhaps (a tolerant thought) the price had recently risen, and he was still adjusting to it, the eye seeing one thing while his voice said another. Perhaps the coin of the realm was in some ways a foreign currency. The woman with the pigtail kept shouting for him, in Welsh, and appending his name – 'Ion!' In the room next to this bar young men were playing at a billiard-table, while others fed coins into machines which whirred and clicked galactically or now and then clattered forth a few coins as a reward. Hadn't the owner *back then* been a major? Weren't there copies lying around of *Country Life* and *The Field*? Now, on the walls of the bar, framed photographs of boxers were hung. Several people sitting in the bar seemed to be from cars that had simply stopped at this point on a journey. The Oakeley Arms was now a roadhouse. And yet I wondered if my recollection of the inn was distorted. Perhaps Roger and I, coming down from our stark life in the clouds at Bron Merion, had assumed for The Oakeley Arms a charm and distinction it had never had.

Ion brought a steak-and-kidney pie to my small table in the bar. There had been an elderly waiter. Could the dining-room have been where the games room was now? A young woman with a purple streak in her hair entered, looked around the bar, and went out again. I suddenly remembered sitting in the bar one night with Roger and some fishermen guests – it must have been the other, smaller bar – when a woman came in, creating a bit of a stir. She was in her forties, with tangled hair. She wore a dusty-looking coat,

carried a cloth bag crammed lumpily, and approached the
bar in a way that was at once shy and defiant, as though she
might have been expecting to be refused service. She asked
for a half-pint of shandy. After consulting a menu, she
ordered some food. When she had gone into the dining-
room, carrying her drink, the Major – who had been
standing at the bar – said to Roger and me, 'The question is,
has she got the money to pay for it?' Apparently she was a
stranger. The next arrival was a man who might have been a
bank manager or solicitor and was clearly a regular customer.
While this man – let's call him Roberts – went through the
dining-room to the men's toilet, the Major set up his usual
whisky. When Roberts returned, he was looking worried.
He said, 'That woman – the one on her own in the dining-
room.'

'Bets are being taken on whether she can pay,' said one of
the anglers, ungallantly.

'How long has she been here?' Roberts went on.

'Oh, five minutes or so,' said the Major.

Roberts picked up his whisky and took a reflective sip.

'What's the matter?' asked the Major.

'I've just driven from Ffestiniog.' He turned to Roger and
me. 'There are two roads you can take down the valley to
here from the bridge at Talybont – the road north of the
river which winds around a bit and the main road south of
it, which is faster. I used the main road.'

His audience took this in.

'The thing is – I saw that woman, twenty minutes ago,
just before I reached the bridge. I drove past her. She was
walking this way. No other car overtook me on the road
here.'

We looked at one another. The Major said, 'There is the
upper road. In distance, there's not much in it.'

Roberts said, 'It swings well around the back of this place.
And she got here before me.'

'Maybe she got a lift in a sports car,' said Roger.

'Are you sure it was her?' asked the Major.

'It was,' said Roberts. 'As my car approached, she turned and looked at it – she looked at me. The headlights lit her up.'

The subject lapsed. The Major wanted to know how Roger had enjoyed doing his National Service in Hong Kong. Perhaps forty minutes went by before the elderly waiter came in and beckoned to the Major, who went over for a quiet word. When the Major returned, he said, 'Well, this is a new one. Owen tells me she asked for the bill. She had one dish that wasn't on the set meal, but he didn't charge her for it. Decided she was hard up. Good old Owen! Anyway, the bill he gave her, including the half of shandy, was for eighteen shillings and seven pence. She got out an old purse and emptied all the money on the table. She counted it out, coin by coin. It came to eighteen shillings and seven pence. Not a ha'penny over.'

'Is she still here?' asked Roberts, straightening his back as if repressing a shiver.

'No. She's gone.'

Roberts said, 'I wouldn't be surprised if she was in Harlech by now.'

As I went to bed at The Oakeley Arms, I thought of Roger and me walking back to Bron Merion that night. We must have sung with more than our usual gusto in order to hold at bay the surrounding darkness and the strange spirits abroad in Wales.

It was a perfect morning. Turning my back on the limpid Vale of Ffestiniog, I followed the minor road Roger and I used to take uphill toward Rhyd. This led me past the gatehouses guarding one of the drives up to Plas Tan-y-Bwlch, the Oakeley mansion that is now a study centre for the Snowdonia National Park. Travelling in these parts in the 1830s, Thomas Roscoe visited Plas Tan-y-Bwlch and was impressed by 'magnificent specimens of the rhododendron, of nearly thirty years' growth, and more than forty yards in circumference'. 160 years later, one of the main problems of the National Park being studied here is the rhododendron – specifically *rhododendron ponticum*, the purple-pink flowering shrub which was brought to Britain from the Mediterranean in the eighteenth century and planted in the gardens of numerous country houses like this one. The lovely rhododendron enjoys high rainfall and poor, acidy soil. And it has turned out to be a demon coloniser. One flower head produces between 3000 and 7000 seeds a year; one large shrub may produce several million seeds. These are widely dispersed by the wind. Once established, even in soil only an inch or so deep, the shrub is hard to eradicate. Cut fiercely down to ground-level stumps, it soon shoots forth new growth. Uprooting it may get rid of the shrub but endangers the topsoil, which thus loosened is easily washed away. The rhododendron is now occupying more and more of Snowdonia, making life impossible for other trees and other shrubs, and restricting the grazing of animals. Its dense shade creates conditions in which no other plants will grow. It is poisonous for most mammals, birds, and insects – and hence whole chains of life are wrecked by it. No heather, bilberries, bluebells, ferns, toadstools; no pied flycatchers, wheatears, woodpeckers, wrens, buzzards; no voles, shrews, and woodmice.

For the moment none of these deadly beauties were visible among the handsome roadside trees; the invaders had apparently been repelled from the place that had first welcomed them. A sign put up by the National Trust, which owns some of the land on the north side of the road, informed the passerby that these woods were 'largely sessile oak, relicts of once widespread woodlands of Wales'. I walked alongside Llyn Mair, a small, tree-enclosed lake, with a number of duck and little grebe swimming on its green leaf-reflecting waters. Mair was the name of a girl from the Welsh north coast town of Rhyl whom I met while in the army at Eaton Hall. We went dancing. I wrote at least one poem because of her. Although I would be reluctant to read that verse again, the name Mair still conjured up for me the giddy feelings one has for girls at nineteen.

I passed under a bridge of the Ffestiniog Railway. This narrow-gauge line had once been used for transporting slates from Blaenau Ffestiniog to Porthmadog on the coast. Closed when Roger and I were in these parts, it had since been revived by volunteers, and I hoped to have a look at the operation when I reached Porthmadog. I stayed with the road to Rhyd, half a dozen houses and no longer a village store. At one spot I could see well up the rough old slopes of Cnicht, which mountaineers call the Matterhorn of Wales, and to the even higher peak of Moelwyn Bach, on whose lower flanks I thought Bron Merion must have stood. But these were extensively swaddled with conifers, which changed the landscape annoyingly. I'd been sure I would see the cottage and recognise it. Now there were all these look-alike trees.

Disappointed, I turned south-west on an old foot track downhill to the town of Penrhyndeudraeth. The sun was hot. I changed to a lighter shirt. The hillside was bumpy, with close-cropped turf between patches of lichen-covered smooth grey rock and a million bluebells just waking up. As I came over a brow of the hill I had a view of the blue Glaslyn estuary with the tide up. My path ran through a plantation of dead trees, twelve to twenty feet tall – their grey trunks apparently charred by fire. The path then descended alongside the Ffestiniog railway, whose narrow single track lay between sharp-topped stone walls. As I walked downhill a train came huffing and puffing uphill from Penrhyndeudraeth. It was being hauled by a curious-looking double locomotive – a push-me pull-you engine with a boiler and stack at each end (the stacks belching charcoal-grey smoke) and a double driver's cab, facing front and back and articulated in the middle. The driver tooted his horn as he passed and a few passengers looked out from the ascending carriages at the walker with his backpack.

Then Penrhyndeudraeth, its slate roofs gleaming like alligator scales. At a railway crossing on the edge of the little town, the bearded gate-keeper wore a bright yellow bib to make him visible to traffic. When I asked about the trains, he fetched a timetable for me from his tiny hut beside the track. 'If you're going tomorrow, remember it's Sunday, so there's no ten-forty-five from Porthmadog,' he said. On the right hand side of the street many of the residents had left their front doors open to let in the morning sunshine. On one front step a black Labrador stood, wistfully watching me pass and clearly wishing he was going for a walk. (This, at any rate, is a sample of a dog-owner's feelings after a few weeks away from his own dog.) One doorway in the town centre had a brass plaque announcing the modest offices of the Snowdonia National Park, so I knocked and went in. I asked some questions, and Marion Rees, an elegant blonde woman who was the Park authority's information officer, gave me some answers.

Snowdonia, she said, was one of ten national parks in England and Wales, of which Wales has three. It was one of the first national parks to be so designated, in 1951, an area of 840 square miles of mountainous north-west Wales reaching out to the less developed parts of the coast. Its objects still are to preserve natural beauty, provide access for people to the countryside, and help maintain the local way of life – though there can be conflicts between those demands. The Park has its own planning department which attempts to encourage appropriate building in the area and prevent what Marion Rees called 'madcap developments'. It tries to look after those parts of the Park that are under pressure from visitors – half a million people on Snowdon every year – and it tries to look out for the visitors who get into trouble, on the beaches and peaks. Its wardens rescue walkers who become lost and injured, and they recover sheep that now and then get stranded on mountain ledges.

'We have a difficult balancing act to perform,' Marion Rees continued. 'A national park pursues an ideal of conservation and public enjoyment, but it also needs to ensure a functioning community. One of our problems is that many people involved in tourism here don't have deep roots in the area. Some want developments that are just too big. Not a car park for fifty cars but one for two thousand. We have about a thousand abandoned mines and quarries. If the price of those minerals goes up, there may be pressure to re-open them – but we have to take into account dust, noise, and waste. We have to protect hill-farming – it's the bedrock of Welsh culture, and it can't be diversified. If you're not careful, you've frittered away your true heritage. We have problems with applications for theme parks set up at old mines – we've turned down an application for a cable-car operation to get visitors in and out at one because of the

effect on the landscape. But of course tourists are important.
We want people to come and walk and climb and breathe
our air – and about eleven million visit this part of Wales
every year. We also want to improve the chances of jobs for
our young, who will otherwise move away. We need small
factories to handle products like meat and wood, which we
grow. We have about twenty-five thousand people living in
the Park. We used to be able to say that nine out of ten were
Welsh-speakers, but we are getting more and more retired
people who are mostly English. The Welsh Office recently
declared that when we consider planning applications the
effect of the proposal on the Welsh language can be a factor.
That's a step forward. Our blood – our Celtic blood – is still
something to contend with. Considering everything, I think
it says a lot for us Welsh that we're still here and not letting
the outside world roll over us.'

It was just a bit too early for lunch in Penrhyndeudraeth and
I stepped quickly along the road westward. I passed through
the little village of Minffordd, notable for having two train
stations, handily adjacent – one for British Rail's Cambrian
Coast line, the other for the Ffestiniog railway, whose track
is carried over BR's by a bridge. Past Minffordd I turned
south along a lane which led through parkland – rhododendrons flourishing – and past a castellated mansion called
Castell Deudraeth to Portmeirion, a folly village.

Portmeirion arouses strong emotions, for and against. Mr
Davies at The Nodffa in Harlech had mentioned the recently
refurbished Portmeirion Hotel and snorted, 'A hundred
pounds a night!' Marion Rees had said, 'Oh, you have to go
there.' Admission – £1.90 – is charged to enter the village
which was the offspring of Sir Clough Williams-Ellis, architect and sailor. Claiming descent from Grufydd ap Cynan, a
prince of Gwynedd who built the original Castell Deudraeth
here (mentioned by Gerald), he bought from an uncle land
on this then overgrown headland in 1925. Williams-Ellis was

a practising architect from 1904 to 1978, when he died; he was an early supporter of the garden city movement and the first chairman of Stevenage, one of the new towns built to take London 'overspill'. To some, in the words of *The Times*'s obituary, he was 'his own best work'. He used to dress in plus-fours, yellow stockings, yellow waistcoat, and brash bow-tie. Portmeirion, only slightly less flamboyant, was built in two stages, pre- and post-Second World War, and though first inspired by Portofino in Italy, came to embody various styles and structures that took Sir Clough's fancy. All represented what he called his 'light-opera approach' to architecture. Escapist might be another term. Working to a larger scale than the enthusiast on the Corris hillside, he collected buildings – had them taken apart, removed to Portmeirion, and there reassembled. He liked to paint them in pastel mediterranean colours, yellows, pinks, and blues, which are a surprise this far north. The last structure he acquired was a colonnade, brought in from Bristol, which he got the philosopher Bertrand Russell to open at a ceremony in 1957.

From the start, Sir Clough invited friends and the theatrical quality of the place attracted numerous visitors. The Duke of Windsor often stayed at Portmeirion in the 1930s. Noel Coward came by train in May 1941 with a woman friend, Joyce Carey (no relation to the novelist Joyce Cary), who was writing a play about Keats. Coward wrote later:

> We arrived on a golden evening, sighed with pleasure at the mountains and the sea in the late sunlight, and settled ourselves into a pink guesthouse. The next morning we sat on the beach with our backs against the sea wall and discussed my idea exclusively for several hours. Keats, I regret to say, was not referred to. By lunchtime the title had emerged together with the names of the characters, and a rough, very rough, outline of the plot. At seven-thirty the next morning I sat, with my usual nervous

palpitation, at my typewriter . . . The table wobbled and
I had to put a wedge under one of the legs. I smoked
several cigarettes in rapid succession, staring gloomily out
of the window at the tide running out. I fixed the paper
into the machine and started: *Blithe Spirit. A Light
Comedy in Three Acts.*

Coward worked on his play daily from eight to one and
from two to seven. He finished it on the evening of the sixth
day and knew it would be a success. He thereafter cut only
two lines. Five weeks after he finished the play it opened in
Manchester and two weeks later in London. The audience –
Coward noted – had to walk across planks laid over air-raid
rubble in order to get into the theatre to see his light comedy
about death – and there they laughed at his splendid creation
Madame Arcati, who has the power to raise spirits and
manages, disastrously, to bring back Charles Condomine's
deceased wife, Elvira. *Blithe Spirit* ran throughout the war
and into 1946. Coward wrote: 'I am prepared to say . . .
with the maximum of self-satisfaction that those six days in
Portmeirion in May 1941 were not wasted.'

Portmeirion has since been the location for various films
and television programmes, most notably a 1960s thriller
series called *The Prisoner*. This obtained some banal sub-
Piranese effects from the Williams-Ellis *mis-en-scène* and now
provides the basis for an exhibit there. But Portmeirion's
artifice is not inevitably aggravating. As I wandered downhill
through the village I found myself charmed by many things:
no traffic; lots of cobblestones; little gardens, rockeries, and
miniature piazzas; a small campanile (I was reminded of the
even smaller work of the Corris fantasist); the faded but
earth-warm Etruscan red stucco façade of the so-called Town
Hall; a recumbent stone lion; a giant Buddha (left behind by
a film company); and a carved head used to lighten the
earnest practicality of a petrol pump.

I had lunch on the balustraded terrace of the self-service

café. Chaffinches and sparrows flitted through the openings of the balustrade, upon the coping of which a fluffy tortoise-shell cat lay sleeping in the sun. Then I walked the last few yards to a quayside in front of the hotel, where a wedding party was just spilling forth – formal dress; photographer; confetti. The quay looked as if it would be a good place to moor a boat at high tide. Now, the tide was just flooding back over the soft sands from the distant channel. Across the perfect hill-surrounded estuary, Harlech Castle rose on its rocky perch. At the quay Sir Clough's old boat, a black-and-white trading ketch named *Amis Ré-unis*, had found its last resting place – had in fact been filled in and built into the quay, its deck now a stone and cement surface on which the visitor can walk.

As I did so, I felt disturbed by the failure to feel wood – its old springy life – under my feet. I could see how reactions might once again be forcefully prompted here. You might find this petrified vessel amusing, a crowning piece of Williams-Ellis whimsy. Or you might be annoyed that a shell had been preserved from which all purpose and spirit had fled. I stand with those who say that one should – when their sailing life is absolutely done – burn one's boats.

By meandering paths I made my way across the neck of the peninsula on which Portmeirion stands. At one point I took counsel from a farmer who was working on an old Datsun in his yard. 'Turn right at the fence,' he said with a friendly smile. 'Then straight on!' Here were pastures with sheep, small copses, and a wooded hillside awash with bluebells, which flourish in moist climates and old woods. Brimstone butterflies, with yellow undersides, fluttered among the bluebells. The stile over which I climbed to rejoin the main road near Boston Lodge – a station on the Ffestiniog railway – was made of a local material, namely railway sleepers. From there the single-rail track and the road proceeded side by side across a narrow causeway to

Porthmadog. The estuary lay to the south; the Glaslyn river wound down from the mountains to the north.

In the days before this causeway – which locally is called the cob – was built, the river was tidal a good way inland. In the early nineteenth century an enterprising man named William Madocks set about reclaiming much of the river valley and building two towns, Tremadog and Porthmadog. Madocks, of Welsh descent, was a Londoner, a barrister, and a member of parliament. Port Madoc and Tremadoc were the original spellings of the towns named for their founder; but in time versions that are more 'Welsh' have been adopted. Some find further justification for the names in the notion that a former island in the river, now a wooded knoll between Tremadog and Porthmadog, was the spot from which Prince Madog sailed in the twelfth century to reach America. (This voyage, whether actual or legendary, was put to use in Elizabethan times by the scholar, magician, and propagandist John Dee – another London Welshman – who thought it helped with England's claims to the New World, Madog well pre-dating the explorers of Portugal and Spain. Madog's voyage also lay behind the belief that Welsh-speaking Indians – 'the Lost Brothers' – had been found in the form of the Mandan tribe living west of the Missouri river. This belief took hold with the aid of Iolo Morgannwg, the gorsedd enthusiast, and helped encourage early nineteenth-century emigration to the United States from Wales. I don't know if anyone has ever pointed out that the Mandans also had coracles – round wicker boats with hide coverings – though this no more made them of Welsh descent than it did the makers of similar craft in Spain and Iraq.)

Madocks received financial support in his venture from a number of idealistic investors. One was the nineteen-year-old poet Shelley, who with his young wife rented Madock's home, Tan-yr-Allt, near Tremadog. This house was said to have a ghost – a gentleman farmer who wore an eighteenth-century tricorn hat and a long cloak. However, on one

occasion it may well have been a real farmer who was seen.
Certainly Shelley thought someone tried to break into the
house and shoot him. He seems to have made himself
unpopular with the local shepherds by killing (presumably
for compassionate reasons) any sick sheep he found when
out walking.

I set forth across the cob. A faded sign at the toll booth
guarding the way dictated tolls for horses, carriages, convey-
ances, and pedestrians who were to be charged 'a sum not
exceeding two pence'. But although cars now pay five pence
of our reformed decimal currency, pedestrians go free. It
may have been a slight headiness caused by this benefaction
that got the better of me here, for I ignored the fact that the
cob roadway was extremely narrow, had no footpath, and
passing cars were likely to bump my elbow or carry away
my backpack and me entangled with it. Fortunately a
Ffestiniog train came steaming along the raised embankment
and one of the trainmen yelled down at me, 'The footpath is
up here!' I waved an acknowledgement and retreated to the
tollbooth, where I found steps I had missed up to the railway
embankment and path.

Up there was not only safety from traffic and a proximity
to trains but a splendid view of the estuary and the river
valley. Madocks's reclamation scheme had channelled the
Glaslyn more strictly, with a sluice in the cob that kept the
tide out of the upper reaches but allowed the river to flow
through and scour the approach from Cardigan Bay to
Porthmadog deep enough for the schooners which carried
away slates. Even so, at low tide the estuary seems to be
almost entirely sand banks. I walked along daydreaming
about keeping a dory or cat-boat here, in which I would
explore the creeks and rills of the estuary and be not at all
unhappy when, on the ebb, my small craft took the ground
and I was forced to put my feet up or walk on the sands till
the tide turned. The slate trade by sea ended at the beginning

of this century and from what I could see of it Porthmadog harbour was now given over to yachts.

I strolled exceedingly slowly through the terminus of the railway. 'Let your childhood dreams come true,' exhorted a platform poster – and there appeared to be a number of people who were doing just that, whether by waiting for a train or standing entranced by steam, smoke, and clanking sounds from the carriages being shunted into place at the platform. My childhood dreams were unexceptional in this respect – how I miss the 'Caerphilly Castle'! – but for the moment I was firm with them and walked on into Madocks's town, which was full of Saturday afternoon shoppers. It didn't take long to find the Oxfam shop. Here, amid used clothes, kitchen utensils, books, and bric-à-brac being browsed over by customers – elderly ladies for the most part – looking for bargains and examining each item with more care than if it cost a great deal, I was offered a cup of tea by the woman volunteer in charge, whose name was Margaret Reynolds. I took off my backpack and placed it on the floor by the counter. 'Don't put it there!' she said. 'Someone will buy it.'

Margaret had been proposed by her sister, the wife of a friend in Greenwich, as willing to put me up if I got to these parts. She was originally from Scotland and now lived with her two teenage daughters in Criccieth, on the coast six miles west of Porthmadog. Over tea in the tiny back room – part office, part crowded store-cupboard – she told me that she and her former husband had first come to Wales to run an outdoor training centre for London youth. More recently she had been working on a local oral history project for the Caernarfon archives and helping manage this Oxfam shop. She said, with her slight Scots accent which here sounded foreign, 'Oxfam is an extraordinary thing. It needs its helpers and many of its helpers need it. Quite a few doctors prescribe working here as an antidote for loneliness and depression. Naturally we also get some volunteers who just want to play shops. In fact there's a good deal of hard work though we

have our exciting moments. Not long ago a local woman
left us the complete contents of two houses. Yesterday we
sold a clock for a hundred pounds. I wouldn't have had it in
my house it was so ugly, but the chap *wanted* it – and he paid
cash. We're still reeling. We get some things to sell that have
never been used or worn. Most of our customers are women,
and it's amazing the rate at which some of them buy clothes.
But I know this kind of shop can be hard to resist. They're
fun to explore in the hope of making a real find. Of course
one or two customers make a fuss about the cost of objects
we've marked at one pound, and which are probably worth
a lot more. Some even want to haggle. They're not thinking
about where the money will go, to feed people in Ethiopia
and Sudan. We're proud of the fact that this shop made
£47,536 last year.'

I thanked Margaret for the tea and told her I would show
up in Criccieth by early evening. I retrieved my pack from
behind a clothes-rack and resisted the offer from another
woman helper of an only-slightly-used waterproof jacket.
What I needed was a broad-brimmed hat against the sun. It
was a cloudless afternoon, the temperature around eighty
degrees Fahrenheit. (Although we have officially adopted
centigrade in Britain, it is noticeable that when it gets really
warm, everyone reverts to Fahrenheit whose higher figures
are more expressive of great heat.) On my way out of
Porthmadog, I traversed several former slate quays and
passed through a boat-yard where owners were happily
slapping red anti-fouling paint on the bottoms of their craft.
I walked around a cove at Borth-y-Gest where children were
making sandcastles on the dried-out beach and splashing in
tidal pools – it was like a photograph from my own
childhood, half a century ago. I started off around the next
headland by way of the beach but gullies of soft mud sent
me up along a winding path. Rough turf and gorse. I passed
a red woollen cardigan on the ground and a few minutes
later came on three late-middle-aged ladies at the top of the

headland, sitting on the grass and looking out to sea. A
sailing dinghy was drifting up towards Porthmadog on the
flood.

'Anyone lost a sweater?' I asked.

'No,' said one.

'No,' said another.

'Why – yes!' exclaimed the third.

While the grateful owner went to retrieve her cardigan, I
was offered the balky camera of one of her companions as
my next good deed. I attempted to make it wind on or wind
back, but didn't succeed. The path provided good exercise
as little headland followed little bay, with scrambles up and
scrambles down, and there were striking coastal juxtapo-
sitions of unspoilt scenery and caravan parks. I lost my way
in one of these. I asked a bare-chested moustached man in
shorts, who was taking the sun in a deckchair beside his
mobile holiday home, where the continuation of the footpath
was. He got up.

'I'd better show you,' he said. 'It's hard to find.' He led
me on an in-and-out route through the caravans while
explaining that he was an ex-scoutmaster and had hiked the
Pennine Way. He pointed out the overgrown entrance to the
continuing path. He said, 'It gets a bit confusing where it
crosses the golf course, but you'll be OK.'

I was OK, dodging the glares of a few foursomes and
evading a ball that passed not far overhead on its way to the
seventh hole – it was followed by a forlorn, rather tardy cry
of 'Fore!' I kept going through an extensive settlement of
summer cottages and caravans and reached Black Rock
Sands, an immense flat beach. The pleasure of walking over
these firm sands was somewhat moderated by cars, which
had access to the beach, and some of which were being
driven by youths bent on demonstrating why such surfaces
are used for attempts on the world motor-speed records.
Despite these hazards elderly couples were strolling hand in
hand toward the distant water. One stout old gentleman,

crossing my track with a Yorkshire terrier, greeted me with
a hearty West Riding "Ow do.' A young couple, lying on
the sand alongside a bright yellow Mini, had bright yellow
and bright orange hair, both streaked with green. Glory be
to God for dappled things!

At the western end of the Sands I made a detour around
Graig Ddu, the dark rocky headland that gives them their
name. There are caves here and other nearby burial-chambers
that testify to the old popularity of this coast. I walked across
a boggy meadow alongside the British Rail tracks. My
landmark was Criccieth Castle on its short hill a mile or so
to the west, seen in black silhouette with the sharp late-
afternoon sun behind it. It was six-thirty as I came into
Criccieth, which gave the impression of being a well-
behaved, properly-spoken small place. It had a tiny harbour
behind a breakwater, a sequestered little square, and a park
between the castle and station where the elderly residents
were playing bowls on nicely-kept lawns while children –
not too noisily – swung on the swings. I bought some made-
on-the-spot ice cream at a shop called Cadwalladers and a
bottle of Muscadet in a store which combined the functions
of pharmacy and off-licence (an infrequent but sensible
combination). With these offerings, and with a face lobster-
red from the sun, I arrived at the Reynoldses', the end house
of a tall terrace near the station. After a fine supper with
Margaret and her mother, down from Scotland for a stay, I
found my eyes closing as I sat with the Reynolds girls, Fiona
and Alison, watching the televised Eurovision Song Contest.
There was – I determined – no Welsh entry. I have no
memory of who won.

Sunday: a day for leisurely back-tracking. I walked to the castle, which is a good deal more ruined than Harlech's. From a tower flew the Welsh flag – a red dragon on a white and green field. This was a *Welsh* castle from the start and hence simpler than the Anglo-Norman model. The Welsh not only had less money and less skilled labour for such constructions but didn't wish to attract royal attention by building great fortifications. Llywelyn the Great began it around 1230. It was, however, taken over and improved by Edward I, who established the 'borough' at its foot. Glyndŵr captured it in 1404 and then sacked it. An earlier visitor to these parts was the chronicler Gerald, on his way in April 1183 to Nefyn on the north shore of the Llŷn peninsula and as usual avoiding the mountains as best he could. He wrote that at Nefyn he 'discovered the works of Merlin Silvester, which I had long been looking for'. Unlike his predecessor Geoffrey of Monmouth, who was satisfied with one Merlin, Gerald seems to have thought that there were two: one called Merlin Ambrosius, who was associated with Carmarthen in south-west Wales and who made prophecies at the time of Vortigern, the early-fifth-century British king who encouraged the Saxons to settle in England; the other called Merlin Silvester, also a soothsayer but with Caledonian origins, who lived at the time of Arthur nearly a century later, 'went mad . . . and fled to the forest where he passed the remainder of his life as a wild man of the woods'. Gerald doesn't explain how this Merlin's works came to be in Nefyn, although by then the Merlin story – in bits, pieces, or together – had become part of the legendary matter of Wales.

The ruined castle casts an atmospheric shadow over Criccieth (which the Welsh spell Cricieth) but more important for the modern town was the arrival of the railway in 1865. It brought summer visitors, as it did to Barmouth. One such tourist was Rider Haggard, the novelist, who stayed as a paying guest at Morwin House with the family of Richard Lloyd, a shoemaker and Baptist preacher. Here also lodged Richard Lloyd's widowed sister, Elizabeth George, and her son, David Lloyd George. Young Lloyd George had been born in Manchester, where his Welsh father was a schoolmaster, but on his father's death he and his mother returned to live with the Lloyds, first in the village of Llanystumdwy, by the river Dwyfor a little to the west of Criccieth, and then in Criccieth itself in 1880. At the age of sixteen, Lloyd George was articled to a firm of solicitors in Porthmadog. In 1884, just twenty-one, he set up his own practice in Criccieth. He went on to become Member of Parliament for Caernarfon – a position he held for fifty-five years – and Prime Minister from 1916 to 1922. Three months before his death, in March 1945, he was ennobled as Earl Lloyd George of Dwyfor. However, although he kept a home for some years in Criccieth and then a farm near Llanystumdwy, these seemed to be places for his wife Margaret to live, while he stayed at his other house in Surrey. As a radical and liberal politician before the First World War, he gave the impression of believing in Home Rule for Wales as much as for Ireland, but in the course of his long political career the use he made of his own Welshness seems often to have been opportunistic. On one occasion, at a trial in a London law court, he wrote a letter in Welsh, but this was so that lawyers sitting near him couldn't understand what he was writing. His biographer John Grigg says pithily that Lloyd George was 'a man who loved the idea of Wales but rather disliked the reality'.

I caught the train to Porthmadog. I then walked from the British Rail station on the Tremadog road through the town centre to the Ffestiniog railway station at the head of the harbour. I bought a third class return ticket to Blaenau Ffestiniog twelve miles away at the other end of the line. Before boarding one of the red and cream painted carriages, I had a look at the little engine which would be hauling the train. Its name was *Mountaineer*. One of the three men in the cab – their overalls held up by braces – told me that it had been built in the United States; he and his colleagues were volunteers, members of the society which had restored and now operated the railway; others like them, men and women, not only drove the trains but worked the signals and maintained the rolling-stock and track. As for *Mountaineer*, it seemed to have an animal naturalness. Steam like breath was being exuded from various upper ports and valves, while water spurted from orifices beneath. Rectangular watertanks were fastened pannier-fashion on each side of the cylindrical boiler. The tall funnel sent upwards a hearty plume of coal-grey smoke. I dashed back to a carriage when I heard the cry, 'All aboard!'

A young guard with sideburns, a grey waistcoat, and black peaked cap was shutting carriage doors. He would have passed for a soldier in the US Civil War. Another similarly outfitted was checking the couplings between the carriages – a reassuring sight for anyone who remembers movies, often about the same period, in which carriages become uncoupled and roll back down the mountain. I found a window-seat in a well-filled carriage and briefly stuck my head out of the slide-down window. Steam was now bursting forth from *Mountaineer* as from a pressure cooker. The engine's wheels skidded for an instant on the tracks, then caught hold. We lurched forward, rattling and shaking as only a proper steam train seems to, picking up speed across the cob.

The two-foot gauge railway was first opened in 1836, with wagons carrying slate down from Blaenau Ffestiniog under the power of gravity and horses riding along, too, in order to haul the empty wagons back up. But this system couldn't handle the booming slate trade from Porthmadog; Welsh slates were in demand all over Europe, as in Hamburg, for instance, where until the RAF and USAF disturbed them during the Second World War all the roofs were of Welsh slate. Steam locomotives were introduced in 1863 and a passenger service soon followed. In this century the railway declined along with the slate business. It closed in 1939. Its reopening in recent years is a testimony to the power of enthusiasm. Much of the track had to be restored, with a major effort needed to build a new spiral 'deviation' and tunnel to get around a section of the old line that had been flooded by the reservoir of a pumped-storage power station. Women operated power-digging machinery alongside men wielding spades.

My train halted for a few moments at Minffordd, where large trees grew out of the platform and the guard called 'Min – ffordd! Min – ffordd!' Some stations had little gardens full of wallflowers and tulips. Some had posters that put forth a good line in fundamentalist exhortation: 'Be Sure Your Sin Will Find You Out.' In the nearby fields the sheep paid absolutely no attention as the train rattled by. The engine-driver leaned out of his cab as we steamed above the back gardens of Penrhyndeudraeth, and people in the gardens and at the level-crossings looked up and waved; unlike the sheep, they apparently never tired of watching the trains go by. As we rattled onwards and upwards, a young waiter took orders for drinks – he soon brought me a reasonably-priced half pint of beer. (I later realised that Porthmadog is 'dry' on Sundays, but the Ffestiniog Railway's trains are free of such restrictions, which may have accounted for the fairly full load of passengers aboard.) The train also provided ever-changing views: one moment, stone walls close at hand; the next, a far vista across the vale; here a glimpse of Llyn Mair and The Oakeley Arms way below; there an even-further prospect of Trawsfynydd power station. Sometimes there was no view at all except thick woods and steep hillsides right next to the train. At some very sharp bends, as on the new deviation, you could see both the front and the back of the train. Before level-crossings and tunnels there were trackside signs saying WHISTLE and whistle we did. In the tunnels the carriages seemed to fill with smoke and smuts – but apparently not to the stifling extent they did in former days, when a smaller bore allowed little air space around the train and passengers occasionally thought they were about to suffocate.

From a railway booklet I learned that Porthmadog museum housed a special railway van converted to carry bodies down from hill-farms to cemeteries near the line, like that at Minffordd; that the Oakeley family had the right to stop trains at their private halt at Plas Tan-y-Bwlch; and that the watertank near the line above the mansion used to be filled with sea water from a tank-wagon, so that Plas residents could enjoy brine baths. I read that the cottage on the left of the line just past Garnedd Tunnel was once rented as a holiday retreat by H. St John Philby, the famous Arabist and father of Kim, the famous spy. Did they, too, drink at The Oakeley Arms? At Blaenau Ffestiniog, the end of the line, the entire town seemed to be slate, surrounded by slate quarries and mountains of slate-mining debris. I got out with the other passengers and had a five-minute stretch before reboarding the train for the less laborious run back down to Porthmadog.

In recent years Porthmadog's main claim to attention has been that in 1984 it was the epicentre of the most powerful earth tremor to shake the British Isles within living memory.

But very little was jumping in town on this particular Sunday evening. This area of Dwyfor was one of two parts of Wales – indeed, the only two in Europe – that retained a ban on Sunday drinking in pubs, hotels, and restaurants. At this writing it is the only one. At a referendum in November, 1989, when Ceredigion in Dyfed by a narrow margin voted wet, the voters here showed that a majority of them would not be swayed by a campaign of local inn-keepers, seeking the profits lost by Sunday-closing, that proposed that the public should have a new choice in how to spend its leisure time, either with an alcoholic beverage in hand or not. The prior choice remained: if they wanted to, those with their own transport or a train or bus ticket could get out of Dwyfor for a Sunday drink. Those of us on foot, who were unaware of the restriction, had to make a sudden adjustment, as I did in Porthmadog's Harbour Restaurant when I asked for the wine list and received instead a practised recitation from the woman who had already given me the menu. 'Five miles from here you can get a drink . . .' I gathered that a courteous explanation of the local custom, and the suggestion that one could get around it by travelling out of the locality, was generally enough to make the customer set aside his immediate peevish demand, 'Why can't I have what I want?' Some, thwarted and thirsty, might just storm out, but the Harbour Restaurant's lady quickly followed her explanation with an offer of mineral water or juice. I at any rate was overtaken by a trusting and hopeful lassitude, in which smells coming from the kitchen played a part.

Gerald, 800 years ago, noted the frugality and parsimony of the Welsh. 'You must not expect a variety of dishes from a Welsh kitchen,' he wrote. Apparently in lieu of feasting 'they spend the dark and stormy nights in observing the movements of their enemies'. The medieval Welsh poets were overjoyed to find, and sing the praises of, any lord who provided them with food and wine in plenty. Let us now then praise the Harbour Restaurant, Porthmadog – its excellent leek soup; its succulent lamb chops; its splendid rhubarb pie; and its friendly atmosphere, which had a number of customers (Dutch, English, and Welsh) talking with one another across the tables, perhaps first about the bizarre rules which had them drinking Malvern water instead of Claret and Blanc de Blanc, but then about the Kalverstraat and Offa's Dyke and whether visitors better appreciated the grandeur of mountains than did the allegedly over-accustomed natives.

I caught the last British Rail train of the evening back to Criccieth, bearing a box of fudge marked 'A Gift from Wales' for the Reynolds family, and at some point noting that the small print on the back said the fudge was 'made in Blackpool'. Once again, you might say – For Wales, see England. But Alison said realistically, 'It's the fudge that counts.'

Although the thrust of the next day's walk was northward, I took a jog two miles to the west to start with. A lane through shady woods, past the grounds of a rifle club (safely silent), brought me to a minor road and Llanystumdwy. On the edge of the village, where the river Dwyfor passes under a bridge, the morning sun filtered through the trees on to a memorial to David Lloyd George. The statesman's sole formal education took place at the village school here but in his diary for 10 May 1880, when he was seventeen, he wrote that he had left Llanystumdwy without regret, remorse, or longing. Nevertheless, in Llanystumdwy he is remembered. The open-air memorial, by Sir Clough Williams-Ellis, is remarkably simple: stone walls; a wrought-iron gate set in a plain gateway; plaques giving no titles or honours but merely Lloyd George's name and dates of birth and death; and for a centre-piece an irregular boulder set in a bed of pebbles. As a place for reverie about life, death, and the transience of fame, it is a good deal more satisfactory than many a more pompous monument.

I walked upriver across water-meadows and through blue-bell carpeted woods, heeding a sign that told me it was forbidden to swim, to boat, or to throw stones and admiring a pale lilac painted stucco and stone farmhouse that sat on a hillside with a view of the river. The Dwyfor was beautiful. It twisted and tumbled down little falls, hastened over inconsequent rapids, and paused to catch its breath on its way through wide calm pools. It seemed constantly to surprise itself about its direction, taking sweeps from one side to the other, sending out a long feeler which threatened to become an independent stream but then abruptly changing its mind and darting back to join the main flow again. The path, which looked as if it was often flooded, had been surfaced by nature with flat stones and what was now dry crinkly mud. Exposed tree roots had to be cautiously stepped over. Numerous cabbage-whites and butterflies with orange-yellow wing tips attested to the lepidopterous benefits of the spot.

I walked eastwards on a lane to Gell, a place almost bereft of houses, and then turned north-east toward the mountains. Two elderly ladies in a small car stopped and asked me the way to Porthmadog; they were heading in the wrong direction and I turned them round. I next encountered an old gentleman wearing a panama hat and being towed out of his garden gate by a black-and-white springer. He wanted to know where I was going and when I told him said, in a chirpy Lancashire accent, 'Ooh, you're on the wrong road to Caernarfon!' 'I know,' I said. 'But I'm taking a long way round. And I don't mean to get there until tomorrow.' 'Well, then,' he said, sagely, 'I don't expect you will.' In one place rhododendrons grew on one side of the lane, gorse on the other. In the pastures some sheep had been shorn; they looked like a different species of animal, knobbly and bald. In one field next to the road I saw two ewes, all their wool intact, lying flat on their sides, with feet stiffly stretched out and what seemed to be blood on their chins. A lamb stood near one, apparently unconcerned. I whistled at the prostrate sheep. I made encouraging noises. But they didn't stir; it looked to me as if the ewes were dead. Was this the dread staggers or bloat? A farmhouse was not far away. In that case, where was the boy who looked after the sheep? Deciding, perhaps from cowardice, that Shelley had estab-lished good reasons for strangers not to interfere in agricul-

tural matters, I walked on. Beyond a hamlet called Golan I
crossed a river – the Dwyfor again, younger but in strenuous
form. I followed its valley north to higher ground.

Up here, at another place called Llanfihangel-y-pennant –
which was one farmhouse and a chapel with many gravestones – I sat by the river, in the shade of a tree, and had
lunch (Margaret Reynolds be thanked). Here, too, I had a
small ceremony: the changing of maps. I put away Sheet 124
and got out Sheet 115, 'Snowdon & surrounding area'. This
was my seventh map and the last I expected to need. I
examined the valley on the map and then looked up at the
actual terrain to the north, the river-bottom pasture slowly
narrowing as the valley floor rose and the enclosing hillsides
became steeper and higher. It was the most serious mountainous landscape I'd yet encountered. The massive presence
of Moel Hebog loomed on my right hand, with a range of
mountains stretching ahead of me and back down to the left.
The valley down which the Dwyfor ran, and up which I
intended to proceed into this mountainous horseshoe, was
named Cwm Pennant.

For several miles the track – trying for the shortest distance
– switched from side to side of the river as the Dwyfor
wiggled down the valley. What seemed to be the end of the
road for most vehicles was marked by a gate and a collecting-
box, in which a farmer was hoping fifty pence 'for pasture
damage' would be placed by drivers of vehicles going
further. Just before the gate a car was parked. An elderly
man wearing a windcheater and blue beret was sitting in a
folding chair on the turf, taking the air, a black dog in
attendance. Twenty yards away, facing the old man but
clearly *at a distance*, an elderly woman sat, also in a folding
chair, rather bundled up and behind dark glasses. He
returned my greeting; she did not. Some sort of private, tacit
argument seemed to be going on in which I had been picked
for one side rather than the other.

Or were they the *genii loci*, the guardians of the spot? For

a while thereafter I had a sense of being in a place where few
nowadays penetrated – the glorious valley surely led to some
Shangri-La. Up here the lambs on the flanks of the mountains were newer, their legs still splayed out. Tall craggy
cliffs closed in the upper reaches of the cwm. No other
human being was in sight. Towards the upper end, where
the valley was a deep and narrow cleft, I began to climb the
steep right-hand slope, zigzagging up to an abandoned
roofless farmhouse and the track of a former tramway, that
had once carried slate down to Porthmadog. At one point,
where the sharply ascending ground was saturated by a
stream, I slithered, slipped, and tumbled over. I would have
sat there to recover my breath if the wet hadn't immediately
begun to penetrate my trousers. I climbed for another twenty
minutes and found a slim lake, the source of the stream, in a
dip at the base of a merciless grey cliff. At the head of the
lake were stone steps and the shells of buildings. I clambered
up a huge stone ramp, nine feet wide. For a moment it was
as if I'd come across the remnants of a lost civilisation which
had gone in for human sacrifice. For all the sunlit splendour
of the surrounding landscape, there was something in the
funereal stones and the empty black-shadowed doorways
that spoke of misery – of cold rain and cold rock. The chill
reached into me.

And yet, in so far as they had a choice of jobs, men
worked willingly in remote slate mines and quarries like this,
reached by arduous paths from villages and small towns that
were by no means close by. The men might well work a six-
day week. They crammed explosives into hand-drilled holes
and – after a bell was rung or bugle blown – fired them to
loosen the rock. The slabs were split and trimmed by hand
to roof-slate size. There were occasional strikes and lock-.
outs, and constant danger to life and limb. Of every hundred
quarrymen and miners of slate, three or four died each year;
from six to ten were injured. They developed silicosis from
slate dust, TB, pneumonia, and typhoid, as well as colds,

chills, and back problems that were generally referred to as lumbago. All were part of a slate worker's lot. Many of the serious ailments went undiagnosed by quarry doctors, who talked of the beneficial properties of slate dust and blamed the workers' illnesses on their propensity for wearing the same flannel underclothes for a month and drinking too much tea. There was no romance in the slate business unless it was in some of the names given the various sizes to which the slivers of metamorphic rock were trimmed: ladies, countesses, marchionesses, viscountesses, and princesses among them. It was a slow haul gaining recognition of unions, reasonable working hours, recognised holidays, and a working wage. And even as these were achieved the slate trade began to decline. There was competition from other roofing materials like tiles and cheaper artificial slates. Wages fell. Men were laid off. They went to work in the South Wales coal field. They went to war in Flanders and France. The few highly mechanised mines and quarries that remain open have a captive market in Snowdonia – where planning regulations require Welsh slates on local roofs – but they help out their profits by charging visitors who want to look at underground caverns and watch slates being split.

I climbed over a ridge above the derelict quarry, following a track that many a quarryman must have trudged. Ahead, to my left, a peak named Y Garn presented its jagged profile to the sky. On the far side of the ridge the ground fell away to a forest over which, to the north-east, rose the great bulk of Snowdon, whose 3560 foot high peak the Welsh call Yr Wyddfa. The story is that this comes from Gwyddfa Rhita, Rhita's Cairn, the summit mound of stones placed over the body of a giant named Rhita who collected kings' beards. Or did until he tried to cut off King Arthur's head along with his beard and, failing, had his own head cut off by Arthur.

I paused to get my bearings at the edge of the forest. This was a large Forestry Commission conifer plantation that stretched south-east a few miles to the little mountain resort town of Beddgelert. Here too a grave – bedd – is involved in the name. Generations of visitors to Beddgelert have been shown a grave which they were told was that of a dog named Gelert, which belonged to Llywelyn the Great. As he lay alongside the cradle of the prince's infant son, Gelert one day surprised a wolf about to attack the baby. The prince returned, saw the bloodshed resulting from the struggle, and thinking the dog had killed his child, impetuously drew his sword and slaughtered the faithful animal. Then he found the dead wolf and his son asleep under the blankets. He made the only amends he could, giving his dog a noble grave. It seems that this tale is quite common in the folklore of various European countries and was first tried out in Beddgelert by an enterprising man named David Prichard, when he took over the Royal Goat Hotel in 1784 and was drumming up business. (You'd have thought he'd have gone the whole way and renamed his hostelry the Royal Dog.) Scholars suggest that a more likely origin for the town's name lies in a priory there that was dedicated to a holy man named Celert.

Eschewing Beddgelert, I followed a path of loose slate chippings through a part of the forest which had been partly cleared and thus retained the view of Snowdon as I descended. A lake appeared to the right, Llyn-y-Gader, fed by several streams that came down the bare flank of Y Garn. I had to jump one and thought of the redoubtable Dr Johnson. He was in North Wales in 1774, with the Thrales and without Boswell, and though he penned only the sparsest of diaries, Mrs Thrale also kept a record of some of his doings. 'Dr Johnson . . . asked of one of our sharp currents in North Wales – Has this BROOK e'er a name? – Why, dear Sir, this is the RIVER Ustrad. – Let us, said he, turning to his friend, jump over it directly, and show them how an *Englishman* should treat a *Welch* RIVER.' At the next stream I stopped and drank. This was what water tasted like straight from the mountain!

It was just after four in the afternoon when I came to Rhyd-Ddu, a village about two and a half miles west of Snowdon's peak and nearly 3000 feet lower. In the post office-shop I inquired about bed-and-breakfast in the vicinity, just in case the youth hostel I was heading for, a couple of miles on, was full. 'Oh, it wasn't full last night,' said the lady of the place, with reassuring certainty. 'But in case you get stuck, there are two people here who'll put you up.' I walked on northwards, once again sucking orange juice through a straw from a small carton, purchased at the shop as quencher of thirst and tiny tribute to the place. I walked at the edge of the road – lightly trafficked – which brought me to a mile-long oval lake called Llyn Cwellyn. Halfway along its northern shore I reached my intended destination for the night, the Snowdon Ranger youth hostel. It was just five o'clock, opening time. The bearded warden said he had room for me – although, after only eight staying last night, there would be thirty-eight tonight, almost a full house. I was glad I didn't have to tramp back to Rhyd-Ddu. I told myself that even if the thirty-eight included a school party, they *had* to be quieter than those at Llwyn-y-Celyn, the night after I came over Pen-y-Fan. (This could be taken as evidence of the fact that memory, ever optimistic, fails to retain painful experience.)

The Snowdon Ranger, one of only a few buildings along the lake, was a well-appointed hostel. There were bunk beds for ten hostellers in the room I was allotted. After a hot shower and change of clothes, I sat in the common room, still uncommonly all mine, where the warden had lit the log fire and books about the place were on hand. I read that one of the routes up Snowdon started here, following for much of the way a path that had been used in the eighteenth century for carrying down copper ore in panniers from mines on the other side of the summit. Borrow came by in

1854, on his way from Caernarfon to Beddgelert, and encountered two men. The younger and more talkative of the pair told Borrow that he was a slate miner, spent six days of the week at the mine, and Sundays at home here with his wife and father-in-law. The lake had plenty of trout, pike, and char (a small kind of trout), he said, and though it was shallow by this shore, on the far side below Mynydd Mawr it was 'so deep no one knows how deep it is'. Borrow cleverly drew the older, more taciturn man into the conversation by asking the younger man if his father-in-law was a fisherman.

'Fisherman!' said the elderly man contemptuously, 'not I. I am the Snowdon Ranger.'

According to the younger man, their house was named after his worthy in-law. There the older man entertained gentlemen 'who put themselves under his guidance in order to ascend Snowdon and see the country'.

Borrow, by judicious flattery – refusing to compare his own walking on level ground to mountain ranging, or his pacing along a road to springing up crags like a mountain goat – elicited from the Ranger an invitation to 'a glass of something', which he declined. The Ranger then felt the need to make sure Borrow understood his good fortune in being where he was. '"The place to ascend Snowdon from is my house. The way from my house up Snowdon is wonderful for the romantic scenery which it affords; that from Beth Gelert can't be named in the same day with it for scenery; moreover, from my house you may have the best guide in Wales . . ."'

Borrow (who had already gone up the mountain from the other side some days before) then supposed aloud that the Ranger was acquainted with 'all the secrets of the hills', and was rewarded with an appropriate amount of hokum for tourists. Borrow then bombarded the Ranger and his son-in-law with more information about the locality than they possessed, in particular about the origins of some local names. But this didn't embarrass them. In fact, by his own account, he left them pleased as Punch.

'"What a nice gentleman!" said the younger man, when I was a few yards distant.

'"I never saw a nicer gentleman," said the old ranger.'

Three years later, *Hormon's Practical Steamboat, Railway and Road Guide to Snowdon and Around* included an advertisement for the Snowdon Ranger Hotel, situated at the foot of Hamer's Ascent to the summit – 'the shortest and best' – and offering bed and breakfast for two shillings and sixpence, dinner at two shillings, and ales, wine and spirits 'equally moderate, of the best quality'. At the turn of the century the hotel had become a religious retreat; monks were in residence. Later it was a hotel again. The YHA bought it in 1937. The present warden told me that when he first took it over, twenty years ago, a bed for the night cost one shilling – the coin which became five new pence. Although he had – by my rough reckoning – presided over an inflation ten times worse than the national average, he did not seem a worried warden. Of course, the YHA price in 1969 was less than that of the Snowdon Ranger Hotel in 1857.

I wasn't the only guest for long, though I remained by at least twenty years the oldest – a predecimal man! Three young Australian men turned up by car; they gave the impression of having travelled for too long with one another, at one point commencing an interminable debate about imperial and metric measurements, how many litres there are to a gallon and how many pounds in a hundredweight. The school party arrived in mini-buses – about twenty-five boys and girls, sixteen and seventeen year olds, and three teachers, two men and a woman. They were from Cowbridge, a prosperous small town west of Cardiff, and were on a geography field trip. The students seemed – I was glad to note – well-behaved. They did the fetching and carrying at supper. One of them put the Aussies right about litres and gallons. I sat with the teachers and a young climber who had just come over Snowdon; the talk was about the ground and various elements, of water and metals like aluminium found in it, of rocks and gases – no radon in these parts, apparently; you need granite for that. I was asked about my trip. One of the male teachers, possibly a shade envious that I had been walking for three weeks and, even more importantly, did not have to have daily contact with school-children, said to me, 'I think you've been away from real life for too long.' Had I? Real life, whatever that is, sometimes seems utterly unreal to me. Unreal life – if that is what these weeks were – often manages to be a good deal less illusory.

After supper, while the students were receiving their post-prandial instruction in compass work, map reading, and the dangers of bogs and precipices, I played table-tennis with the youth who had spent the day climbing and took a mild pleasure in whacking him two games out of three. Then I walked across the road and down to the lake. There was still a hazy silver light at nine-fifteen, though all the colour had been washed out of the landscape. The lower part of the wooded ridge on the far shore, a section of Beddgelert Forest, was intensely dark. The lake itself, under that brooding mountainous brow, was like a gleaming grey eye slowly closing with sleep.

'How did you sleep?' asked one of the Cowbridge teachers at breakfast – a friendly question.

'Poorly,' I said.

'I hope our lot didn't disturb you.'

'Mmmm.' I searched for words that wouldn't seem discourteous. What came forth was, 'Well, they did.'

Is it all the late evening talk of compasses and maps, the descriptions of crevasses and peat bogs, or simply the effect of a long road journey, no exercise, and warm food that produces these bursts of nocturnal restlessness in teenagers? There was much rampaging in the hostel corridors, banging doors, laughing and shrieking, as the boys raided the rooms of the girls, or vice versa. Although the merriment ceased not long after midnight, I had by then passed through the period of being ripe for sleep into a grumpy wakefulness. I had a prolonged sneezing fit, which seemed antisocial in a room with five others, although three of them were snoring. I spent some time finding by touch an aspirin in the depths of my backpack. When I tried to sneak out of the room to get some water to wash it down, the automatic door-closing device took control, refused to let me shut the door quietly, and did so at its own speed with a loud conclusive thud. The same going back into the room. Bodies stirred. I lay in my bunk, hoping my streaming nose was an allergic reaction to the YHA pillow rather than a head-cold setting in. In the small hours, the anxieties of the sleepless become annoyingly repetitive – and among my recurring considerations was the thought that this night was a re-run of that at Llwyn-y-Celyn. How similar even was the name to Llyn Cwellyn! Surely an omen I should have heeded. What was it going to be like, climbing Snowdon, the snowy mount, after three hours sleep?

Breakfast somewhat improved my mood. The cold didn't seem to have materialised. I did my chore (washing several window-sills), said goodbye to the warden who returned my YHA membership card, and made for the Snowdon Ranger path, which began next to the road a hundred yards away. I paused only to tear up the YHA card and drop the pieces in a litter bin. This – I trusted – would not be a costly gesture at this stage of my walk. I told myself I would rejoin when the YHA introduces strict, sound-proof segregation of weary hostellers, who arrive on their own feet, from vehicle-assisted school-children. Possibly an Adult Hostel Association would fit the bill.

It was going to be a warm day. There was just a little haze and hardly any wind. The first stage of the Snowdon Ranger path zigzagged above me up the open hillside, with sheep here and there nibbling the grass to an altitude, about halfway, where the pickings became too sparse to be worth the climb. There are seven traditional routes up Snowdon. The Snowdon Ranger – although not the most difficult in mountaineering terms – starts from relatively low ground (about 460 feet above sea level near the lake) and, climbing to 3560 feet at the summit, covers a greater vertical distance than most of the others. On this particular morning, on this flank of the highest mountain in England and Wales, not another person was to be seen. At about 800 feet I stepped carefully around a golden-brown furry caterpillar that was wriggling slowly across the path. Before long, sweat was running freely from my forehead. I stopped for a breather and looked back down at Llyn Cwellyn, whose surface reflected the dark-green forest beyond and hid depths, toward the far bank, I now saw from the map were known to be roughly one hundred feet – a fact Borrow would no doubt have surprised the Ranger and his son-in-law with, if he had known it. Directly above me, several larks were competing in aerial bouts of song.

Climbing again, I followed a straight path which ascended above a small lake, a slate-blue saucer of water called Llyn Ffynnon-y-gwas and up on to a curving, rising ridge – Clogwyn Du'r Arddu – which forms the north side of a deep semi-circular valley around which several spurs of the mountain bend. Snowdon seen from several thousand feet above (or seen on a map) looks like a petrified sea monster, a misshapen starfish perhaps, stretching out five contorted limbs – some sprawling, some knife-edged – which cradle five bays of lower ground. These hollows, valleys, or partial craters are sided with banks that occasionally rise into steep cliffs. The surface varies between turf, loose stone or scree, and bare rock. Numerous streams run into the valleys and could often be heard before they were seen. I stopped at one, which had stones for stepping over it, and scooped up water to cool my brow. Parts of the mountainside are boggy; some streams, as I'd found elsewhere, took the easy option of coming down the track. After an hour I was a little less than halfway to the summit but dark ramparts looming ahead showed that the serious part of the climb was still to come. The sun was also ahead of me; the mountain was *contrejour* and all the more impressive for that reason. I sat down for a while on a rock slab, a perfect bench, on which a previous climber had inscribed his name, FRED. When I got going again I heard myself utter a few words of cheerful encouragement: 'Up we go!'

The next section had much loose slate and rock; it was an uneven staircase worn into the mountain and stepping up it I had to lift my knees high. To my right the ground fell away sharply and I didn't let my gaze linger there. Then I was up on the crest of one of the limb-ridges that buttress the central mass of Snowdon. I could see into the valley on the other side of the ridge and was suddenly aware that, on that side, to the north, the ground fell away nearly vertically below me. A sheer drop. I stayed away from the edge. I have no special fear of heights, but like many am afraid that I'll be seized with an irrational desire to spread my arms, my proto-wings, and hurl myself forth in a burst of Icarian enthusiasm over the abyss. My father had to climb Snowdon during an army training exercise during the Second World War; he is nervous of leaving ground-level – dislikes going up ladders or staying in hotel bedrooms above the second floor. He says that the only way he managed the ascent of Snowdon was by keeping his gaze firmly fastened on the haversack of the man in front of him.

The valley I was looking into stretches north to the town of Llanberis. From there the Snowdon Mountain Railway climbs the longest and most gentle of the ascents to the summit. Its track, rising along the far side of the valley, would have been hard to see three-quarters of a mile away, but a train drew my attention to it. It was a single carriage pushed by an engine. I could also hear the occasional plaintive 'floot floot' of its whistle as it puffed laboriously upwards. I had been trying to put out of my mind the fact that Snowdon has a railway. It was discouraging that while I was climbing under my own steam, others were getting to the top with mechanical assistance. However, the railway was still at a distance, and didn't seem to be getting its passengers up much faster than I was climbing.

By now the grass was getting thin; not a tree or shrub was to be seen; sizeable loose rocks and small pebbly stones covered the slopes. I was above the lark-line. Thirty minutes' exertion brought me to a point where, looking around, I decided the hard part was behind me. A more gradual ascent led to the railway track, two rails between which ran a dentillated rail for a cogged wheel on the engine. As I walked alongside the track, I soon realised that I wouldn't have to

worry about meeting a train. Despite the day's heat, snow
several feet deep lay undisturbed in a shadowed gully
through which the track climbed; the summit station was
evidently still a stop too far this early in the season. Some of
the passengers who had come up in the train I'd seen and got
off at the penultimate station were walking up the Llanberis
path, which more or less follows the railway. So, too, were
other climbers who were arriving by other paths from the
east, such as the so-called Pig Track and the Miners Track
which come together for the last stage up to the summit.
Here, as at Pen-y-Fan, there had been no other human being
in sight for several hours and now, approaching the summit,
a small crowd had appeared. Several groups had dogs with
them. A few, having reached the summit earlier, were going
down; one young woman in trainers jogged downhill past
me at the edge of the track. I stooped to touch the no-longer
spotless snow, which felt like the rough ice you shave from
a freezer in need of defrosting.

About two and a half hours after leaving the Snowdon
Ranger, I reached the little plateau which sits just below the
summit. Here is a station of sorts. A rectangular shed, two
concrete platforms, a café – all shut, the café windows
shuttered. There has been some sort of facility for visitors to
the top of Snowdon for more than a century. At one point
there was a small inn which called itself a hotel. As far as
Borrow was concerned it was 'a rude cabin, in which
refreshments are sold, and in which a person resides throughout the year, though there are few or no visitors to the
hilltop except during the months of summer'. Here his
stepdaughter Henrietta had some excellent coffee while
George and the guide shared a bottle of 'tolerable ale'. A
German called Julius Rodenberg who, about the same time
as Borrow, was in Wales collecting fairy tales, climbed
Snowdon in a thick mist and took shelter in the inn. He had
there 'a warm fire, a glass of grog, and as much humour as a

man can have who is 3571 feet above the sea in a mist, for which he would not have walked ten steps on the flat!'

Our good friend Gerald of Wales had of course something to say about Snowdonia but gives the impression of having viewed the mountains from a safe distance on the north coast. The Snowdonia range was called Eryri by the Welsh – in other words, the haunt of eagles – and Gerald had heard of a remarkable eagle which lived in the mountains and fed on a human corpse every fifth feast day when 'it thinks war will break out'. Gerald also tells us of one mountain-top lake with a floating island, on which sheep are sailed around by the wind, and another lake in which all the fish have one eye only, the right not the left. In recent centuries more diligent observers have made a thing of actually climbing the mountain, among them many botanists and naturalists. The late-seventeenth-century scientist Edward Lhuyd, who recorded for the first time many British flowers and ferns, found on what he called 'the highest rocks of Snowdon' a bulbous plant with rush-like leaves which has the scientific name *Lloydia serotina* but is most often called the Snowdon Lily. Dr Johnson, with the Thrales, climbed 'with great labour' only a few hundred feet above Llanberis ('I was breathless and harassed,' he wrote in his diary), but he helped the ten-year-old Thrale daughter Queeny spot goats on the mountainsides – her short-sighted father had promised her a penny for every goat she could see. ('Queeny's goats, one hundred and forty-nine, I think,' the great man noted.) The Romantic Age, with its cult of the picturesque, its attraction for the Sublime and 'the Finely Horrid' (as one late-eighteenth-century writer termed it), brought numerous enthusiasts to the peak. Wordsworth climbed Snowdon by moonlight and wrote about it in his long autobiographical poem, *The Prelude*: 'There I beheld the emblem of a mind/That feeds upon infinity . . .' Others did so to watch the sunrise. For a sample of the Picturesque School in full, late flood, here is Thomas Roscoe (1838):

'. . . these British Alps partake sufficiently of the magnificent to impress the beholder with feelings of awe and
admiration. If not on the largest scale, they can yet boast
almost every variety of the noblest characteristics of
mountain scenery – even to the terrible. In their darker
hour, when the storm is up – when the torrent pours its
hoarser music with the autumnal blasts, and the near voice
of the thunder, and the deep rolling masses of mist, convey
the impression of some region seated among the clouds –
no traveller of other lands will pronounce Snowdon desti-
tute of images at once fearfully beautiful and sublime.'

By the early nineteenth century travellers were beginning
to complain about the number of other people they found
on the mountain-top. Most visitors of that period went with
guides. Thomas Pennant in 1773 had recommended Hugh
Shone as 'a most able conductor', and seems to have ridden
a horse until 'the ascent becomes very difficult on account of
its vast steepness'. Borrow went up the easy way from
Llanberis with Henrietta and a young lad for guide. While
Mrs Borrow stayed at the inn in Llanberis, George and
Henrietta climbed (according to Borrow) 'arm in arm,
followed by the lad, I singing at the stretch of my voice a
celebrated Welsh stanza . . . "Easy to say, 'Behold Eryri,' /
But difficult to reach its head."' At one point Borrow
thought that Henrietta 'would be obliged to give over the
attempt; the gallant girl, however, persisted'.

Above the station and the café the mountain comes to a
peak in the natural mound that attracted the name of
Wyddfa's cairn. On the very top of this stands a stone and
concrete pillar, about four and a half feet high, bearing a
triangulation marker and forming an ideal support for the
climber who has reached this final point and stands there
surveying the scene. This is as high in Wales as you can get.
I found half a dozen other climbers here and took my turn
by the pillar. From this 'exalted situation', as Pennant called

it, a prospect of much of Wales, all of Anglesey, some of
Cumbria and Shropshire in England, even of Ireland across
the Irish Sea, is promised on a pristine day. But mountains
attract cloud; even in seemingly clear conditions, as Pennant
pointed out, Snowdon 'becomes suddenly and unexpectedly
enveloped in mist'. On this particular sunny day, haze if not
mist filtered the view. It made vague the further distances
and softened the perception one had of immense abysses and
blade-sharp ridges. Small puffs of cloud produced stippled
shadows on the ground below, breaking up the harsher
outlines of chasms and craters. The many lakes lying in deep
bowls between the outstretched buttresses of the mountain
were muted mirrors – receptive pools into which it seemed
one might safely plunge. The haze changed the scale, blurred
one's sense of the dreadful and dangerous. I had that slightly
disembodied confidence one has when gazing down from
the window of an aircraft at 32,000 feet on the beauty of
creation.

Angelic reflections soon followed by human needs. It was
just as well I'd brought emergency rations. I sat at the base
of Wyddfa's cairn, drinking water and munching a sandwich
left over from the day before. Nearby, a young Australian
with a giant backpack but no provisions was complaining to
the other climbers about the unopen café. Summits seem to
enhance the need of some to speak their minds. Borrow, not
shy on any occasion, claims that at the top of Snowdon he
let go with an etymological and poetic harangue 'to which
Henrietta listened with attention, three or four English, who
stood nigh, with grinning scorn, and a Welsh gentleman
with considerable interest'. The young Okker, clearly feeling
hunger pangs, told all within hearing about sundry gastron-
omic experiences from his recent past until someone gave
him a cheese roll and he shut up.

Eating and drinking was in any event made difficult by
the presence of thousands of blackfly and midges. No
account, ancient or modern, that I'd read about Snowdon

warned of these insects. It was a plague. They climbed over
bread and water-bottle and had to be brushed or blown away
before one took a bite or swallow. They crawled over one's
arms and face and got in one's hair. When one insect took
off, several more landed. Movement was the only answer –
and rapid movement at that. There was no sign of any of the
legendary eagles; the last golden eagle is thought to have
nested here several centuries ago. Although choughs and
ravens are said to frequent these heights, the only birds I saw
were four herring gulls, gliding in great circles and hardly
needing to stir their wings to stay aloft in the rising currents
of air as they kept a look-out for scraps of food dropped by
climbers.

I moved down to a natural terrace of rock just below the
station, where flies, midges, and fellow climbers were fewer.
Looking out over the landscape, it was easy to see how
earlier peoples imagined something other-earthly about it. I
did not take sides on whether this was – as Defoe conjectured
– because the mountains made people believe the Devil lived
hereabouts, or, as Belloc declared, because Snowdonia had
once been inhabited 'by the gods . . . whom our God has
ousted'. David Jones suggests that Plutarch envisioned this
as the spot where Cronos slept, like Arthur, in order to come
again. Certainly this is the place where Welsh legends are
most at home. Looking to the east I could see the gap in a
saddle called Bwlch-y-Saethu, the Pass of the Arrows.
There, and not at the usually accepted 'Camlaum', according
to some of the old Welsh stories, Arthur joined in battle for
the last time – fighting with the assistance of his remaining
knights against the villainous Mordred and a force of Saxon
invaders. It was there that Arthur was fatally wounded,
though he managed to kill Mordred with Excalibur as he
fell. The sword was thrown by Sir Bedivere into the waters
of nearby Llyn Llydaw. The last knights took refuge in a
cave in the face of the ridge Y Lliwedd, which overhangs the
lake, and where they are sleeping until Arthur – *rex quondam*

et futurus – summons them again. The name Arthur was
given by the Tudor king Henry VII to his eldest son, who
died before succeeding to the throne. Perhaps not to tempt
fate, it has since been reserved for royal princes who have
not been in the first line of inheritance, or has been given to
princes as a middle name. The fights that take place near
Llyn Llydaw nowadays are quarrels between conservation
groups and the Central Electricity Generating Board about
pipelines which carry water down from the lake to a hydro-
electric power station and disfigure the mountainside –
making arbitrary scars on the wrinkled old skin of the Welsh
earth.

Turning southwards, I looked down the long sharp spine
of another ridge which obscures another lake, Llyn Dinas,
and a wooded foothill of Snowdon called Dinas Emrys. On
this hill, a mile or so from Beddgelert, are the remains of a
fort associated with Vortigern, the British king who made
the mistake of inviting over the Saxons of Hengist and Horsa
in 449. This is where Vortigern apparently decided to build
an impregnable fortress with the magical help (so the legend
goes) of a boy called Merlin. Merlin also made for the king
handy prophecies about battles between a red dragon and a
white dragon, prophecies which neatly forecasted events in
the struggle between the British/Welsh and the Saxons/
English, particularly in respect to the red dragon winning
for a while – as the British did in Arthur's time – before it
began to tear itself apart. This may seem (in the Shakespear-
ian phrase) skimble-skamble stuff or part of the poetic matter
that lies within history: legends that possibly illuminate the
obscure details heaped up by the ninth-century Bangor cleric
Nennius in his *History of the Britons* and that were improved
on by such early medieval popularisers as Geoffrey of
Monmouth, whose Latin was soon translated into Welsh.
Among Merlin's prophecies, as recounted by Geoffrey, is
one that sounds surprisingly up-to-date: 'The balance of
trade shall be torn in half; and the half that is left shall be

rounded off.' This utterance, like that of many modern economists, seems to mean whatever you want it to. According to Pennant, the Roman Catholic Church in the mid-sixteenth century took time from its long labours at the Council of Trent in defining the legacy of medieval scholasticism and opposing the new Protestantism to forbid the repetition of Merlin's prophecies.

THE WAY TO BANGOR PIER

DO MOUNTAIN CLIMBERS find summits anti-climatic? I suspect that the ascent and descent matter most and in retrospect form an all-inclusive experience in which the period at the summit figures only as a necessary way-station: a point you have to pass on the journey between going up and going down. After forty minutes at Snowdon's summit I set off downwards by the path to Rhyd-Ddu. This would lead me on a more roundabout return route but did not require me to retrace my upward steps. It was also a steeper route than the Snowdon Ranger path for a while, requiring more concentration than exertion – though energy was involved in finding the right foothold and putting one's feet down in a way that didn't jar muscles and tendons. In places I walked on the sharp topmost edge of the ridge, with the ground falling away for several thousand feet on each side. I passed several small groups of people panting upwards. On the lower slopes I paused to allow the passage of a flock of sheep being worked across the mountain-side by a black-and-white sheepdog and a shepherd who was alternately shouting and whistling. After a long whistle, he shouted 'Woooh! Weeeya! Jack!' He then gave a long and a short whistle. The dog, so directed, sloped around the fringes of the flock. The shepherd, the commanding officer, stood on a little knoll. Occasionally a rapid salvo of shouts and whistles made me think the movement operation was on the brink of going wrong. But then all was calm again, the shouts and whistles unflustered, the sheep hurrying along over crag and turf as they were told.

From Rhyd-Ddu I followed the road to and along Llyn Cwellyn that I had taken the day before to the youth hostel. From the Snowdon Ranger it was a little more than seven miles to Caernarfon and gently downhill all the way. I walked along the former roadbed of the Welsh Highland Railway, which once ran from Caernarfon to Porthmadog. Although the ties themselves were long gone, the path was corrugated in grassy ridges over the chippings which had lain between and under the ties. The main A4085 road and the river Gwyrfai followed more or less the same course northwestwards toward the coast. Moel Eilo was the name of the last bare-faced mountain on my right, Craig Cwmby-chan that on the left, and then abruptly I was out from between them, out of Snowdonia and on the coastal plain. It was like a geography lesson. Ahead, across the Menai Strait, the island of Anglesey – Ynys Mon – spread out flat and green. The hills of the Llŷn peninsula ran off to the left, looking like the hills in a Mediterranean painting by Turner, out of which Polyphemus or R. S. Thomas might suddenly appear, hurling boulders at intruders. When the old railway track became impassable because of missing or partly dis-mantled bridges I took to the road. This, now branching away from the river, passed through scrappy country and strung-out villages. The map reminded me that it had been a Roman road, Helen's *via* again; it brought me at the end of the afternoon to the outskirts of Caernarfon and the Roman fort of Segontium.

Set among suburban houses is a park-like plot: behind a little museum, stone foundations stand out from the neatly-mown grass, with the exposed floors of what once were barracks, workshops, granaries, forage stores, bath-house, and headquarters buildings covered with gravel. Visitors can see the channels of the heating system which conducted warmth and fumes under the floors and up flues in the walls.

After the fort was founded in AD 78 a cohort of roughly a thousand men, part infantry, part mounted, was garrisoned here. Towards the end of the second century the legionaries were those of the first cohort of Sunici, which had originally been recruited from a Rhineland tribe, but had been stationed in Britain for some time before it reached Segontium. The fort's last regular garrison is thought to have been withdrawn by the usurper and general Maximus at the time he was raised to the purple. His Welsh wife Helen had a reputation for piety. The imperial palace she and Maximus had in Trèves was said to have been given up by her to be made into a church, while here at Segontium she had her own chapel. Their son, Publicius or Peblic, was believed to have retired from the world to take a religious habit. The church near the fort – Llan Beblic – is dedicated to him.

I walked on into Caernarfon. A pedestrian underpass beneath a roundabout provided a grotty modern urban introduction to the town that fortunately proved uncharacteristic. Caernarfon is both old and Welsh in feeling. Many ancient churches, houses, shops, and inns line narrow streets within well-preserved defensive walls. The town grew at the junction of the river Seiont with the Menai Strait – the broad channel that divides the island of Anglesey from the mainland. The mouth of the river is dominated by a huge castle, another of Edward I's constructions intended to keep the Welsh in check – though in 1284 the townspeople were sufficiently annoyed by a tax the king had imposed to seize one of his constables, Sir Roger de Pulesdon, and hang him from one of the castle loopholes. Nevertheless the king's son and heir Edward II was born here and in 1301 presented to the natives as the first English Prince of Wales. A later Prince of Wales, the present Prince Charles, prepared for his investiture here in 1969 by a term at the university college in Aberystwyth, where he is thought to have been the first English Prince of Wales to acquire a working knowledge of the Welsh language. The investiture was a grand ceremonial occasion, described by the *Guardian*'s reporter Nesta Roberts as 'an audio-visual out of Froissart'. When the Prince's mother, the Queen, passed through the town in her royal coach, someone threw an egg.

I wasn't unhappy to find that the castle had closed for the day. I admired its turrets and battlements from without, inspected the nearby Seiont quayside with its fishing boats and yachts, and made my way to The Black Boy inn. My room looked out on the town walls and a playground – though the walls themselves provided a chance to climb or play war games that most children enjoy. In the snug bar of the inn several small groups of men, evidently pub regulars, were talking in Welsh. Although one broke briefly into English to exchange banter with some American visitors, the Welshmen gave the impression of being comfortably insulated in their own language, secure from alien intrusion. They could overhear and understand us; we could overhear but not understand them. They might as well have been talking Albanian.

After dinner I walked to another Caernarfon pub to meet a man who had agreed, a little reluctantly, to talk to me in English. We sat in a quiet corner. Owain kept his voice low. This may have been partly because he didn't want to be heard by his compatriots speaking to an Englishman in the Englishman's language; mostly it was because we were discussing illegal action: the fire-bombing of English property in Wales. The campaign by Meibion Glyndŵr, the Sons of Glyndŵr, against those they call 'colonialists' and 'white settlers', has now gone on for more than a decade. There have been arson attacks on 200 homes, shops, and offices, mostly in North Wales. Several million pounds worth of damage has been caused. Estate agents in England who deal with Welsh property have been attacked as have the offices of building societies which provide mortgages for second homes; a Right-Wing think-tank in London; a visitor's car in Snowdonia; yachts moored at Caernarfon, Bangor, and

Conwy; and a Liverpool firm which runs adventure holidays in Wales. Devices used have included acid-filled condoms and containers of petrol mixed with washing-up liquid. Some victims have installed asbestos-lined letter-boxes; others have got rid of their letter-boxes altogether and collect their mail from the post office. So far, despite several buildings being completely burned out, no one has been killed. So far, despite a police announcement of a £50,000 reward for information leading to the conviction of the arsonists, there has been no conviction. The police seem to believe that only a dozen or so people are involved – people with educated Welsh accents and hence 'respectable back-grounds', judging from a few anonymous warning calls that have been received. Some Welsh people believe the arsonists live in England. One woman executive told me, 'They must come from outside, place their bombs, and clear out. I can't think they live in Wales.' However, small parades have taken place in North Wales where groups of Meibion Glyndŵr men have marched through villages in dark glasses and berets – similar to those worn at IRA paramilitary demonstrations; a recent display of this kind was at a commemoration of the deaths of the two men blown up by their own bomb at Abergele on the eve of the investiture of the Prince of Wales in 1969. The only arrests the baffled police have made to date have been of an actor and singer Bryn Fon and his girlfriend for possible possession of explosives; but the pair were soon released, uncharged.

Owain wouldn't say if he was a member of Meibion Glyndŵr. 'I support the effort, though. I think they're brave people, facing the possibility of years in prison – English prisons – if they are caught. I fully understand R. S. Thomas when he says that he deplores killing but goes on to ask "What is the life of one English person compared to the destruction of a nation?" There's a councillor and school teacher in Pwllheli, Alwyn Pritchard, who's come out with similar remarks – he has also resigned from Plaid Cymru in

protest against the call of the Plaid MP Dafydd Ellis Thomas
for more resources to be given to the police so they can catch
the arsonists. A lot of people in this part of Wales support
the aims of Meibion Glyndŵr even if they don't approve of
violence. You can buy badges with the motto "*Taniwch dros
Gymru!*" – Strike a Light for Wales! There are coffee mugs
with a picture on them showing a dragon breathing fire on a
cottage. Many people can see it's a last-ditch fight for a
Welsh homeland – and for that, the English influx has to be
halted. It may be that there's no other way of doing it except
by burning houses. That very fact makes us angry. But do
you expect us to lie back and calmly accept our own
extinction?'

Back in my room at The Black Boy, I switched on the
television. The two-and-a-half hours of Welsh-language fare
on this particular night included a children's comedy programme; the news; a woman singer introducing her favourite
songs; a round-up of topical events; hymn singing; and a
late-night meditation. Many of the commercial advertisements between these programmes were in English. The
meditation was preceded by half an hour of '*Snwker*'. The
screen confirmed that this was indeed snooker, a game
evidently transcending national differences; being shown was
a championship televised in Sheffield with a Welsh commen-
tary for Welsh-language viewers. I watched the cues glide
and the balls cannon and sink into the pockets, a calming
sight – whatever the language attached to it – that made one
ready for meditation or, in my case, slumber.

Caernarfon to Bangor – the last serious walking day. Bangor, for several reasons, had gradually become my final destination. It wasn't absolutely as far north as you can go in Wales – the Isle of Anglesey stretched several miles further toward the pole, as did two promontories, Great Ormes Head and the Point of Ayr, between which lie the seaside resorts of Llandudno and Rhyl and numerous retirement havens for northern English incomers. But Anglesey was flat and separate; it used to be known as 'the Mother of Wales' because it provided so much cattle and grain; and I felt its offspring was sufficient unto this walk. Moreover, Bangor like Cardiff was an ancient city, with a university. 'Cardiff to Bangor' had a symmetry, to my mind, which 'Cardiff to Llandudno' did not.

I would like to have gone forth full of brio on this day – three weeks and two days after I'd set off. But the head-cold, heralded by sneezes at the Snowdon Ranger and fought off the day before, had arrived. The weather was grey and cool. I set off, snuffling, wearing a sweater, out through the town walls and the somewhat ramshackle light industrial eastern outskirts of Caernarfon. I avoided the main road, walking instead on a former railway right-of-way not far from the muddy foreshore. To my left, the Menai Strait at this state of the tide seemed to be mostly sandbanks. To date, most of the pedestrians I'd encountered near towns had been young mums pushing infants or pensioners with their dogs – here an elderly man accompanied by a sheepdog, similarly retired, advised me to head inland, on the inshore side of the main road, since I would find the old railway blocked by a factory, the Ferodo brake-lining works, in a mile or so. 'But you're doing the right thing, walking,' he said. 'I spend more of my time walking with the old dog than I do anything else.'

I thanked him for his approval, ignored his kind advice, and kept going along the track, which immediately got difficult. A farmer, perhaps anxious for the security of his sheep in the adjacent fields, had done his best to make it impassable with barbed wire. I scrambled over and under these impediments. Where the fields were ploughed rather than under grass, the soil exposed was red, both here and on Anglesey across the water. The overgrown path had pleasant surprises as well as obstructions: rabbits hopping away at my approach; and an owl flying suddenly out from a deep chink in the masonry of a ruined bridge as I walked under it, big brown wings beating close to me, making me duck. The Ferodo works, a vast cream-painted factory, seemed to be the source of a pungent smell that made one think of cars, though less of their brakes than of burning tyres or batteries being overcharged. I detoured briefly to the main road. Back on the track the next obstacle was less noxious, more threatening: five white beehives planted in the middle of the path. From them rose a hum like that of a small power station, and I took a moment or two to decide – go on, or retreat? But courage was summoned. Full of trepidation, I sneaked past, almost on tiptoe. What if I sneezed? But the bees stayed within their loud honey factory.

A third, unexpected ordeal had to be faced. The footpath, now clearly marked on the map in red as a public right-of-way, crossed meadowland near Llanfair Hall to a farmhouse. The path passed between house and farm-buildings. Lying across the path was an aged black dog, tethered on a long piece of line. From under lowered eyelids he watched my approach. He began to growl. I looked at him, trying to convey telepathically that I was a dog owner and in general felt admiration for his species. He started to bark, though not too fiercely. I assumed a poise as confident as I could manage and proceeded – show no fear, is what you're always told. The dog stirred, rose to its feet, and jumped, actually *went for me*, putting his worn old teeth to my shins, one shin (moving, needless to say) after another. Once again I regretted not having mastered the Welsh for 'Down!' 'Sit!' and 'Leave off!' At least his tether held; the ancient hound of Glyndŵr was unable to pursue me. And no cloth had been penetrated or blood drawn.

The peaceful parkland that followed made up for these annoyances. Cows, out of Cuyp or Constable, grazed in lush fields. The Strait here looked like a river, and on Anglesey a steepled church stood in meadows without any visible village to provide it with a congregation. I came to some woods and a stream in a little ravine that required careful negotiating. Then I was forced up to the main road as it entered the village of Port Dinorwic. The road was being worked on; only one lane was open, and traffic lights controlled the restricted flow; a file of vehicles heading toward Bangor moved forward very slowly with frequent long halts. I had to cope with the self-satisfied feeling that arose from overtaking the trucks and cars, trying not to look too smug as I passed the drivers stretching impatiently and tapping their fingers and noticing me with my pack striding along. But the exhaust fumes from this congestion in Port Dinorwic's narrow main street forced me to forego the pleasures of pedestrian hubris and descend a sidestreet. I walked around an empty stone-sided tidal harbour and then along a dock basin with a lock which had once let in ships to carry away slate. Now the basin was a marina for yachts. I exercised the privilege of a sailor ashore to look in passing at each vessel as if I might sail it on a long voyage, approving the rig of one or disapproving the cockpit layout of another. I bought a cup of coffee in the marina café, self-service but

not cheap. The staff were unresponsive to my conversational
pleasantries. They looked over and around me, not sure of
what I was – a tramp? an alien? Certainly *not* a yachtsman.
Three weeks of walking had no doubt given me the appearance of having been out in all weathers, a look which
effectively camouflaged clues of education, income, and class
– and which therefore might be bothersome to those (met
more often in England than in Wales, I think) who are
uncomfortable unless they can promptly slot a stranger into
a category.

Perhaps I was simply coming back to the demanding
urban world. I walked to the head of the basin and crossed
an entering stream by a footbridge made of a fifteen foot
length of slate, about three inches thick and a couple of feet
wide. The ordnance map showed what seemed to be a skein
of tracks and lanes extending through the grounds of a
country house toward Bangor; but at the first gate, complete
with a gate lodge, was a sign: PRIVATE – ACCESS ONLY. This,
I thought, could be construed to mean access for walkers. I
began to walk in. A man with a large dog popped out of the
lodge so quickly he must have been waiting to see what I
would do. He said, with a Lancashire accent, 'Can I help?'
He didn't sound helpful. The dog shared his suspicions.

I said that I was making for Bangor and wanted to avoid
the main road. Wasn't there a footpath I could reach through
the gate?

'Well, I wouldn't go that way,' he said. 'The estate's been
sold off. Various private owners. The big house belongs to
some *Welsh* and they're very keen on their privacy.'

I asked him to recommend a route which didn't intrude
on anyone. And so I found myself taking a swing inland,
along a lane which climbed away from the main road, with
the small red flowers of Herb Robert growing at the base of
the hedges. The view south was of Snowdonia and I was
taking a last look at the mountains when a pair of horses
came by, their riders greeting me in a way that somewhat

assuaged my recent hurts. Then I went downhill into
Bangor, crossing the A5 trunk road near a complicated
junction which reminded me of the M4 interchange outside
Cardiff – these concrete arteries of mechanised mobility that
also form our cities' moats and curtain walls.

Bangor, a 'city' by virtue of having a cathedral, 'the Athens
of Wales' according to the Wales Tourist Board, is a university town of 16,000 people. It is on the coast and yet, except
for one small section, is set apart from the water. In fact it
seems more like a stretched-out village, set in a long valley
that points toward the eastern end of the Menai Strait, with
wooded hills on either side sheltering its buildings and
streets. Two famous bridges on the northwestern outskirts
connect Wales to Anglesey – Telford's Menai Suspension
Bridge, which when finished in 1826 had the longest span of
any bridge in the world and carries across the Strait the
London-to-Holyhead A5 road; and Stephenson's box-girder
Britannia Bridge of 1850, generally described as tubular,
built solely for railway use but since 1979 carrying a second
deck for road traffic as well. It was in Bangor in the early
ninth century that the scholar Nennius wrote his History of
the Britons and made precious mention of Arthur as *dux
bellorum*. When Archbishop Baldwin arrived here three centuries later, accompanied by Gerald, he put Gwion, the
Bishop of Bangor, under such pressure that 'in the end there
was nothing for it but that he himself should take the cross'.
The congregation on hand, continued Gerald, 'wept and
wailed very loudly'. The present small cathedral, St Deniol's,
begun in the mid-thirteenth century, was judged by the
industrious Pennant as having 'nothing remarkable within,
except a few tombs'; it was much done over in the nineteenth
century. More noteworthy is the cathedral garden which has
a Bible Walk whose trees, shrubs, and flowers are of types
all mentioned in the Holy Book: rather prudishly, a fig tree,
not an apple tree, provides the reference to Adam and Eve.

Recalling Dr Johnson's difficulties in Bangor in 1774, when he and the Thrales had trouble in finding lodging and he was forced to put up in 'a very mean Inn . . . in a room where the other bed had two men' and where he had 'a flatulent night', I had made inquiries in a Welsh-language bookshop in Caernarfon. There a woman had recommended that I stay in Bangor at The British Hotel. Whether she did this tongue in cheek, out of a sense of irony, or because she genuinely thought I would like it, I never discovered. The hotel was Bangor's largest. A slight suggestion that the sun which had set on the British Empire, and on the ancient Britons, might also have set on it caused me to ask if I could see the not inexpensive accommodation I was offered. A large bathroom and capacious bath apparently made up for the small bedroom, but I told the young woman at the reception desk that something would have to be done about the bed, which might as well have been a hammock. She said it would. I was largely submerged in the bath, happily steaming off the remains of the head-cold, when there was a knock on the bedroom door. Betowelled, I opened it. A portly out-of-breath porter stood there with a large and heavy plywood door. I told him to leave it outside for the moment, since there didn't seem to be room for it and both of us in the room at one time. After another ten minutes in the tub, I dressed and wrestled the door on to the bedframe and under the mattress. I tested it and decided it would make the necessary difference between firm sleep and possibly permanent curvature of the spine.

Food and drink further improved my mood. The British Hotel staff were friendly. As I ate, I thought about 'Britain'. Clearly for some Welsh the older, pre-English Britain still furnished an important prop – they felt, in Tony Conran's words, that 'their country is essentially the Island of Britain as a whole, and the fact that they now occupy only that fraction of it called Wales is no more than an unfortunate historical accident'. But for more Welsh people, I suspected, a different, modern Britain filled their lives at the expense of that older one. Their identity as citizens of the United Kingdom involved interests and preoccupations that were basically the same as those of people living in England, like taxes and television, snooker or snwker.

Even so, Bangor provided a final spokesman for Welsh Wales. During the evening, I talked in the hotel bar with a young man named Elwyn Vaughan. He had worked in a bank for several years and was now a mature student of Business Administration in Welsh at Bangor Normal College. His father had a large hill-farm not far from Dolgellau. Elwyn told me that he combined his studies with work for Plaid Cymru and Cymdeithas yr Iaith Gymraeg, the Welsh Language Society. I asked him if he thought the prognosticators were right who declared that over the next twenty years the Welsh-speaking proportion of the population would continue to sink, possibly as low as five per cent.

'We're going to go on fighting to prove them wrong,' said Elwyn. 'The age of the chapel is over – this is the age of television. We have to get more airtime for Welsh-language TV and radio, which has a spin-off effect for independent Welsh programme makers. We also need an English-language channel specifically for Wales, to help non-Welsh-speaking people here find their Welsh identity through the medium of English. Youngsters have to realise that Welsh is interesting if it's to live. A North Wales pop group, The Alarm, has done some benefit concerts for the Welsh Language Society – their lead singer, Mike Peters, is learning Welsh. And people my age have to be able to live in Wales. The singer Dafydd Iwan, one of the founders of the Welsh Language Society, has helped set up a cooperative housing association – it now has several hundred houses it rents to Welsh people at prices they can afford. Some of our members have occupied empty houses to protest against the way they're sold at high prices as holiday homes to non-Welsh-speaking immigrants. But we know we have to *sell* Welsh, create a higher profile for it. Well, we've got the road signs and the bus timetables and children going to Welsh nursery and primary schools. We now have to get Welsh companies to use Welsh in business, in marketing. I say to the forecasters – "You're mistaken. We're going to double the number of Welsh-speakers by the end of the century." '

Elwyn bade me a cheerful goodnight. I thought he would have a splendid career in business and hoped only that what I feared would be disappointment in the language struggle would not weigh too gloomily on him. I felt it, for a moment: after a thousand and some years of Welsh tales and poems, after millennia of speech, the pain of loss to come. I recalled 'The Gododdin', the morale-boosting poem by the late-sixth-century bard Aneirin, which takes the form of a series of heroic elegies on three hundred Britons – warriors of the Gododdin tribe – who fell in an attempt to recapture the stronghold of Catraeth from the English. The warriors spent a year in preliminary feasting and drinking of wine and mead; the subsequent attack was a disaster. The poet, writes Tony Conran, 'shows us a people with its back to the wall'. The poem tries 'to mitigate the futility of the exploit . . . by stressing its heroic glory'.

And after the revelling, there was silence.

A bright and blustery morning. My cold had retreated. I walked down through the town by way of the partly pedestrianised High Street and a little neighbourhood in which the front windows of the terraced houses displayed bright orange posters: not NO BARRAGE, as in Cardiff's Butetown, but NO SUPERMARKET – DIM ARCH FARCHNAD. I assumed the householders were not complaining about their lack of a supermarket but the possible imposition of one in their quiet streets. Long live the corner store! I arrived at a muddy bay and Dickie's Boatyard, where many sailing boats sat in their cradles awaiting launching, wire halyards impatiently pinging against metal masts. A street beyond the boatyard led out to the Garth – the north-facing promontory where Bangor finally reaches the Menai Strait. Here was Bangor Pier, over 500 yards long. I bought a ten pence admission ticket and strolled out on its wooden deck more than halfway to Anglesey.

I like piers. My great-grandfather John Bailey was one of the partners in a consortium which built the pier at Shanklin, on the Isle of Wight. A few miles away at Sandown, where my mother and father took me for summer holidays before the Second World War, I used to play on the beach near Sandown Pier. I admire the old cast-iron pillars like Victorian grand-piano legs supporting the deck, the swell rising and falling beneath the deck planking to the sound – is it only in one's head? – of accordion music, and the tawdry theatre often to be found at the seaward end where little-known artistes play in musical revues. I like the under-furnished and ill-stocked bars and the 'amusements' where distorting mirrors produce Francis Bacon-like reflections and a coin in a machine gives a short tenancy of a miniature crane and grab with which to try to pick up a plastic whistle or a chewy sweet wrapped in faded cellophane. I like perhaps most of all the feeling piers give their customers of being out at sea. Before the war, in fact, you could not only obtain the sea air and marine sensations on a pier, you could catch a boat from it. At the wharf-like staging at the seaward end of Shanklin and Sandown piers, excursion steamers would drop and collect passengers, their big paddle-wheels thrashing the water into foam.

Bangor Pier was built in 1896, toward the end of the half-century in which most British piers were put up. Although it looks like a third, thwarted attempt to bridge the Strait, the intention was simply to get across the mud flats to deep water where ferries could land trippers, particularly from Liverpool – who would then spend their holiday money in Bangor. Shipping companies like Cunard brought their employees on annual outings. The pier also provided a place where the townspeople could promenade, having paid their penny fee at the turnstile. There was entertainment on the pier: competitions for brass bands, fancy dress, and best-decorated prams; walking and swimming races; regattas with greasy-pole contests and soot-fights from small boats. On the pier, despite the lack of a proper pavilion which meant that rain drove everyone ashore, there were dances and gramophone concerts, electrograph shows, and performances by pierrots, comedians, and conjurors. The pier had its knocks – in 1914 a coaster rammed it and caused considerable damage; at the beginning of the Second World War it was intentionally broken in two so that it wouldn't be useful to German invasion forces. By the mid 1970s, like many another pier around the coasts of Britain, Bangor Pier had become derelict and dangerous, needing costly repairs.

Fortunately Bangor had civic leadership. George Gibbs, the town clerk, and Jean Christie, the Mayor, plotted and bargained. The pier was bought by the town from the district council for a penny, 'listed' as a structure of special architectural interest (which meant it couldn't be demolished out of hand), and made the object of numerous begging proposals. Grants and gifts were gathered in. A firm of consulting engineers donated a full structural survey and estimate for repairs. Most importantly, a government programme to help remedy long-term unemployment provided a solution to labour costs. During a period of five years, the Manpower Services Commission paid for several hundred otherwise out-of-work men to work for a year at a time rebuilding Bangor Pier. In May 1988 it was re-opened, looking brand-new again – an object lesson for sceptics, an exemplar of what can be done by enthusiasm and local pride.

As I walked the pier, I enjoyed a slight bounce from the planking underfoot. I admired the little kiosks with oriental gingerbread woodwork that were modelled on the Pavilion the Welsh architect John Nash built at Brighton for the Prince Regent – some onion-domed, some with tented roofs, and selling sweets and handicrafts. Billy Burges would have loved it. I took note of plaques which honoured the institutions and individuals who had coughed up the cash for kiosks, girders, planks, and seats. The Shell oil company had chipped in for the new open-air end-of-pier pavilion. John Lindsay, former mayor of New York City, paid for a plank. One seat was 'Sponsored by Mrs Mary Brown – who came back home to Wales.' Another was 'Sponsored by Jess Stevenson – who loves Wales.' At the far end, I leaned over the railing and looked down at the white caps: wind against tide in the Strait. Several men were angling there. I asked one, a stocky man in his late forties, what sort of luck he was having. 'Not much this morning,' he said. He went on to say that he had worked on the restoration of the pier; he was clearly proud of it.

'We had to watch the tide all the time, you know. It had to be low water when we dug out the mud from the base of the legs – and that sometimes meant six in the morning. It could be cold, wet, and dirty. That mud down there is eight feet deep. And then it would suddenly be under fifteen feet of water. We had safety boats, and lifelines, but some of the lads fell in. You'd forget where you were, take a step back to admire your work, and, whoosh, splash! No one drowned, though one lad got hypothermia. I did all sorts of jobs, scraping barnacles, painting, putting up scaffolding, sandblasting, cutting up old pieces of pier. We worked in all weathers for a pretty average wage but we felt chuffed by the work we did. It was a pity the MSC rules only let us work a year, then they let us go and brought in new men. It was to get people back to work, that was the idea. Mind you, it was useful training, and you've got to admit the pier looks good. Bangor is lucky – it got an almost new pier at half-price. I come out here most mornings with a rod, and most mornings I catch a few fish.'

He reeled in his line. There was nothing on the hook. He drew the rod back, flicked it forward, and the line shot out, weight and hook splashing into the water. He was going to keep trying until he landed a fish – or landed a job. I turned and looked down the long alley of the pier to the houses on the Garth, the wooded ridge behind Bangor, and, in the further distance, the unchanging grey mountains with grey cloud around their peaks. I was in two minds about walking back toward the station and the London train. I felt like a lone sailor at the end of a voyage, wanting to go ashore and yet dreading the loss of independence and the cessation of onward movement; looking forward to going back home but knowing it would involve having to live with the urge to set off again.

BIBLIOGRAPHY

Cardiff and the Valleys, John B. Hillings (Lund Humphries, 1973)
Cardiff and the Marquesses of Bute, John Davies (University of Wales Press, 1981)
When Was Wales?, Gwyn A. Williams (Penguin, 1985)
A Cambrian Way, Richard Sale (Constable, 1983)
Lothair, Benjamin Disraeli (Longmans, Green, 1870)
The Journey through Wales and *The Description of Wales*, Gerald of Wales (Penguin, 1978)
The Mabinogion, edited by Gwyn Jones and Thomas Jones (Dent, 1974)
Wild Wales (1862), George Borrow (Collins, 1955)
The History of the Kings of Britain, Geoffrey of Monmouth (Penguin, 1966)
A Tour through the Whole Island of Great Britain (1724–6), Daniel Defoe (Penguin, 1971)
Merthyr, Rhondda and 'The Valleys', A. Trystan Edwards (Hale, 1958)
Epoch and Artist, David Jones (Faber, 1959)
One Saturday Afternoon, R. Meurig Evans (Nat. Museum of Wales, 1984)
The Valley of the Shadow, John H. Brown (Alun Books, 1981)
My Lamp Still Burns, Robert Morgan (Gomer Press, 1981)
Welsh Verse, translated and edited by Tony Conran (Poetry Wales Press, 1986)
Victim of the Beacons, R. D. Raikes et al. (Brecon Beacons Nat. Park, 1978)
The National Question Again, edited by John Osmond (Gomer Press, 1985)
The Matter of Wales, Jan Morris (OUP, 1984)
The Drovers' Roads of Wales, Fay Godwin and Shirley Toulson (Whittet, 1987)

The Celts, Nora Chadwick (Penguin, 1970)
Wales: The Land Remembers, Gwyn Williams (Faber, 1977)
The Icknield Way, Edward Thomas (Constable, 1913)
The Break-Up of Britain, Tom Nairn (NLB, 1977)
Mysterious Wales, Chris Barber (Granada, 1983)
The Welsh Extremist, Ned Thomas (Gollancz, 1971)
Planet magazine, various issues (Aberystwyth, 1986–91)
Angles & Britons, J. R. R. Tolkien (University of Wales Press,
    1963)
Selected Poems, R. S. Thomas (Hart-Davis MacGibbon, 1973)
Poems, Gerard Manley Hopkins (OUP, 1948)
Gerard Manley Hopkins, Paddy Kitchen (Hamish Hamilton, 1978)
Obstinate Cymric, John Cowper Powys (Druid Press, 1947)
Walks and Talks of an American Farmer in England (1852), Frederick
    Law Olmsted (University of Michigan Press)
Harlech and Lleyn, Michael Senior (Gwasg Carreg Gwalch, 1988)
Tours in Wales, Thomas Pennant (H. Humphreys, 1883)
The Snowdonia National Park, W. M. Condry (Collins, 1966)
Wanderings and Excursions in North Wales, Thomas Roscoe (C. Tilt
    and Simpkin, 1836)
Bangor Pier, Ian Skidmore (Gwasg Carreg Garmon, 1988)
Guide to Field Archaeology in Britain, Eric S. Wood (Collins, 1968)
The Journey into North Wales, Samuel Johnson, in Vol. V of
    Boswell's Life of Johnson edited by G. B. Hill & L. F. Powell
    (Clarendon Press, 1964)